READING ANGEL

READING ANGEL:

The TV Spin-off with a Soul

EDITED BY STACEY ABBOTT

I.B. TAURIS
LONDON · NEW YORK

Reprinted in 2005 by I.B.Tauris & Co Ltd
6 Salem Road, London W2 4BU
175 Fifth Avenue, New York NY 10010
www.ibtauris.com

In the United States of America and Canada
distributed by Palgrave Macmillan a division of St Martin's Press
175 Fifth Avenue, New York NY 10010

First published in 2005 by I.B.Tauris & Co Ltd

ISBN 1 85043 839 0
EAN 978 1 85043 839 7

A full CIP record for this book is available from the British Library
A full CIP record is available from the Library of Congress

Library of Congress Catalog Card Number: available

Typeset in Palatino by JCS Publishing Services
Printed and bound in Great Britain by TJ International Ltd,
Padstow, Cornwall

CONTENTS

ACKNOWLEDGMENTS

Editing this book has been a true labour of love and has only been possible due to countless people who have offered their support and guidance along the way. I must first thank each of the contributors to the collection for their intelligence, enthusiasm and professionalism by providing insightful and exciting new scholarship on *Angel* in what was a very tight schedule. They have been a joy to work with, making this a true collaboration and my role as editor a pleasurable one. I would also like to thank all of those whose proposals I could not include in the book. I was overwhelmed by the response to my call for papers and excited by the diversity of interesting work that is being done on *Angel* around the world. I hope that this means that *Reading Angel* is only the beginning of the discussion about the series.

To all those at I.B. Tauris who have seen this book through to its final publication, I express my gratitude. I owe the greatest of thanks to Philippa Brewster for having confidence in me as an editor and *Angel* as the subject of an edited collection. We all owe Philippa our appreciation for recognizing the significance of popular American television as a subject for study and creating a space for this work. I would like to thank Janet McCabe and Kim Akass for their encouragement throughout this project and Janet for convincing me that I could edit this book in the first place. I wouldn't be writing these acknowledgments if it weren't for her.

In the area of *Buffy* Studies, I would like to thank Roz Kaveney for her influential work in both versions of *Reading the Vampire Slayer* as well as Rhonda Wilcox and David Lavery for their publication *Fighting the Forces* and their encouragement throughout this project. All of us working within this area owe Rhonda and David a great deal of thanks for providing an outlet for research on *Buffy the Vampire Slayer* and *Angel* both through the online journal *Slayage* and the international conference held in Nashville in May 2004. It was an inspiring few days. I would like to thank the British Academy for funding my attendance at the conference, enabling me to deliver the paper 'The Comic Stylings of Wesley Wyndam-Pryce', an early version of my chapter in this book, and receive incredibly helpful and enthusiastic feedback from those who attended my presentation.

Over the past year, a number of people have offered almost daily encouragement. My regular Wednesday morning emails with Karen Myers, to analyse the previous night's episode of *Angel*, has been an enjoyable opportunity to discuss the series and work through many of the arguments that have informed my thoughts on the show. I would also like to thank Karen for all of her insightful comments about *Buffy* and *Angel* over the years, for reading and re-reading my work on the subject and finally for devoting a good deal of her busy schedule to proofreading this book. Thanks too to SavingAngel.org for their design inspiration.

Of my husband Simon Brown, I can only say that his unwavering belief in me has been an incredible source of strength throughout this project. It has been a difficult and challenging year for both of us, and despite his own very heavy workload, he has always taken the time to listen to my ideas, problems and insecurities, offering advice, help or simply a shoulder to lean on. He is and always will be my partner in all that I do.

To my siblings, Glenn, Leslie, Jeff and Joanne (aka: 'super cyber sibs') I thank them for their daily emails which always bring a smile to my face and remind me that there is more to life than work. They are my family and my best friends. To my mother, Joan Abbott, I owe everything I am to her. She, who has faced and overcome unwarranted adversity throughout her life, has shown me that we can do anything if we set our minds to it.

Finally I must express my deepest gratitude to my father, Stanley Abbott, whose passing this year has been a truly devastating loss to my family and myself. While he could not really understand my excitement over a TV show about a vampire with a soul (this seemed a bit silly to him), he was very pleased when I began to work on this book and would have been proud to see the results. What he never realized was that throughout my life, he remained my inspiration. Through our countless discussions about film, television, politics etc, he taught me to be fearless when expressing myself and to take pleasure in discussion and debate, all of which has influenced my work. It is therefore to my father that this publication is dedicated.

IN LOVING MEMORY
STANLEY CHARLES ABBOTT
17 APRIL 1924—12 MAY 2004

CONTRIBUTORS

Stacey Abbott is a Lecturer in Film and Television Studies at Roehampton University, where she teaches courses on textual analysis, world cinema and genre studies. She has written on the horror genre, *Buffy the Vampire Slayer* and *Angel*, and is on the editorial board for *Slayage: The Online International Journal of Buffy Studies*. She is currently writing a book on the modern vampire in film.

Stan Beeler is Chair of English at the University of Northern British Columbia, Canada. His areas of interest include popular culture, television studies, comparative literature and Renaissance literature. He is currently co-editing a book on the *Stargate-SG1* television series.

Phil Colvin graduated in English and Creative Writing from the University of East Anglia in 2003 where he worked as a film and TV features editor on the acclaimed student newspaper, *Concrete*. He is currently working at the University of Bristol and trying to write a first novel without stealing too much dialogue from Joss Whedon.

Janet K. Halfyard is a Senior Lecturer at Birmingham Conservatoire, UK, where she teaches courses in film music as well as twentieth-century and contemporary music. Her publications include papers on contemporary vocal technique (which she performs as well as researches) and on film and television music. She has written several essays on music and performance in *Buffy the Vampire Slayer* and *Angel*, and has recently completed a monograph examining Danny Elfman's 1989 score for *Batman* for the Scarecrow Press Film Score Guide series.

Janine R. Harrison, raised in Chicago's south suburbs, is a writer and educator. Career highlights include: editing for *Chicago Advertising & Media*; writing speeches for the Coordination Council for North American Affairs; and re-writing/editing *Don't Let the Accent Fool You*. Janine was a 2003 *Post–Tribune* memoir contest winner.

Matt Hills is the author of *Fan Cultures* (London: Routledge, 2002) and *The Pleasures of Horror* (London: Continuum, 2005). He has recently written on cult TV for edited collections such as *Teen TV* and *The TV Studies Reader*, and has contributed fan studies to the journals *American Behavioral Scientist, Mediactive* and *Social Semiotics*. Matt is a Lecturer in Media and Cultural Studies in the School of Journalism, Media and Cultural Studies, Cardiff University.

Benjamin Jacob has taught English and American Literature at the University of York. His work has appeared and is forthcoming in magazines, books and journals.

Roz Kaveney is a freelance editor, writer and literary journalist. Her books include *Reading the Vampire Slayer* (editor), *From Alien to The Matrix – Readings in SF Film* and the forthcoming *Teen Dreams*.

Tammy A. Kinsey teaches 16mm film, digital video production and a variety of cinema studies courses in Film/Video at the University of Toledo. Obsessed with all things visual, Tammy enjoys exploring images in detail. Other research interests include film censorship and alternative approaches to filmmaking. Her paper '"I Wish I Had the Blue": Cinematic Language in "The Body"' was presented at the *Slayage* Conference on *Buffy the Vampire Slayer*.

David Lavery is Professor of English at Middle Tennessee State University, where he teaches courses on science fiction, modern poetry, popular culture and film. He is the author of over eighty published essays and reviews and editor/co-editor of books on *Twin Peaks, The X-Files, Buffy the Vampire Slayer* and *The Sopranos*. With Rhonda Wilcox he co-edits *Slayage: The Online International Journal of Buffy Studies*.

Michaela D. E. Meyer is an Assistant Professor in the Department of Communication at Christopher Newport University. She specializes in critical examinations of young adult programming, particularly on the Warner Brothers network. Michaela would like to thank Brianne Meyer and Li Wang for their helpful suggestions on this piece.

Matthew Mills read Music at Christ Church, Oxford, and subsequently attended Trinity College of Music, London. He now maintains a busy schedule of playing, conducting, composing, teaching and research, and is completing a PhD in Composition at Royal Holloway, University of London, under the supervision of Simon Holt. Forthcoming projects include a chamber opera, performances of music by Beethoven, Chopin and Ligeti, and an article on music in *The Talented Mr Ripley*.

Jennifer Stoy is a graduate student in English at the University of California, Santa Barbara. Her first article on *Angel* was published in the second edition of *Reading the Vampire Slayer*.

Sharon Sutherland is Clinical Instructor in Dispute Resolution at the University of British Columbia Faculty of Law. Sharon's primary teaching subjects are mediation and negotiation, and she practises as a child protection and community mediator. Sharon's current research explores the intersection of law and theatre.

Sarah Swan is a recent graduate of the University of British Columbia Faculty of Law, and a judicial law clerk at the British Columbia Supreme Court.

Sara Upstone is an AHRB-funded research student researching spatial politics in the postcolonial novel at Birkbeck

College, London, where she also teaches. She has published articles on subjects ranging from J. R. R. Tolkien to Toni Morrison. Her research interests include postcolonial, twentieth-century and contemporary literature, cultural and spatial theory and popular culture.

Rebecca Williams is a PhD student at the School of Journalism, Media and Cultural Studies at Cardiff University. Her research topic is genre, fan practice and hierarchy. She has had work published in *Slayage: The Online International Journal of Buffy Studies* and *The European Journal of Cultural Studies*.

Rhonda V. Wilcox is Professor of English at Gordon College in Barnesville, Georgia. She is the author of numerous essays on popular culture, including '"There Will Never Be a Very Special *Buffy*": *Buffy* and the Monsters of Teen Life', in *The Journal of Popular Film and Television* (1999). With David Lavery, she is the editor of *Fighting the Forces: What's at Stake in Buffy the Vampire Slayer* (Lanham, MD: Rowman & Littlefield, 2002) and *Slayage: The Online International Journal of Buffy Studies*. Her forthcoming publication *The Art of Buffy the Vampire Slayer* (London and New York: I.B. Tauris and Palgrave) is due to be published in 2005.

CAST LIST

A Great Cast is Worth Remembering

ANGEL INVESTIGATIONS

Angel	David Boreanaz
Winifred 'Fred' Burkle/Illyria	Amy Acker
Cordelia Chase	Charisma Carpenter
Doyle	Glenn Quinn
Charles Gunn	J. August Richards
Lorne (The Host)	Andy Hallett
Spike	James Marsters
Wesley Wyndam-Pryce	Alexis Denisof

FRIENDS AND FOES (OFTEN BOTH)

The Beast	Vladimir Kulich
Connor	Vincent Kartheiser
Justine Cooper	Laurel Holloman
Darla	Julie Benz
Drogyn	Alec Newman
Drusilla	Juliet Landau
Eve	Sarah Thompson
Faith	Eliza Dushku
Groosalugg	Mark Lutz
Hamilton	Adam Baldwin
Holtz	Keith Szarabajka
Jasmine	Gina Torres
Harmony Kendall	Mercedes McNab
Knox	Jonathan M. Woodward
Kate Lockley	Elisabeth Rohm

Holland Manners	Sam Anderson
Lindsey McDonald	Christian Kane
Lee Mercer	Thomas Burr
Lilah Morgan	Stephanie Romanov
Merle	Matthew James
Linwood Murrow	John Rubinstein
Nina	Jenny Mollen
Gavin Park	Daneil Daekim
Gwen Raiden	Alexa Davalos
Nathan Reed	Gerry Becker
Sahjhan	Jack Conley
Skip	David Denman

Kicking Ass and Singing 'Mandy': A Vampire in LA

STACEY ABBOTT

Los Angeles. You see it at night and it shines. A beacon.
People are drawn to it. People and other things. They come
for all sorts of reasons. My reason. No surprise there. It
started with a girl.

('City Of', 1:1)

Right from the opening words of the first episode of
Angel, producers Joss Whedon and David Greenwalt acknowledge the series' link to its parent show
Buffy the Vampire Slayer (*BtVS*) as well establishing its unique
new vision. Angel's claim that he came to LA because of 'a
girl', reminds fans that it was the doomed love affair between
vampire and slayer that forced Angel to leave Sunnydale, and
introduces into Angel, the character and the show, a hint of
melancholy and tragedy. He is a man escaping a dark past, a
fact that is emphasized through the series regular use of flashbacks. While *BtVS* is a series that, like its characters, is firmly
set in the present, *Angel* is haunted by his past, reflected in the
series' debt both visually and narratively to film noir. The
noir-style voice-over, matched by an equally noir-ish opening
montage of the bright urban lights of Los Angeles, informs us
that this will not simply be an extension of *BtVS* but rather a
series with its own style, narrative and thematic preoccupations. The dark LA landscape makes it clear that the new
series has moved on from the confines of a high-school and
small-town setting and it is the evolution of the title character,

Angel, the vampire with a soul, together with the team he builds along the way, which is its primary focus.

The characters on *BtVS* were portrayed as 'normal' people placed in extraordinary situations but trying to maintain the semblance of normality. The ending of the series has Buffy achieve this aspiration when she finds herself in a situation where she is no longer alone responsible for saving the world, but now one among many, free to pursue a normal life ('Chosen', B7:22 – *BtVS*, Season 7, Episode 22). On *Angel*, however, each of the characters, Angel, Cordelia, Doyle, Wesley, Gunn, Fred and Lorne, has been expelled from normality. They are damaged and looking for redemption, belonging and purpose to help them heal their wounds and find meaning in their lives. Their work for Angel Investigations (AI) puts them on the path to achieve their desires. In the big city, *Angel* reminds us, these aspirations are, however, difficult to achieve and as a result the characters are constantly straying from their path and finding themselves at war with each other as much as with their enemies. Yet they continue to return to the team and resume the good fight, reinforcing the existential theme of the series that it is not winning the battle that matters but simply taking part in the fight, as Angel himself realizes after his own crisis in Season Two when he tells Kate, 'If nothing we do matters, then all that matters is what we do.' ('Epiphany', 2:16)

The final sequence of each series captures much of the differences between the two shows. Where *BtVS* ends with the team united on the bright expanse of the open road considering their future, *Angel* ends with the team standing together cramped in a dark and rainy alley, preparing to face an army of demons from hell. Buffy ends with the unanswered but hopeful question, 'Yeah Buffy, what are we gonna do now?' as the camera tracks in to a close up of Buffy as she begins to smile. Angel, however, ends with the team choosing to undertake a hopeless battle and continue the good fight by answering Angel's call to arms, 'let's go to work', before the final episode cuts to black ('Not Fade Away', 5:22). Angel's ending is equally hopeful but not by suggesting a positive future for Team Angel but rather by seeing the characters resume their mission and go out fighting ... or do they? From the first shot to the last shot, *Angel* declared its difference.

ANGEL/ANGELUS AND MORAL AMBIGUITY

What defines *Angel's* distinctiveness as a series? To answer this question we must begin with the man/vampire himself. On *BtVS*, Angel came to represent a form of moral ambiguity, a metaphor for a boyfriend who could torment and break your heart.[1] His cruel nature, however, became increasingly separated from his good side through the polarization of Angel and his vampiric alter ego Angelus. In *Angel*, on the other hand, the distinction between his good and evil sides became increasingly ambiguous. As I have argued elsewhere, the process of moving Angel from peripheral love interest to central protagonist of his own series enabled the writers to examine the many ways in which Angel and Angelus merge, and this is largely because we now see Angel, not through Buffy's love-struck eyes, but through his own subjective experience.[2] He cannot escape who he is. This new series constantly reminds him and the audience that Angelus lurks just beneath the surface and can, as in 'Eternity' (1:17), emerge at a moment's notice.

Furthermore, the series takes great pains to demonstrate that it is the combination of Angel and Angelus that defines Angel and gives him his strength and power. When cured of his vampirism and made human in 'I Will Remember You' (1:8), Angel discovers that he has been released from the cosmic battle between good and evil and is no longer of use to Buffy. He must become a vampire again in order to continue the good fight. 'Are You Now, or Have You Ever Been' (2:2), a flashback episode to Angel's post-ensoulment but pre-Buffy life, presents Angel as a character that is a curious hybrid of Angel and Angelus. He smokes, a key signifier of Angelus, and seems cold and empty, with little regard for humanity. The bellhop of the hotel in which Angel lives claims that Angel gives him the heebie-jeebies, because when you look into his eyes 'there's nothing there'. Yet it is in this episode that we see Angel's first attempt, albeit a failed one, to engage with humanity and help those in need. In the Pylea episodes of Season Two, ('Over the Rainbow', 'Through the Looking Glass', 'There's No Place Like Plrtz Glrb', 2:20–2) Angel is trapped within a dimension that separates his human and demon sides to their most extreme incarnations. As a man he can walk in the sunlight and see his reflection, but when his demon is released he turns into an uncontrollable monster, far more brutal and animalistic than Angelus. In these episodes it becomes clear that these are the polar extremes of Angel's hybridity, with Angel and Angelus hovering in between, more like shadowy sides of each other than opposites.

To further evoke the darker side of Angel, there is an increased emphasis within the series upon Angel's vampirism. On *BtVS*, his vampirism made him a powerful ally for Buffy, but more significantly introduced a doomed love affair into her life, as summed up by Giles: 'A vampire in love with a slayer. It's rather poetic … in a maudlin sort of way' ('Out of Sight, Out of Mind', B1:11). On *Angel*, however, the audience is constantly reminded of the reality of Angel's vampirism by the emphasis upon a dark visual style to the interiors and the dominance of exterior night sequences. He is after all a creature of the night who will burn up in the sunlight. There is also an increased emphasis upon Angel drinking blood. Cordelia and Wesley often refer to Angel's liquid diet, for example, when making brownies Cordelia explains that Angel can't have any because they are full of 'nutty goodness. Not red blood cells.' ('I've Got You Under My Skin', 1:14) Similarly, in 'Are You Now, or Have You Ever Been' Cordelia spices up Angel's blood with a hint of nutmeg. This shift in emphasis between *BtVS* and *Angel* is not surprising since to Buffy Angel's vampirism was, even after her encounters with Angelus, largely an obstacle to their being together, while for Angel vampirism is something he struggles with on a daily basis as he resists the urge to give in to his bloodlust and life as Angelus.

In other episodes these references to blood drinking serve as more than a simple reminder that Angel is a vampire but also of the constant threat of him drinking human blood. In 'Somnambulist' (1:11) Angel dreams of hunting and killing his victims and explains to Cordelia that the dreams weren't nightmares, he enjoyed them. In 'The Shroud of Rahmon' (2:8) he pretends to kill Kate Lockley by drinking her blood in order to stop another demon from attacking her. While his intentions were good, the episode ends with him sitting in the dark, vividly remembering the experience. In 'Sleep Tight' (3:16) his blood is spiked with the blood of his son, which awakens his thirst and causes him to describe Connor as smelling like food. Most significantly, the two final episodes of the series, 'Power Play' (5:21) and 'Not Fade Away' show Angel drinking human blood twice. In the penultimate episode, he kills and feeds off Drogyn, a friend and champion being offered to Angel as a sacrifice to prove his commitment to the evil 'Circle of the Black Thorn', a moment that is specifically designed to make the audience, along with Team Angel, suspect that Angel has indeed been corrupted. In the finale, when Hamilton, the liaison to the Senior Partners tells Angel that he cannot be beaten, as he is a part of Wolfram & Hart, 'their [the Senior Partners] strength flows through my veins. My blood is filled with their ancient power', Angel calmly replies 'can you pick out the one word there you probably shouldn't have said?' before vamping out one last time and drinking Hamilton's blood. Here, unlike the scene with Drogyn or the Season Two episode with Kate, he is not feeding as part of an act, nor is he being tricked into it as with Connor. He recognizes that his strength at this moment is as a vampire and this provides him with an advantage over the powerful but human Hamilton. This moment sums up much of the contradiction of Angel, which is that, in order to be a true hero and atone for his murderous life as a vampire, he must embrace his vampirism and accept that he is a combination of Angel and Angelus. This also leaves him at the end of the series with the blood and power of the Senior Partners flowing through his veins. The impact of this is left untold.

Perhaps he can slay the dragon he faces at the end of 'Not Fade Away' or maybe he has further tests ahead of him, along his road to redemption.

CONTRADICTION AND SELF-PARODY

As the title of this introduction indicates, *Angel* is about contradiction. A vampire with a soul, not to mention a creature of the night living in a state known for its sunshine, seems oxymoronic. Similarly, kung fu and singing Barry Manilow's romantic ballad 'Mandy' are two seemingly incompatible actions and yet are both strongly identified by fans with the show's hero Angel. This is more than simply a penchant for the perverse, but establishes the series' commitment to character and narrative complexity. On *BtVS*, Angel, with a few exceptions, had to play the character as a straight romantic lead with little opportunity for humour. In *Angel*, the character is an action hero who is able to lampoon himself by revealing his failings, a fact that series star David Boreanaz found particularly attractive about the role:

> The best position to put Angel in is an uncomfortable position when he's around other people and he's embarrassed or he has to sing and he's horrible. Those are funny moments […] if you have a moment like that, there's always a transition to a dark place, attacking a demon or faced with a life or death situation. The show lends itself to that. It's a nice balance.[3]

This balance does more than simply oscillate the actors between performance extremes but enables the writers to undermine expectations constantly and present the characters as recognizably human. It can also at times suggest something far more transgressive. The pinnacle of the series' lampooning of Angel came in 'Smile Time' (5:14), in which Angel, investigating a children's television programme that is having a life-threatening effect upon its young viewers, is magically transformed into a puppet. One of the absolute masterpieces of the series' five-year run, this episode mercilessly parodies Angel's superhero status by having him reduced to a 'wee little puppet man' whose nose comes off, laughed at by his colleagues, mocked by Spike and even ripped apart by his werewolf would-be girlfriend. As if this weren't enough, the episode then goes on to satirize not just the man but the representation of the 'hero' by featuring an iconic shot of Team Angel exiting Angel's office in unison, shot in slow motion, as the camera cranes down to reveal the Angel-puppet leading the way, brandishing a broadsword over his head. Later in the episode, in classic form, the Angel-puppet even vamps out in a fight scene to demonstrate that he is so much more than felt and stuffing. While it is easy to view this episode as a comic interlude pastiching its own generic forms before the heightened emotion of Fred's death in 'A Hole in the World' (5:15), the episode also features some of the series' darkest and most disturbing imagery.

The television puppets that suck the life out of their viewers represent more than the mind-numbing effects of television, itself a bold statement for any television show, but evoke themes of paedophilia and sexual abuse. In the episode's pre-credit teaser, a young boy sits and watches a children's television programme, 'Smile Time'. On screen one of the puppets waits until the boy is alone and then approaches the screen and talks to the boy directly: 'OK Tommy, you know what to do.' When Tommy, not surprised that a television character is talking to him, refuses, the puppet is more insistent while maintaining its innocent voice and language: 'Tommy you should never break a promise. You don't want to be a bad apple do you? Come on, you know "Smile Time" isn't free.' Before speaking the next line, however, the puppet's brow furrows and his tone becomes aggressive and commanding. 'Now get over here and touch it.' Tommy acquiesces and places his hands on the television set and the puppet begins to moan and say: 'that's it Tommy. Touch it. That's it ... oh yeah. Good boy Tommy', before the boy collapses and the puppet returns to conventional behaviour. The allusion to sexual abuse by a seemingly benign and trusted figure is clearly conveyed through the 'performance' of the puppet and the hesitance of the child. It is a disturbing opening that sits in creative tension with the innocence of the episode's humour. While we laugh at Angel's predicament and how his transformation plays with our perception of him as hero, the humour does not undermine the actual threat they are facing as the puppets are portrayed as one of the series' most horrific villains. It is through contradictions, such as 'monstrous puppets' or a ballad-singing superhero, that the show is regularly able to explore dark themes around abuse, treachery, self-doubt, the purpose of heroism and the meaning of masculinity.

GENERIC HYBRIDITY AND ANGEL'S VISUAL STYLE

The visual style of the series is also defined by contradiction. As previously mentioned, the film noir night-time urban setting establishes the tone for the series, but rather than be defined by a singular genre, *Angel* draws upon a range of generic references to create a distinctive and coherent hybrid form as demonstrated by the extensive discussion of genre in this book. This commitment to genre does not simply inform the series' narrative but brings together seemingly disparate iconography, from genres as diverse as horror, the detective film, 'hood films, comic-book superheroes, musicals, melodrama, martial arts, comedy, and office and courtroom drama. The visual signatures of these genres are integrated with the noir landscape to create *Angel*'s distinct and cinematic visual style through which the series' narrative and themes are expressed. The visual is absolutely fundamental to our understanding of *Angel*.

From the first episode, the show established its distinct visual style by emphasizing the hybridity of film noir landscape with a superhero narrative.[4] While Buffy is also a superhero (or 'champion' in the vernacular of the Angelverse), the nature of the series, both narratively and visually, emphasized that despite her powers and skill, she is a normal girl, and in fact *BtVS* ends with her realization that she is no longer alone and unique. The visual style of *Angel*, however, constantly reminds us that Angel is so much more than a man. The noir conventions begin with the series' opening montage of Los Angeles and continue when the montage ends with Angel in a bar, drunkenly talking about the girl he left behind. However, as a group of men accompanied by a couple of young women exit the bar, the camera tracks past Angel in close up as his eyes follow their movement and, losing the drunk act, he gets up to follow them. The sequence then cuts to a low-angle shot of Angel walking towards the camera in slow motion with his long coat flowing behind him like a cape. In this shot we shift from the aesthetics of a noir detective drama, the dingy bar, the ceiling fans loudly whirling above, to the superhero genre, the low angle, slow motion and flowing coat. Joss Whedon specifically credits this stylistic moment to the influence of John Woo's visual style, best captured in his *hero* dramas *Better Tomorrow* (1986), *The Killer* (1989) and *Face Off* (1997).[5]

The iconography of the superhero genre continues in the following sequence, when Angel attacks the men, now revealed to be vampires, with Batman-like gadgetry. The scene ends with Angel leaving the alley, walking away from the camera in a low-angle shot, coat still flowing behind him. This is the iconic shot of the series used within the credits. This sequence visually establishes that Angel, in this new series, is to be a mix between noir hero and superhero. Aesthetically, this hybridity is evoked through the series' constant opposition between a high and low view of the city. Michael Walker argues that in film noir the city is itself a character but specifically 'the seedy underside of the city', a characteristic of the genre that is evoked when Angel circulates within the labyrinthine tunnels, sewers and demon haunts of LA.[6] These images are, however, usually counterbalanced with images of Angel standing on the rooftops, watching over the city and acting as its guardian.

The fusion of film noir and superhero is but two of the series' generic influences. In the show's second season the musical is introduced into the mix. *Buffy the Vampire Slayer* broke all conventions of television drama by staging a full-blown musical episode, 'Once More With Feeling' (B6:7), in which a demon uses a spell to transform the town of Sunnydale into one big musical, with everyone regularly bursting into song and expressing all of their feelings of insecurity and doubt, even thoughts of suicide. *Angel* also plays with the conventions of the musical. Rather than devote one specific episode to the musical genre, the entire season arc is built around the introduction of a new narrative and musical space, Caritas, a demon karaoke bar.[7]

That the musical is absolutely fundamental to the second season of *Angel* is demonstrated by the fact that the opening of 'Judgement' (2:1) begins with the performance of the song 'I Will Survive' and the final episode of the season ('There's No Place Like Plrtz Glrb') ends with Angel returning home from an adventure in a demon dimension quoting the classic line from *The Wizard of Oz* (Victor Fleming, 1939), 'there's no place like home'. That the musical has been thoroughly integrated within the dark, hybrid world of *Angel* is made clear by the fact that 'I Will Survive' is sung by a green-skinned, red-horned demon and that Angel's elation at returning home is undercut when he opens the door to find a downcast Willow, in town to tell him of Buffy's death.

The musical, though, does more than top and tail the season. Aesthetically it introduces bright colours to a series that has been dominated by dark blacks, blues, greys and browns. The new location, Caritas, is atmospherically lit with electric-blue backdrops and pink neon behind the bar. The demons tend to be a range of colours, vibrant green being the most prevalent and the Host, the aforementioned green-skinned demon, is not only colourful because of his skin, but also because he wears increasingly vibrant and daringly coloured suits from episode to episode. Suddenly, the glitter, spectacle and glamour of the musical regularly seep into the series. At first this seems an intrusion. The shift between the noir world of Angel Investigations and the musical world of Caritas is designed to be shocking and incongruous. Wesley informs Angel that he has been expanding his network of contacts, which includes a safe haven for demons, a likely place to find informants. He wants to take Angel and Cordelia there but warns that 'it's a little outside the box'. These words are followed by a cut to a demon singing the Pointer Sisters' classic 'I'm So Excited'. Wesley's words do more than warn Angel, they also prepare the audience that the show is about to step outside its own generic box by entering the world of the musical.

Through Caritas, the introduction of the musical also becomes a natural extension of Angel's world. In the musical, characters express their hearts' desires through song. *Angel* takes this further by having the characters reveal their souls and destinies through song, interpreted by the Host. This enables the musical to integrate with noir and superhero narrative by providing the team of Angel Investigations with yet another tool in their fight against evil. Caritas, however, is more than a narrative convenience but rather contributes to the series' move away from episodic case of the week to the greater narrative arc around personal introspection and existential angst as each of the characters question their place within the 'good fight'. Season Two is a season of identity crisis and the musical offers the characters a means of questioning identity. Through song they do more than bear their souls, they search their souls.

Genre on *Angel* therefore does not simply act as a shorthand of signs utilized to simplify the narrative. Instead, the generic hybridity of *Angel* is used to signal the complexity of its narrative construction. Genres are not abandoned but are increasingly integrated into the series, creating a tapestry of generic references that define the *Angel* landscape and its distinctive visual style. This tapestry mirrors the narrative construction of the Angelverse, which has developed out of five years of *Angel* story arcs and three years of *Buffy the Vampire Slayer*, covering, through flashbacks, the 250 years of his vampire existence, all woven together to tell the story of the vampire with a soul.

ABOUT READING ANGEL

What I have attempted to do in this introduction is outline some of the many ways that the creators of *Angel* have signalled its difference from *BtVS* by developing new themes specific to the series and creating a path for Angel that would have been impossible had he remained a peripheral character on *Buffy the Vampire Slayer*. While there has been much great work about *Angel*, much of it has tended to consider the series as an extension of the Buffyverse. The aim of this collection, however, is to consider what makes *Angel* a distinct television series in its own right. The authors who have contributed to the book are united, along with the many fans of the series, by their enthusiasm for *Angel* as a dynamic show with unique style, narrative arcs, characterizations and themes. The book is therefore broken into four sections, each reflecting characteristics of the series that are distinct to *Angel*. It begins with a section discussing the specifics of *Angel's* production aesthetics and contexts before moving on to explore the significance and impact of relocating Angel, the man and the series, to Los Angeles. Part Three examines how the corporate Big Bad Wolfram & Hart allows the series to explore a more insidious global evil that extends beyond Angel Investigation's nightly street-level confrontations into the corporate office, boardroom and courtroom. Finally, Part Four highlights the series' preoccupation with issues of masculinity, often explored through the manipulation of genre itself a major concern, that stands in contrast to Buffy's role as a feminist text. While the series has come to an end (or has it?), this publication is not intended to be the last word on *Angel* but rather the beginning of a discussion. As Angel tells us in 'Not Fade Away' 'let's go to work'.

It's time to begin investigating *Angel*.

NOTES

1 For further discussion of the moral ambiguity of supernatural
   television series, see Beth Braun, 'The *X-Files* and *Buffy the Vampire Slayer*: The Ambiguity of Evil in Supernatural
   Representations', *Journal of Popular Film and Television*, 28: 2
   (2000), pp. 88–94. For a discussion of how *BtVS* uses monsters as
   metaphors for adolescent issues, see Rhonda V. Wilcox, '"There
   Will Never Be a Very Special *Buffy*": *Buffy* and the Monsters of
   Teen Life', *Journal of Popular Film and Television*, 27: 2 (1999), pp.
   16–23.

2 Stacey Abbott, 'Walking the Fine Line Between Angel and Angelus', *Slayage: The Online International Journal of Buffy Studies*, 9
   (2003), at http://www.slayage.tv/essays/Slayage9/Abbott.htm.

3 David Boreanaz, 'Angel Light?', interviewed by Joe Nazzaro,
   Starburst Angel Special, 57 (2003), p. 15.

4 For a discussion of the series' use of film noir see below, Benjamin Jacob, 'Los Angelus: The City of Angel' (Chapter 5) and
   Jennifer Stoy, '"And Her Tears Flowed Like Wine": Wesley/Lilah
   and the Complicated(?) Role of the Female Agent on *Angel*'
   (Chapter 11); for discussion of the significance of the cinematic
   superhero to the series see Janet K. Halfyard, 'The Dark
   Avenger: Angel and the Cinematic Superhero' (Chapter 10).

5 Joss Whedon, DVD commentary for 'City Of', *Angel Season One
   DVD Collection*, 20th Century Fox Home Entertainment (F1-DGB
   22830DVD) Region 2.

6 Michael Walker, 'Film Noir: Introduction', in Ian Cameron (ed.),
   The Movie Book of Film Noir (London: Studio Vista, 1992), p. 12.

7 For a further discussion of Caritas as a significant musical space
   in *Angel* see Matthew Mills, '*Ubi Caritas*?: Music as Narrative
   Agent in *Angel*' (Chapter 2); For a discussion of both Lorne and
   Caritas as representing LA's entertainment industry as well as
   gay community see Stan Beeler, 'Outing Lorne: Performance for
   the Performers' (Chapter 6).

PART ONE:

*'It Was a Seminal Show
Cancelled by the
Idiot Networks':*

*Narrative and Style
on* Angel

1

Angel: *Redefinition and Justification through Faith*

PHIL COLVIN

I n February 2000, midway through *Angel's* first season, the announcement was made that the show was to be renewed for a second season by the Warner Brothers (WB) network. Early renewals are often something of a coup in American network television, especially for a new show whose ratings had so far been respectable, but considerably lower than those for its lead-in on the WB network, *Buffy the Vampire Slayer*. Speaking on the renewal, Joss Whedon gave a hint of what was in store for the next season. 'We're looking to build up the ensemble a little more, but you'll see fewer stories that are peripheral to Angel [...]. We initially saw Angel as being more of a guardian for other characters, but we found the audience was much more emotionally invested in Angel, so we'll be staying closer to home and exploring his character.' In other words, although *Angel* was coming back for a second season it wasn't going to be precisely the same show. Whedon, and co-creator David Greenwalt, were making adjustments to the show's format that had convinced the network that it was worth investing in for a second year.[1] Following the announcement, the final episodes of *Angel's* first season were produced. All of which, as we shall examine later in this essay, made contributions to the show's readjustment.

Three years later, during the fourth season, the producers were talking about redefining *Angel* once again, but this time under very different circumstances. The show, although now critically lauded, was approaching the end of the season with no decision made upon its future. It had been operating without *Buffy* as a lead-in for two years and its ratings, although consistent, were lower than at any other time in its run. Greenwalt, now a consulting producer, described the new direction the *Angel* producers were cooking up as '*Angel* meets *West Wing* meets *LA Law* [...]. It's not going to be dreary and dark. He can walk in the sun. I am so sick of this no-sun thing [...]. To me, it's like a brand-new show.'[2] The 'new show' was premiered in the Season Four finale 'Home' (4:22) and, consequently, the show was renewed for a fifth season.

When examining *Angel* on a season-by-season basis, much emphasis is placed on Mutant Enemy's tradition of planning each year's plot as an arc to be resolved by the following summer, whilst contributing to a larger story of the series. Reading the structure of the series, therefore, could be seen as simply relating each episode into its relative season context. However, although this may be the impression produced by *Angel*'s fine plotting, it pays no attention to the fact that *Angel* is, first and foremost, an American network television series that finds itself influenced by a multitude of industry factors in the course of a ten-month production season. Most critical, as far as this essay is concerned, are the demands of the networks who produce and air *Angel* because, when it comes to deciding whether to renew a series, the strength of plots and critical acclaim are not the criteria on which such decisions are made. In 1974 Martin Seiden suggested that television drama was not really controlled by programme makers, or indeed the networks, so much as by Nielson Media Group's analyses of programmes' viewer ratings. In 1980 Muriel Cantor concurred that there was 'little controversy that the Nielson ratings are a powerful force in American broadcasting'.[3] Higher ratings mean a series can draw increased revenue from its advertising, but a low-rated series can effectively lose money for its network. *Angel*, like genre television in general, did not attract immensely high viewing figures. Networks, though, still make a specific demand on genre series: audience upside. This is the ability for shows, especially those that have run for several years, to increase their viewership. So if the current season has failed to consistently attract new viewers, then it doesn't matter how steady its ratings are: the series is still unlikely to be recommissioned.

This viewer/advertising relationship is most critical during 'sweeps' periods. These come in November, February and May when Nielson collects demographic viewing data from sample homes in every one of the 210 television markets in the United States.[4] Networks will set their advertising rates by how high viewership is in these periods. To viewers, the sweeps have become synonymous with heavily promoted episodes often featuring big-name guest casting or, in the case of a spin-off like *Angel*, crossovers of popular characters. Putting aside those who later become regulars, the *Buffy* character with the most appearances in sweeps episodes is Faith, the troubled slayer turned killer and villain. In many ways she represents Buffy's dark side and, therefore, her crossover to *Angel* may appear to be a standard sweeps promotion. However, Faith and Angel established a connection on *Buffy* on account of their shared experiences of darkness. In 'Consequences' (B3:15), several months before Angel's move to LA, Faith's soul became the first which he tried to save.

As I will demonstrate, Faith's status as Angel's first 'client' serves the series as a chance for redefinition. Her appearances in Seasons One and Four allow not only the showcasing of a popular character and plenty of action sequences, but also give an opportunity to reaffirm *Angel*'s original mission. Once affirmed, the format by which that mission is carried out can be radically changed. Whedon and company may be praised for their forward planning but, I argue, the true success of *Angel* has been its ability to react to outside influences and, when facing an uncertain future, its willingness to completely reformat itself around its original creative vision. The business of producing sweeps episodes on network television can be a cynical one but, for *Angel,* the character of Faith has made the process much more proactive and, arguably, the greatest strength of the series' structure.

Faith's first season appearances, 'Five by Five' (1:18) and 'Sanctuary' (1:19), mark *Angel's* third and fourth direct cross-overs with *Buffy* after 'In the Dark' (1:3) and 'I Will Remember You' (1:8). All these episodes share certain structural patterns. A Sunnydale resident arrives in LA to act as an antagonist to Angel. He does something to undermine their objectives, forcing them to return to Sunnydale unfulfilled and allowing Angel to assert his independence as a character and, therefore, a series. *Angel's* very conscious identification with LA plays a key role in this. Both Spike in 'In the Dark' and Buffy in 'Sanctuary' are told by Angel that LA is 'my town' and 'my city', the latter instance being particularly important since Buffy describes Sunnydale as 'hers'. The ending of 'Sanctuary' is the most complete, with Angel emphasizing to Buffy not just a difference of location but also of mission statement, marking the final appearance of Buffy in *Angel*: 'This wasn't about you, it was about saving somebody's soul. That's what I do here, it's nothing to do with you.'

Faith, however, does not fit into this established pattern. In 'Five by Five' she arrives in LA and is duly set up as the antagonist for the episode when she is hired by Wolfram & Hart to assassinate Angel. By 'Sanctuary' this plan has failed but Faith does not leave the city, even with the threats posed by Buffy and the Watchers' Council. Faith decides to remain in LA, serving a prison sentence for her crimes, with Angel, as we see in 'Judgement' (2:1), watching over her.

The significance of this plot to both series is not simply the crossover of Faith's character, but that in LA she is able to find the home that she could not in Sunnydale. Faith's last appearance in Sunnydale is in 'Who Are You?' (B4:16) where she switches bodies with Buffy and sets out to destroy her life. However, Whedon, who wrote the episode, comments that by its conclusion Faith 'actually wants to be Buffy'.[5] This is something Faith can't achieve, because Buffy refuses to see her in any other way than as an enemy. And, in matters of the mystical, Buffy alone embodies Sunnydale moral authority, as she comments to Xander and Willow in 'Selfless' (B7:5) when faced with the prospect of killing Anya:

> *Buffy:*   It's always complicated. And at some point, someone has to draw the line, and that is always going to be me ... There's no mystical guidebook. No all-knowing council. Human rules don't apply. There's only me. I am the law.

Faith may also be a slayer but, having abused her powers, betrayed her friends and committed murder with no remorse she has broken the law of Sunnydale and so must be destroyed. Sunnydale is a place of absolutes, not one that recognizes the need for redemption and 'saving someone's soul'. That place is Los Angeles.

Angel performs many of the same duties as Buffy in LA, but occupies a very different moral space. He is a champion, and is described as such on numerous occasions, but he does not possess any moral authority because he has committed numerous crimes in his past life. He helps people not because he is anointed to do so, but because he wants to atone for his past sins even though, as he comments to Faith in 'Sanctuary', that may be a hopeless aim: 'The truth is, no matter how much you suffer and how many good deeds you do you'll probably never do enough to balance out the cosmic scale.' Angel understands the fundamentals of the path to redemption: it's not about short cuts like Faith becoming Buffy (or, in his case, becoming invulnerable in 'In the Dark' or human in 'I Will Remember You') but about taking responsibility for past actions and accepting the guilt that comes with them. By the end of 'Sanctuary', Faith has not gained redemption but she realizes that to find it, she must become its servant. This is something which Buffy cannot understand, and so she must leave LA. Not only has Faith torn Buffy and Angel apart, but she has also torn their two series with them. Crucially, though, we are left on the side of Angel because, in LA, Buffy's Sunnydale morality makes her appear to be a monster:

Angel:	Buffy, let's talk.
Buffy:	Oh, I don't think talk is in order right now.
Angel:	She needs help.
Buffy:	Help? Do you have any idea what she did to me?
Angel:	Yes.
Buffy:	Do you care?
Angel:	She wants to change. She has a chance to …
Buffy:	No. No chance. Jail.
Angel:	You think that'll help?
Faith:	Buffy … I'm sor—
Buffy:	Apologize to me and I will beat you to death.

We are also left, though, with a slightly different interpretation of Angel's purpose. His mission statement thus far in the series has been 'helping the hopeless'.[6] Essentially, this is what he does for Faith. However, whereas every other episode of the series (barring crossovers) has been about Angel solving problems in people's lives, Faith's is the one problem he cannot solve because it is his own. This is emphasized in 'Five by Five' through several motifs shared by the characters.

Faith's arrival in LA is paralleled with flashbacks to Angel's birth (that is, Angelus' ensoulment) in 1898. We watch Angel attack a woman in an attempt to continue being Angelus, but see him fail because his soul will not allow him to simply be a monster. Similarly, Faith tries to convince Angel that she is nothing but an animal. Tormented by her guilt, though, she pleads for Angel to kill her: 'Do you hear me? I'm bad! I'm bad! I'm bad. Please. Angel, please, just do it … Just kill me.' Faith's activities also draw parallels from those in Angel's life. She harms those closest to him just to 'get Angel into the game', reminding us of tactics Angelus used against Buffy in 'Passion' (B2:17). And her torture of former Watcher, Wesley, reminds us of the similar ordeal endured by Buffy's Watcher, Giles, at the hands of Angelus in 'Becoming Pt. 2' (B2:22).

Therefore, although we're watching Faith's commencement on the road to redemption, we're also seeing Angel re-commit to his own. Effectively, 'Five by Five' and 'Sanctuary' together represent a second pilot episode to *Angel*. Not just by reiterating the series' core values but also introducing their own set of new motifs and iconography. Wesley, for example, is reintroduced to us as a dramatic, rather than comedic, character when he shrugs off an offer of forgiveness from the Watchers' Council in order to solidify his allegiance to Angel and earn his own redemption. And the image of Angel cradling a crying Faith becomes a central part of *Angel's* visual iconography by featuring every week in the opening credits.

Perhaps most importantly of all, these episodes see the overarching nemesis of Wolfram & Hart shift from being merely a representation of Angel's struggle against the evils of the big city to becoming a tangible, human threat. Representatives from Wolfram & Hart previously appeared in 'City Of' (1:1), 'Parting Gifts' (1:10) and 'The Ring' (1:16) but always on the periphery of the plot, represented by nameless lawyers, business cards and emblazoned suitcases (i.e. symbols of corporate America) rather than by familiar adversaries. This was an intentional design choice by Whedon and Greenwalt to allow *Angel* to feature a consistent force of evil who wouldn't need to be trying to kill Angel each week to prove to be a threat to him.[7] However, the move to a series mythology centring on Angel himself necessitated a much more personal struggle. Therefore the characters of Lilah Morgan and Lindsey McDonald are reintroduced, the latter as a direct adversary when Angel infiltrates Wolfram & Hart and confronts him for the first time.[8] In terms of the plot of 'Five by Five', their exchange actually serves little purpose. We don't know why Angel goes undercover, he finds nothing in Lindsey's office and the two do not trade anything other than threats and innuendo. However, coupled with his appearances in the final episodes of the season, 'Blind Date' (1:21) and 'To Shanshu in LA' (1:22), where he spurns redemption in favour of power and authority, Lindsey is built into a direct adversary to Angel's mission.

'Five by Five' and 'Sanctuary' mark the watershed when Whedon and Greenwalt rejustify Angel's role from being guardian to becoming the protagonist in a mythology. In the concluding three episodes of the first season we see the new structure of the show begin to take shape. 'War Zone' (1:20) introduces Charles Gunn, designed expressly to become a series regular and 'build up the ensemble'.[9] He reappears in 'Blind Date' and 'To Shanshu in LA', both of which focus on Wolfram & Hart's upper hierarchy, the Senior Partners, continuing the assault on Angel begun by Lindsey and Lilah. They launch direct attacks on the lives of Wesley and Cordelia, and finally resurrect Darla, whose renewed acquaintance with Angel propels much of the mythology of the next three seasons.

Angel's new format, though, did not result in substantial viewer gains and by the middle of the fourth season, several factors were contributing to low ratings and a genuine threat of cancellation. Most notable was the WB's loss of *Buffy* to the United Paramount Network (UPN) at the end of *Angel's* second season. As well as losing its natural lead-in for viewers, *Angel* had no definite place in the WB's schedules. The efforts to find one resulted in moving timeslots three times in a year and a half. *Angel's* move around the schedules didn't actively reduce its core audience (as producer Steven S. DeKnight remarked: 'We were convinced being up against *Alias* [at the beginning of Season Four] would crush us and then we got the same numbers.'[10]), however, it did reduce the ability of casual viewers to follow the series. And none of its new timeslots resulted in a growth of audience for *Angel*.

Arguably, though, the show's stylistic tone in the fourth season also contributed to Angel's inability to attract a new audience. Although Seasons Two and Three had been mythology-based they had both broken up their arcs with stand-alone episodes. After 'The House Always Wins' (4:3), though, the fourth season was entirely based around the ongoing storyline. As producer Jeffrey Bell observed, 'I think if you were inside the umbrella it was the most emotionally satisfying year we've ever had [...]. But if you were outside of it [...] the response was, "I don't know what the Hell is going on, so I'm going to go and watch *The Bachelor*."'[11]

In the middle of the season, the WB asked *Angel's* producers to make a proposal for the fifth. Essentially, Whedon and his team were being asked to concoct another radical format change. The challenge was to balance the network's demand that the series be made more accessible on a weekly basis, whilst still maintaining the strength of the relationships between *Angel*'s large ensemble cast. Those changes were outlined in the season finale, 'Home', an episode designed by writer Tim Minear 'so that it would basically be a pilot for next season'.[12] However, there are several elements central to the act of redefining the series which don't take place in 'Home'. By the time Angel Investigations take their tour of Wolfram & Hart, it's clear that neither Cordelia nor Connor will be joining them. Perhaps most important, though, is the fact that there is no restatement of *Angel*'s original creative vision in 'Home' which, as we saw in 'Five by Five' and 'Sanctuary', is a crucial element of justifying a new series format. These elements had already been laid earlier in the season, once again during sweeps episodes and, again, utilizing Faith.

The beginning of the 'Salvage'/'Release'/'Orpheus' arc (4:13–15) finds Angel Investigations at its weakest. Mid-Season Four LA is a post-apocalyptic world littered with fallen heroes and, significantly, without redemption. With the sun blotted out, the laws of the night operate on a permanent basis. Angel is no longer the guardian of LA as he should be because he has relinquished his soul and become Angelus. Angelus, as we discover in 'Orpheus', regards Angel's mission as torture and so consciously sets himself up to be its antithesis. Whereas Angel helps the helpless, Angelus preys upon them, saving a young girl from vampires in 'Salvage' only to attack her himself. The rest of Angel Investigations have also turned away from their mission. Cordelia is currently possessed by an evil spirit and Wesley, although now basically operating with Angel Investigations, has not had a proper reconciliation with the group after having taken baby Connor and subsequently being rejected by Angel ('Forgiving', 3:17). It is he who, in 'Calvary' (4.12), defines the parameters of the hunt for Angelus that exclude any hope of redemption. 'Our only advantage is that Angelus might think we want to capture him, I think we're all agreed that's not an option anymore […]. Take the shot, any shot you can get.' It's

Wesley, though, who in 'Salvage' begins to reclaim the importance of redemption when he is confronted by his imagined vision of Lilah:

> *Lilah:* For all your supposed darkness, your edge-of-the-razor mystique, there was always a small part of you that thought you could pull me back from the brink of my evil, evil ways. Help me find redemption.
>
> *Wesley:* Redemption ...
>
> *Lilah:* Angel's influence, I suppose. The whole 'not giving up on someone no matter how far he or she has fallen'.

That realization leads Wesley to Faith. She, despite being incarcerated, is the person most suited to saving Angel because she is on the redemption road herself. Wesley does not even have to try and set the guidelines for the hunt for Angelus before Faith makes her feelings on the matter clear:

> *Faith:* I'm not gonna kill him, Wesley ... Don't care what you thought you sprung me for. Angel's the only one in my life who's never given up on me.
>
> *Wesley:* I know. That's why it had to be you.

Faith's words, and most of her actions in 'Salvage', play out like a subverted 'Sanctuary', with Faith taking Angel's role and the more cynical factions of Angel Investigations serving as Buffy. Faith is the one who, despite having been imprisoned for two and a half years, is now affirming *Angel's* mission because she is unwilling to make any compromises on Angel's redemption.

Faith's impact on Angel himself is, most obviously, to help him defeat Angelus and to reclaim his place in the world. However, in doing this she must face challenges to her own redemption. Most notably from Angelus in 'Release', when he tries to goad her into rejecting her humanity and accepting that she, like him, is a monster hidden beneath a soul:

> *Angelus:* Now you know how it feels, forced to be someone you're not. Try to bury the fiend but you can't get the whole demon out ... I could beat you to death

and it won't make a difference, nothing can ever
change what you are, Faith. You're a murderer, an
animal and you enjoy it. Just like me.

Faith: You're wrong. I'm different now. I'm not like you.

This is a conscious subversion of 'Five by Five', where Faith
was forced to admit that in her heart she could not be the
monster she wanted to be. Angelus' 'lessons' are completely
in opposition to those of Angel but in the chaos of 'Release'
even Wesley does not reject them out of hand: 'Angelus is an
animal, the only way to defeat him is to be just as vicious as
he is.'

Angel, therefore, needs to reassert himself to restore order
to the series and he does so in 'Orpheus'. In fact, his first act is
to impart a new lesson to the weakened Faith. She, having
infiltrated Angelus' psyche and watched Angel stand up to
his alter ego, believes she has found her redemption and is
ready to die. Angel, though, must remind her that true
redemption is that which has no end in sight:

Angel: I used to think that there'd be a point where I'd
          paid my dues
Faith: I served my time.
Angel: Our time is never up. Faith, we pay for everything.

By the end of 'Orpheus', Faith is ready to return to Sunnydale
not because she has finally achieved redemption, but because
she has learnt that pursuing it means doing the duty allotted
to her. In her case, that's being a slayer and in Angel's, it's
being a champion.

It is that reaffirmation that is directly challenged by the
offer delivered by Lilah in 'Home'. She offers Wolfram &
Hart's resources to Angel: firstly to secure Connor's future
and then to fight evil. However, what she describes to Angel
is a scenario which completely undercuts the champion status
he and Faith fought for: 'People don't need a champion, they
need a man that can compromise and fight from within the
belly of the beast.' This is not the first time Lilah has offered
Angel the chance to compromise his mission. In her first
appearance in 'The Ring' she offers to buy his freedom from

slavery in exchange for him 'picking the battles [he] can win'. On that occasion, Angel refuses but in 'Home' he accepts.

Wolfram & Hart's offer isn't just limited to Angel himself, however. Indeed, it seems key to Lilah's actions in 'Home' that the firm wants Angel Investigations to join as a team, not just as individuals. The fact that the fractured group of 'Salvage' is able to become the one facing collective temptation in 'Home' owes a lot to Faith. Her most notable contribution is to Wesley who, by in turns tending to her wounds and then assisting her capture of Angelus, reclaims both the mantle of Watcher he lost in 'Consequences' and, more importantly, his leadership within Angel Investigations. As Faith remarks, 'You ran a good show.'

There are, however, two notable exceptions to Faith's restoring influence. Neither Cordelia or Connor make a commitment to Angel's salvation. Cordelia instantly spurns Faith's arrival, calling her 'psycho slayer' and having nothing to do with her. At the end of 'Salvage', she reveals her pregnancy to Connor and forces him into a commitment with her which doesn't extend to the rest of the group: 'We're connected now .... You and me ... forever.' They become the antagonists to redemption when Connor, on Cordelia's orders, tries to kill Angel at the conclusion of 'Orpheus'. Although Faith manages to stop him, he and Cordelia are permanently separated from the group and are not offered the Wolfram & Hart deal in 'Home'.

In terms of series structure, the effect of 'Home' is logical: by removing their central opposition, Angel Investigations can now be justified to fight a number of different battles and foes. And, therefore, justified to move away from the all-encompassing story arc which alienated casual viewers in the previous season. However, that doesn't mean that the series reverts back to Season One's 'guardian Angel' principle. By building Angel Investigations' new operation as both a compromise of the mission Faith fought to reassert in 'Orpheus', and a team effort, a more subtle sort of arc is created. Each individual case can stand alone, but each contributes to Angel Investigations' growing sense of their own corruption. In

'Sanctuary', asserting and affirming Angel's mission allowed for the commencement of a single, focused struggle. In 'Orpheus' and 'Home', reasserting and compromising that same mission allows for multiple struggles, but actually increases the emphasis upon the restructured Angel Investigations.[13]

Angel Investigations began their fifth season having compromised their mission, and the series itself began not knowing how long its latest configuration would survive on screen.[14] Neither they, nor Faith, reached a certain future but they demonstrated the necessity of real change to keep them on the road, whether it be towards redemption or further episodes. What they gain from surviving each crisis point isn't fully fledged redemption or crushing defeat in the face of compromise but something almost as important: justification to keep doing what they do.

NOTES

1 Joss Whedon, quoted in *Sci-Fi Wire* (21 February 1999), at http://www.scifi.com/sfw/issue149/news.html. David Greenwalt commented that the tone of the series had also been adjusted: 'Angel himself is so dark, and the things he's done in his background are so bleak, that we needed to balance the show with some lighter, brighter sides of LA.' *Sci-Fi Wire* (25 September 2000), at http://www.scifi.com/sfw/issue179/interview.html.

2 David Greenwalt, speaking to Zap2It TV, 'Producer Admires *Angel* from Afar' (12 May 2003), at http://tv.zap2it.com/news/tvnewsdaily.html?31560.

3 Muriel Cantor, *Prime Time Television: Content and Control*, (California: Sage, 1980), p. 76.

4 The name 'sweeps' refers to the process by which Nielson mails out diaries to certain households around the country, then collects and processes the diaries in a specific order. The diaries from the northeast regions are processed first and then 'swept up' in a geographical progression throughout the USA, from the south to the midwest and then finally to the west.

5 Joss Whedon, 'Overview Featurette', *Buffy Season Four DVD Collection*, 20th Century Fox Home Entertainment (F1-DGB 22848DVD) Region 2.

 6 At least, that's Cordelia's interpretation in 'I Fall to Pieces' (1:4)
    and it's particularly pertinent to Faith. By 'Darla' (2:7) the phrase
    has become 'we help the helpless'.
 7 Joss Whedon and David Greenwalt talk about the genesis
    behind Wolfram & Hart on their audio commentary to 'City Of',
    Angel Season One DVD Collection, 20th Century Fox Home Enter-
    tainment (F1-DGB 22830DVD) Region 2.
 8 Infiltrating Wolfram & Hart itself becomes one of the recurring
    motifs of the series. Angel returns to the building in 'Blind Date'
    and, by the third and fourth seasons, seems to be threatening the
    senior staff on a weekly basis.
 9 Whedon, *Sci-Fi Wire* (21 February 1999).
10 Steven S. DeKnight interviewed on CityofAngel.com (31 March
    2003), at http://cityofangel.com/behindTheScenes/bts3/
    deKnight2.html.
11 Jeffery Bell interviewed in '*Angel* Evolutions', *Cinefantastique*, 35:
    5 (2003), p. 55.
12 Tim Minear commenting to Zap2It TV, '*Angel* Finale Offers End-
    ings and Beginnings' (26 April 2003), at http://tv.zap2it.com/
    tveditorial/tve_main/1,1002,271|81252|1|,00.html.
13 Spike's addition to *Angel*'s fifth season was due, in part, to Faith.
    Earlier in the fourth season, the two popular characters were
    earmarked to star in a second *Buffy* spin-off. These plans had to
    be put aside, though, after Eliza Dushku signed on to star in
    Fox's *Tru Calling*. As a result, the WB specifically requested
    Spike's crossover to *Angel*.
14 Although *Angel*'s fifth season did succeed in attracting and
    maintaining higher viewing figures, the WB decided not to
    order a sixth. According to WB president Jordan Levin the series
    still 'didn't have a tremendous amount of new audience upside'.
    It was a move which mystified Whedon as much as *Angel*'s fans:
    'I thought that if a show was really good and doing really well
    [in the ratings], it was renewed, I was apparently misinformed.'
    Levin and Whedon, 'Variety, Frog Net's Drama *Angel* Folds
    Wings' (16 February 2004), at http://www.variety.com/article/
    VR1117900126?categoryid=14&cs=1.

2

Ubi Caritas?: *Music as Narrative Agent in* Angel[1]

MATTHEW MILLS

While the literature devoted to the study of film music has increased in recent years, comparatively scant attention has been paid to music used in television. Although there has been some discussion of the use of popular music in comedy/drama series such as *Ally McBeal*, an exploration of music's potential to elucidate the narrative of a medium where the episodes are viewed in separate instalments spread across several weeks (or years) has not yet been attempted.[2] In the television shows of Joss Whedon, however, music is given an uncommonly high prominence, and *Angel* in particular is saturated with themes of musical performance. Its range of musical reference is unusually wide, from traditional nineteenth-century operatic gestures, through local musical traditions (particularly in flashback sequences), to the more recent genres of popular music. Although it is impossible in a chapter of this size to discuss these issues fully, I hope that this discussion will enable the reader to appreciate the artful way in which music contributes to the show's narrative world.

Theorists have tended to categorize the functions of film music roughly as follows: (1) to provide continuity, establish structural boundaries and generate changes of intensity and pace; (2) to imply historical or geographical settings, from either within or without the narrative context; (3) to externalize the thoughts of a character, set particular moods, or function more generally as a signifier of emotion.[3] Music in *Angel* functions in all of these ways. Much of the music accompanying the drama (the 'underscore') is repeated on more than one occasion, and this repetition can influence the way we 'read' the music's meaning. Since we automatically associate what we see with what we hear, a few seconds' worth of music can recall characters and events far more efficiently than, for instance, a flashback. Inherent in this recollection is a comparison between the two situations, and it is by stimulating such comparison that thematic repetition can play an important narrative role. Recurring music gradually accrues meaning as it gathers new associations. Often, different or contradictory associations create a dialectic space, a kind of thematic friction that generates secondary implications for the narrative, further nuancing the viewer's interpretation of characters and situations. For this process to work efficiently, however, the music must work primarily *as* underscore. The challenge for the composer is, therefore, to be sensitive not only to the music's narrative potential, but also to the immediate musical requirements of the scene to be underscored.

Angel makes much use of music as a geographical and historical locator. This might involve using a certain genre or style, as in the 'medieval' music in 'Through the Looking Glass' (2:21), the Mariachi band in the scenes in 'Heartthrob' (3:1) set in Nicaragua, or the Irish fiddle and 'trad. jazz' band in the flashbacks in 'Orpheus' (4:15), set in turn-of-the-century New York and 1920s Chicago respectively. Also, pre-existing music from the time or place in which a scene is set, such as Perry Como's 'Hoop-De-Doo' in 'Are You Now, or Have You Ever Been' (2:2), might be used to evoke the place or period in question. Musical allusion to other genres, or even specific shows, might likewise evoke a sense of location or set the tone of a particular episode. The use of shakuhachi, for instance, as Harmony and Tamika assume martial arts fighting stances with their chopsticks in 'Harm's Way' (5:9) alludes ironically to martial arts films, while in 'Ground State' (4:2), the oboe–piano–string orchestration of the opening sequence recalls

Mark Snow's music for *The X-Files*, matching the teaser sequence's more general allusion to that show, and the jazzy riffs that accompany the heist scene parody the music for *Mission: Impossible* (Brian De Palma, 1996), just as Gwen's entry mirrors Ethan Hunt's break-in to the CIA in that film.

The theme that recurs most frequently is associated with Angel himself (Figure 1). Accompanying scenes of heroism – usually fight scenes – it is often loud, played by brass instruments, accompanied by detached, syncopated rhythmic figures, in the manner of generic 'action music'. In other, more reflective situations, it may be played on wind instruments, strings, or the piano. At a slower tempo, played softly, the same melody has a very different implication.

Figure 1

The process of making a theme's initial associations explicit is vitally important to the technique's success, so it is no surprise that Angel's theme is featured heavily in 'City Of' (1:1). The teaser sequence, showing Angel fighting vampires, is accompanied by stock-in-trade action music: loud, fast, syncopated and rhythmic. On two occasions we hear the melody on brass, first during the fight itself, and then again as Angel leaves, accompanied by sustained chords.

Later, when Doyle challenges Angel – 'are you game?' – to take a more difficult, socially oriented view of salvation, thereby offering him a chance to find the redemption he craves, we hear only the first four notes of his theme. Its last note hovers uneasily, unresolved, the theme's incompleteness mirroring Angel's inability to answer Doyle's question. The use of the clarinet played softly generates a sense of intimacy that maps onto the dialogue, especially Angel's almost confessional line, 'I'm not good with people'. It is particularly through the use of musical recollection of the opening fight sequence that this scene achieves its pathos: the man who walks into a dark alley to save two girls is afraid of having to strike up a conversation with a woman he doesn't know. We hear the theme when Doyle poses the question again. Angel is in a newly socialized environment. His home and (soon to be) office is brighter than in earlier scenes, when it was sombre and uninviting. Musically, there is a brief respite from minor tonality, and the theme is developed sequentially and reharmonized – the first time that it is not simply reiterated in its original form. Its reintroduction in its heroic guise as Angel answers Doyle's question brings a sense of determination to his affirmative answer.

In 'I Will Remember You' (1:8), when Angel visits the Oracles for a second time, a higher-pitched melody reflects the otherworldliness of their domain. The extremely slow tempo, soft dynamic and use of the clarinet – as in 'City Of', denoting intimacy – add emotive weight to the Oracles' sympathy for Angel, as the hierarchical boundaries are momentarily breached. The minor-key closure coincides with the Oracles' description of the results of the temporal fold, the moment of transcendence quickly giving way to a radiant gloom. Heroism, after all, implies sacrifice.

We hear the theme again in 'In the Dark' (1:3) when Angel saves another girl in an alley, in 'Hero' (1:9) as he fights the Scourge, and as he amputates Lindsey's hand in 'To Shanshu in LA' (1:22) – augmenting the association with Angel's destiny, as Lindsey is burning the Shanshu scroll when he loses his hand. Season One is littered with recurrences of Angel's theme, all associated with an aspect of Angel's identity. In 'I've Got You Under My Skin' (1:14), it plays as Seth Anderson tells Angel 'maybe you are an angel'. The idea of Angel as a 'hero-for-hire' is also represented musically: in 'Lonely Heart' (1:2), the theme is played as Angel gives Kate his business card, and in 'I Fall To Pieces' (1:4), we hear it again as Angel says 'Guess I'm going to work'.

The theme occurs less regularly as the show progresses. In Season Two, as Angel's obsession with Darla leads him down an ever darker path, the theme almost disappears entirely.

This is not surprising, given Angel's uncharacteristically amoral behaviour. As Darla observes after he has set her and Drusilla on fire in 'Redefinition' (2:11), 'That wasn't Angel. It wasn't Angelus, either … Who was that?' As Angel's actions belie the qualities his theme has come to represent, so the theme itself disappears from the underscore.

The theme returns, like Angel-the-hero, in 'Epiphany' (2:16): we hear it twice over shots of Angel 'borrowing' Lindsey's truck, again as he saves Cordelia and the others from the Skilosh demons, and a fourth time as he tells Kate of his 'epiphany'. This final statement recalls Angel's connection to the Powers That Be, as Kate reminds him that he entered her flat to save her without an invitation. We hear the theme in 'Heartthrob', as Angel defeats the demon monks, but only infrequently thereafter, until Season Five. It occurs twice in the opening scene of 'Conviction' (5:1), in similar circumstances to its first occurrence in 'City Of', providing both a sense of continuity, and a welcome burst of familiarity in a very different, and not always entirely successful, final season. It makes its last appearance in 'You're Welcome' (5:12), as Angel says to Lindsey 'I'm Angel', reiterating his musical 'identification'. Beyond this, however, little use is made of the theme in Season Five. This is resonant with the morally ambiguous position Angel is seen to occupy, alerting both his team and the viewer to the possibility that Wolfram & Hart's darker powers may have seduced him. In this necessary deception, the music conspires with Angel against us: the underscore could have been used to suggest that Angel-the-hero was still going strong, but it is in Season Five's nature to keep the viewer guessing, and the music reflects that.

Angel's theme is also used as a simple identifier: in 'Guise Will Be Guise' (2:6), it accompanies Wesley's entrance wearing Angel's overcoat, as he announces 'I'm Angel'. In 'Carpe Noctum' (3:4), as Angel (in Marcus' body) looks at himself in the mirror, the score confirms for us that Marcus' spell switched his and Angel's bodies. Similarly, in 'Conviction', when the girl in the alley asks Angel 'Who are you?', the underscore answers her with Angel's theme.

A beautiful theme is allocated to Doyle in the two adjacent Season One episodes 'Hero' and 'Parting Gifts' (1:9 and 1:10). The musical procedures employed are remarkably similar to the treatment of Angel's theme. In a partial flashback sequence, Doyle tells Angel of his previous encounter with the Scourge, accompanied by a haunting wordless vocal solo (Figure 2). Although the music functions as a general 'tragic' theme, its use in flashback, accompanying Doyle's narration, suggests more than that: it evokes Doyle's past and his inability to accept himself as half-demon, which led to his failure to save the Brachen demons from the Scourge. Beyond his immediate horror at what he saw, this theme also gives voice to Doyle's guilt and his need to atone for his failure.

Figure 2

The second – interrupted – statement of the theme invites a comparison. Rieff, pursued by Doyle, ran away from his family in an attempt to escape from his demon roots. When he thinks he sees Doyle's corpse, a parallel situation is immediately established in the underscore. Doyle saw the massacred demons because he could not accept himself; Rieff now sees a 'death' he believes is due to his own failure to accept his demon lineage.

That Rieff's running away almost led to another Scourge massacre, by delaying the departure of the ship, is especially significant for the next occurrence of the theme, which consists of three successive repetitions. The first and third, as Doyle says goodbye and as Angel and Cordelia take in his death, are melancholic; the second is triumphant and heroic as he disconnects the Beacon and dies. By this time, the theme has come to represent not only his own, but also Rieff's difficulty in accepting the legacy of a demon parent. Through his self-sacrifice, Doyle atones for his previous failure, but he also prevents a massacre that Rieff would have been partly responsible for, and so spares *him* a similar guilt. Now understanding how Angel does what he does, he demonstrates a bravery that previously baffled him. Having presented Angel with a chance to atone for his past, he sees a similar chance for himself, and takes it.

In 'Parting Gifts', Doyle's theme is truncated upon each of its three further appearances. The first, as Cordelia tells Barney about Doyle, features only the first four bars, played on the flute. When Angel tells Wesley he had a partner, we hear the first two bars only, as we do when Cordelia frames the picture of her first vision as a memento of Doyle, in both cases played on the piano, accompanied by strings. It is as if Doyle's theme recedes as his colleagues come to terms with his death.

The theme also appears much later, in 'Power Play' (5:21), when Angel tells his team about his planned massacre of the Black Thorn, which is likely to be a suicide mission; it begins as Spike says, 'I'm in'. Such a long-range thematic connection, recalling a character whose departure many fans deplored, demonstrates that no matter how different Season Five is to Season One, the team's fundamental premise is the same. With the hindsight of knowing the series was shortly to end, the musical reminiscence also has a poignant nostalgia – a recollection of the past that emphasizes just how much things have changed, and how radically the show has transformed itself.

Musical repetition can also function as comparator in a much more localized way. For example, in 'The Prodigal' (1:15), the wordless female voice accompanying the flashback of Angelus killing his father is repeated as Angel watches vampires kill Kate's father, powerless to stop them. Similarly, Wesley sings Brahms' 'Wiegenlied' to baby Connor in 'Sleep Tight' (3:16), inadvertently alerting Lorne to his plan. After Wesley knocks Lorne out, the piano plays a distorted version of the Brahms, underlining the unsettling juxtaposition of Wesley's father-like kindness and his sudden violence.

Themes can also be 'interrupted': broken off abruptly, or changed in such an unexpected way that the music the viewer expects is not delivered, emphasizing an unusual situation.

The teaser sequence to 'War Zone' (1:20) exemplifies this technique. As the vampires close in on the girl in the alley, a truck pulls up, the vampires turn round, and their leader sneers 'You!'; Angel's theme begins, the camera tilts up from a man's feet, taking in a long, dark overcoat. As Charles Gunn's face comes into shot, the music breaks off, and he asks 'You expectin' someone else?' – which we were. The sudden abandonment of the theme and interrupted harmonic progression map first and foremost onto our own surprise. But there is more than mere shock involved here. The underscore would seem to imbue Gunn with all of the qualities associated by now with Angel. Gunn appears to be doing Angel's job, and the score at first implies that he is a hero for it. As it turns out, Gunn doesn't share Angel's heroism: he is not *destined* to fight evil in this way, he *chooses* to; nor is he seeking redemption through it; his reason at this stage is left unstated. Moreover, he is also reckless: his sister is sired by a vampire when a similar trap goes wrong, and Gunn is forced to kill her. The interrupted cadence in fact calls into question Gunn's possession of the attributes that the music has helped to identify with Angel. Although the underscore plays to our initial expectations – expectations fostered deliberately through repeated music–image association – its use here is in some senses 'super-narrative', for it invites us to draw conclusions that the characters themselves do not, retrospectively indicating that this man is not Angel, and it makes its point by undermining its most immediate implication, namely, heroism on the part of the character on screen. The statement of this theme in 'Guise Will Be Guise', mentioned above, is interrupted identically, although the effect is rather more comical, as Wesley declares 'I'm Angel', and promptly trips over himself.

There are several 'love themes' in the series, the first of which appears in 'There's No Place Like Plrtz Glrb' (2:22) in the scenes between Groo and Cordy, reprised at the end of 'Double or Nothing' (3:18) as Gunn and Fred kiss. Also, music heard in 'Couplet' (3:14) as Groo and Cordy kiss is used again at the end of the episode as Angel watches them leave together. Finally, music used to represent Buffy and Angel's happiness in 'I Will Remember You' is heard again much later in 'Soul Purpose' (5:10), as the Blue Fairy gives Spike a heart, thereby musically linking the two vampires in their respective moments of joy.

With the introduction of Caritas and Lorne in Season Two, the show's musical focus broadens, initially as each of the characters performs karaoke, but also in the sense that musicality becomes a means of characterization, and takes on metaphorical significance. The use of songs with lyrics is a technique featured on *Buffy the Vampire Slayer*; as has been discussed by Renée Dechert, who also notes the significance of a character's musical taste.[4] In *Angel*, while a character's choice of song is often revealing *per se*, such as Fred's performance in 'That Old Gang Of Mine' (3:3) of Patsy Cline's 'Crazy' (an irony not lost on her colleagues), it is often Lorne's comment on that choice, or its performance, that is most telling. His observation that Harmony would be better named Cacophony, is surely not only a comment on her singing, but also on her intellectual disorganization. The joke is extended to the show's title, 'Disharmony' (2:17). In 'Slouching Toward Bethlehem' (4:4), Cordelia's choice of Whitney Houston's 'The Greatest Love of All' – a number which is clearly close to her heart, since she also sang it in the Season One *Buffy* episode 'The Puppet Show' (B1:9) – horrifies Lorne; he likewise describes 'the so-called musicals of Andrew Lloyd Webber' as one of the downsides to life in this dimension ('Reprise', 2:15). These judgments reinforce our sense of his musical superiority, created largely by Andy Hallett's astonishing vocal performances. This superiority adds weight to the wisdom he offers: the observation, for instance, that music is 'something beautiful, painful, and right', whose existence makes life in this dimension worthwhile ('Over the Rainbow', 2:20). Caritas, as a charmed, 'musicalized' space, is a place of hope, of self-discovery and direction, a place without violence; it is the antithesis of Pylea, a world without music, where violence is an integral part of life in a nation of warriors for whom dance is a necessary form of social expression. As master of this haven, Lorne acquires a distance that always sets him slightly apart from the Angel Investigations team, to which he never truly commits himself as the others do – as he tells Angel in the final episode, 'Not Fade Away' (5:22), 'I'm not a fighter, Angel-wings. I've never had the stomach for it.' He also acquires a narrative distance that is most fully manifested in 'Spin the Bottle' (4:6), where Lorne addresses comments directly to the television audience, even when, as he puts it, 'I know I should be unconscious at this point in the story but, can you believe these mooks?' – standing outside the diegesis to the extent that he even follows a commercial break with 'well, those were some exciting products, am I right?'.[5] He is also distinguished by the anagogic ability that gives him a power over others – be they employees at Wolfram & Hart ('Conviction'), or members of Angel's team (Wesley, for instance, in 'Sleep Tight', 3:16). Lorne's gift makes him susceptible to exploitation, a risk the vision-endowed Cordelia discovers in 'Parting Gifts'. The parallel with Cordy doesn't end there, since Lorne too, despite his power, cannot always help.[6] In 'A Hole in the World' (5:15), as Fred sings 'You Are My Sunshine' to Wesley, Lorne immediately senses Fred's fate, an instant before she collapses. Besides the obvious humour, there is doubtless a hidden meaning in his choice in 'The House Always Wins' (4:3) of 'It's Not Easy Being Green', originally performed by Kermit the Frog.

But if music is both Lorne's strength and his weakness, it is also his weapon: he uses his voice, particularly its extreme upper register, as a means of distracting attackers in 'Happy Anniversary' (2:13), 'Sleep Tight', 'The House Always Wins', and in Pylea uses song (Diana Ross' 'Stop In The Name Of Love'), an alien art-form, to distract the villagers. In 'Not Fade Away', Lindsey says that he couldn't have completed the mission without Lorne's high note in 'MacArthur Park'.

The only other good performances in Caritas come from Darla and Lindsey, neither of whom has Lorne's moral authority. When Lindsey performs 'LA' (written by David Greenwalt) in 'Dead End' (2:18), he accompanies himself on the guitar with his 'evil' hand; only at this point do we learn that he used to be a Caritas regular. Eve's relationship with Lindsey is emphasized by her performance of the same song in 'A Hole in the World'. His talent impresses the others, and arouses the jealousy of Angel, whose own, less polished, performances in the bar provide some of the show's comic highlights. Bearing in mind Simon Frith's observation that '"[s]incerity", in short, cannot be measured by searching for what lies behind the performance; if we are moved by a performer we are moved by what we *immediately* hear and see',[7] it is telling that the most duplicitous, untrustworthy characters are also those whose vocal performances most closely approach professional quality.

Angel's choice of Barry Manilow's 'Mandy' ('Judgement' 2:1) because he knows the words and thinks it's 'kinda pretty', acquires a grislier edge in a flashback in 'Orpheus', when he puts the song on the jukebox shortly before drinking from a fresh corpse – surely something he could not have dissociated from the song later – whereas its adaptation as a eulogy to Jasmine in 'The Magic Bullet' (4:19) is both hilarious and unsettling. The recurrence of particular songs – 'Mandy', 'The Greatest Love of All', 'LA', 'Lady Marmalade' – mirrors the recurring thematic material in the underscore, serving both mnemonic and structurally unifying functions.

As a musicalized space, Caritas throws into relief the other charmed musical spaces, the Tropicana Club ('The House Always Wins') and the theatre ('Waiting in the Wings', 3:13). The exploitation of Lorne's power, using his show as a means of controlling his audience's behaviour in the casino, is similar to the musical masking of the carrier wave from the puppets in 'Smile Time' (5:14). The choice of *Giselle* – the apogee of Romantic ballet, conceptualized by Théophile Gautier to honour Carlotti Grisi, who danced the title role in Paris in 1841 – to tell the story of a magically animated ballet company suspended in time by an impresario in love with his prima ballerina, is apt, to say the least. Furthermore, the ballet's plot – a peasant-girl falls in love with a count who is betrothed to another, when their love is exposed, she goes mad, dies and, as a vengeful spirit suspended in time, saves her lover from death – is mirrored and reversed in the Blinnikov love-triangle implied by Angel and Cordy's encounter in the dressing-room. In this scene, they seem to act out a tryst between the ballerina and *her* lover, rendering Cordy's boredom – 'the magic of the ballet? Not really doing it for me' – rather ironic.[8] Although the underscore to these scenes is not original *Giselle*, it apes the mood and tone of Adolphe Adam's music, conveying the sense that the magic is not restricted to the stage, conflating past and present as Angel and Cordy act out the dancers' secret desires, mirroring their own as-yet unacknowledged attraction.

As even this cursory discussion shows, music plays a pivotal role in *Angel*. It contributes to the unfolding of its narrative structure and thematic nexus as fully, in as many ways and as subtly as a film score, and even more extensively, given the span of time over which thematic connections are developed. It would come as no surprise if, as Warner Brothers' recent press release about the series' cancellation implies, the *Angel* gone from our television screens might reappear in the cinema. That is, after all, where the music has been all along.

NOTES

1 Material presented here was delivered at the London–Oxbridge Graduate Exchange Conference, 17 November 2001, and subsequently at Royal Holloway, University of London, at the Conference on Aesthetics and Philosophy of Art at the University of Warwick, 10–11 May 2002, and at 'Blood, Text and Fears: Reading around *Buffy the Vampire Slayer*' at the University of East Anglia, Norwich, 19–20 October 2002. I am indebted to James Longstaffe, who checked earlier drafts, prepared the music examples and provided useful background information. Chris Wiley's advice in earlier stages of this research was invaluable.

2 Julie Brown, '*Ally McBeal*'s Postmodern Soundtrack', *Journal of the Royal Musical Association*, 126: 2 (2001), pp. 275–303.

3 See Claudia Gorbman, *Unheard Melodies: Narrative Film Music* (Bloomington: Indiana University Press, 1987), pp. 73–91; and

Aaron Copland, 'Tip to Moviegoers: Take Off Those Ear-Muffs', *New York Times*, 6 November 1949, Section VI, p. 28.

4 See Renée Dechert, '"My Boyfriend's in the Band!": Buffy and the Rhetoric of Music', in Rhonda V. Wilcox and David Lavery (eds), *Fighting the Forces: What's At Stake in Buffy the Vampire Slayer* (Lanham, MD: Rowman & Littlefield, 2002), pp. 218–26.

5 This fascinating episode gradually dissolves the distinction between Lorne's opening narration and the flashbacks to the diegetic 'present' which intersect it. Lorne's 'unconscious' comment, made directly to the television audience from within the diegetic 'present' (the 'past' of his narration), starkly accentuates Lorne's narrative and authoritative distance.

6 For instance, when Cordelia – who is voluntarily demonized in order to withstand her visionary gift – is first endowed with Doyle's power, she is kidnapped and only narrowly escapes ocular enucleation ('Parting Gifts', 1:10). In 'To Shanshu in LA' (1:22), she experiences a torrent of paralysing visions; the pain of others, which she experiences during these visions, prompts an enormous self-transformation. She grows increasingly frustrated at 'the cryptic visions' ('Judgement', 2:1), whose misinterpretation leads to calamity, while in 'Epiphany' (2:16), she sees a vision of her own attacker just moments before he strikes.

7 See Simon Frith, *Performing Rites: On the Value of Popular Music* (Oxford: Oxford University Press, 1996), pp. 168, 210, 215, and *passim*.

8 On *Giselle*, see Debra Craine and Judith Mackrell, *The Oxford Dictionary of Dance* (Oxford: Oxford University Press, 2000), pp. 204–5.

3

Transitions and Time:
The Cinematic Language of Angel

TAMMY A. KINSEY

Illyria: 'You ripped me out of linear progression!'
'Time Bomb' (5:18)

A ngel is an anomaly in television. Within the rubric of an essentially traditional narrative, we see many techniques common to experimental film and abstract art: the bright flashes of light, the smeared images of motion, and the odd articulation of space/time are used in many editorial transitions as well as in the visions seen by the characters in the show. The meanings implicit in those brief moments are paramount to the experience of the series as a whole. These transitions compress and expand time, move us both forward and backward in the narrative, and reveal much information in little screentime. One way to investigate the manner in which different methods bring about particular physical responses in viewers is by utilizing editing theory. These concepts provide a means of deconstructing the ways images and sequences are connected throughout the series. Viewers are engaged on levels not readily apparent through the storylines themselves and a careful investigation of this style of filmmaking is absolutely necessary to the understanding of the power (both visual and emotional) of *Angel* for its viewers.

The transitions may be simple flashes of light or elaborate sequences of information revealed through quick cuts. They are always rather short, as is customary for transitional devices designed to move us from point A to point B. They work to indicate a shift in time or place. The visions seen by the characters (first by Doyle, then Cordelia and ultimately Angel himself) are manifestations of things happening in the storyline *now*, in the *future* or (on occasion) in the *past*. The transitions do not always contain information recognizable to the viewer, but they have a definite effect on the experience of the show. The look we see in the first season of *Angel* is continually expanded upon throughout the subsequent four seasons, each with its own aesthetic stamp, yet they are all united by certain stylistic concerns.

The ways in which meaning is ascribed to any visual representation (often without conscious thought) are not accidental. Filmmakers since the early days of the motion picture have been interested in the methods of engendering specific responses in their viewers to various works. The theoretical discoveries of these early film artists are still deeply relevant today. The cinematic design elements seen in *Angel* are absolutely profound in their investigation of the temporal shifts necessitated by both the visions and spatial movements.

The physical experience of sight is paramount to the understanding of avant-garde film and to the manner of transitional abstractions in the series. Afterimages of things seen momentarily remain on the surface of the retina. Ergo, we are 'seeing' without actively seeing; we are seeing things we are not consciously aware of having ever seen at all. This is the reason for the illusion of motion pictures, as well as the way subliminal messages are placed into streams of visual information. One way of further explaining this is by examining the Phi Phenomenon.

The Phi Phenomenon is the manifestation of a perceptual illusion, often called 'apparent movement'. The effect occurs when 'two stationary lights are flashed successively. When the interval between the two lights is optimal [...] then one perceives an apparent movement of light from one location to the other.'[1] Johannes Kepler's *Ad Vitellionem Paralipomena* (1604) 'established the retinal image as the nexus between the world of light and the dark processes of the brain from which our perception of the visual world emerges'. René Descartes' *La Dioptrique* expanded upon this investigation into the operation of the eye and the mechanics of the formation of the retinal image in 1637.[2]

Early studies of the function of the eye and the development of photographic techniques ultimately played a role in the evolution of cinematic technology and theories of production. In the 1920s, Russian filmmaker Lev Kuleshov conducted experiments in the ways in which people responded to various editorial tactics. Kuleshov used a still close-up of the face of an actor, 'juxtaposed to three different frames: a plate of soup, a dead woman in a coffin, and a child playing. As a result of the juxtaposition the audience had the impression that the expression on the actor's face altered',[3] thus showing that meaning is made in the relationships between images. Sergei Eisenstein's approach to Soviet montage evolved as a means of creating greater meaning from the collision of discrete images.[4] This gestalt-like action of the brain provided observations that fuelled editing practice in both traditional narrative and avant-garde films.

Stan Brakhage (1933–2003) is perhaps the most important major figure in American avant-garde film of the modern era. His extremely impressive body of work (literally hundreds of films) is largely dedicated to explorations of vision, studies of light and movement intended to replicate the experience of seeing. In a 1993 interview, Brakhage spoke of his lifelong fascination with sight and the multitude of ways we perceive the world. 'Open-eye vision is what we are directly conscious of, but there's much more going on that we ignore. Seeing includes open-eye, peripheral and hypnagogic vision, along with moving visual thinking, dream vision and memory feedback – in short whatever affects the eyes, the brain and the nervous system'. Brakhage further complicates the notion of seeing by stating that:

Hypnagogic vision is what you see with your eyes closed
[...] It's optic feedback: the nervous system projects what
you have previously experienced – your visual memories –
into the optic nerve endings. It's also called closed-eye
vision. Moving visual thinking [...] occurs deeper in the
synapsing of the brain. It's a streaming of shapes that are
not nameable – a vast visual 'song' of the cells expressing
their inner life. Peripheral vision is what you don't pay close
attention to during the day and which surfaces at night in
your dreams. And memory feedback consists of the editing
of your remembrance. It's like a highly edited movie made
from the real.[5]

It is these various alternative notions of vision itself (human
optical phenomena) that are addressed and engaged by the
unusual aesthetic qualities of many of the transitions on
Angel, as well as (obviously) *the visions* themselves.

Physiological changes occur in the human body due to variations in the visual field, internal and external rhythms of the
shots, and the ways in which the human brain deals with the
information conveyed. These changes are stimulated by both
cinematographic and editorial choices. Variations in camera
movement (both the style and the speed), the length of the
shots themselves, and the manner in which sound and light
are used, all contribute to individual physical responses to
visual information. Each of these is crucial to the look and feel
of *Angel*, the seductive quality of its means of explication that
always leaves us wanting more. While it may seem that the
flash-flash-flashing is a simple visual tactic, one must realize
that it is used for several very specific reasons.

Some transitions are purely time-lapse in nature, employed
to move us from day to night, place to place geographically,
or to show the life of the city. Los Angeles is quite obviously a
character itself in *Angel*, and these basic time-compression
images imbue it with a kind of living, breathing pulse. This is
by far the most traditional use of a transitional element in
Angel. From the first moments of 'City Of' (1:1), it puts us into
both the geographical space and the temperament of the
show. The sun fills the frame with a deep orange tone, rising

and falling to convey the vibrancy of the place and the passing of time. The time-lapse shots of traffic movement are not unusual in themselves, but it is noteworthy that these are the first images seen in the series. We are given the context for the narrative in these recurring sequences of green, red and yellow lines of light signifying the constant flow of humans in cars, anonymous, in this big city.

It seems rudimentary, but the use of the flashes of light makes these shots of the setting sun and the movement of traffic on the highway at once more engaging than simple. The flashing is reminiscent of bolts of lightning or the strobing we see in nightclubs; this kind of flash creates a physiological response in the human body. Such rapid visual shifts engage the synapses in various ways, immediately moving the viewer to take distinct notice of the situation. It strongly calls attention to the moment of the flashing, there is a pause, and then the brain is in a way reset. Taken to an extreme where there are multiple seconds of flashing or variations in light and dark fields, some people may have unpleasant reactions, from headaches or nausea to epileptic seizures. Indeed, the style of experimental filmmaking known as 'flicker film' often carries warnings. It is important to note here that, conversely, many people enjoy very pleasant sensations in viewing those same flickering images. This is akin to a hallucinatory or trance-like state.[6] Filmmakers of the experimental film canon have been interested in the effects of light and editorial pacing on the viewer for some time. Such artists as Paul Sharits and Stan Brakhage have made work predicated on those involuntary human reactions. An examination of the information contained within the rapid-fire edits of certain aspects of *Angel*'s aesthetic reveals a very close relationship to these notions.

The transitions used in Angel reveal much about both the content of the work and the physical presence therein. Whereas most mainstream films and television shows use very traditional methods of cutting between scenes in a straightforward manner, the transitional sequences in *Angel* are more evolved; they are elaborate methods of revealing information, both as visual cues and narrative substance. They move across lines of the abstract and the concrete, leaving marks in the viewer's mind. We do not always know exactly what we just saw, but we intuitively respond to it.

The initial episode of *Angel*, 'City Of', provides solid information about the aesthetic approach of the series. It is in this episode that we experience the opening credit sequence for the first time. This new piece of visual information is loaded with elements that describe the show while presenting an unusual cinematic environment. The title credits for *Angel* are built around images superimposed on others. At the start, Angel is seen overlaid with images of the conceptualized 'helpless' in the series. The use of optical mats as the names of the actors are shown is noteworthy as well. Each character is presented in a smaller rectangle within a larger box that fills the frame. The outer area is different for each character, and the images as well as the colours used in these background mats reveal intricate details about these people. For example, the title sequence for the first season shows a pale blue background for Angel, green for Cordelia and yellow for Doyle. The images seen in these tinted mats hint at entrapment and escape (windows and doorways for Angel), presence in the world (brick wall and street scene for Cordelia), and confidence (desk, hanging up the phone and standing up for Doyle). The situation of each character in each subsequent season is similarly suggested by the image and tonality used in tandem with the text of the actors' names.

In *Angel*, we frequently see transitional sequences comprised of several very brief scenes or images cut together in a rapid-fire manner. An investigation of these sequences shows that they are built from a variety of image artefacts. Frequently we see shots and sequences previously or subsequently seen in the story that are not a part of what I call the 'Narrative Now', referring to the present time in the story. Within the moments of the transitions, time is shaken. A flash of a shot may appear, and that scene may arrive several minutes later in the episode. There is also use of such things as out-takes, production slates, lens flares or 'bloopers'.

In 'The Thin Dead Line' (2:14), as Gunn pulls up in front of the shelter after Wesley has been shot, there is a flash sequence that lasts only a few seconds. It appears to be just a quick bit of flashing and a pulsation of colour. Screened in slow motion, the images in these quick cuts can be absorbed more fully. There is a shot of lightning over a field, a return to the scene itself as a negative image, a flash of light that seems to throb, and a return to the positive image of the scene. This places the viewer in a space of experiencing a forced pause, not unlike the musical notion of a beat. This type of editorial decision leaves an impression on us that is not nameable or knowable, but it affects the way we feel about the subsequent material.

At the beginning of 'Epiphany' (2:16), the viewer suspects that Angel the hero is lost. The structure of the scene and the imagery itself strongly reference the material seen in 'Innocence' (B2:14) when Angel loses his soul. In 'Epiphany', Angel wakes up in bed with Darla, slowly realizes what has happened, gets dressed and thanks Darla for saving him. His soul is intact. As he and Darla talk, Angel remembers the call from the suicidal Kate. He rushes from his house to Kate's apartment. This seems to be a rapid-fire movement from one place to another with some flashes of light and images of traffic interspersed, but it is much more. An investigation of the sequence in slow motion reveals shots of a road, Angel driving his convertible in a tunnel and a surprising out-take in which Angel is smiling widely. This is the last thing seen as Angel arrives at Kate's apartment and begins pounding on her door. The viewer has moved from fear and concern about Angel to a sense of comfort and trust. The subliminal image of David Boreanaz grinning is a part of that.

While not formal transitions at all, the vision sequences usually behave as segues into narrative transitions. When a vision is experienced and subsequently explained to the main characters, they move forward temporally to another place and act upon the information presented by that vision. There is frequently a shift in the speed of the action, so that the visions are often slow-motion sequences. This allows the viewer to absorb the images presented, but it also creates a sense of physical suspension for the viewer. We watch slow motion intently, as it forges a heightened engagement. The visions share the quick cutting technique with transitions, but they deal with time and space in a very different way. They contain images we can recognize and qualify, and as such they act as a visual means of explication. Interior experiences are given concrete form. The images seen in the visions are occurring in the present, future, or even in the past. The experience of the visions, however, is always in the Narrative Now.

'Lonely Heart' (1:2) gives us the first visualization of these skull-crunching waves of information. Doyle's vision here is short and simple compared to the stylistic turns that follow, but it is immediately intriguing. We see flashes, a girl, fast movement and smears of motion. It is over in seconds onscreen, but is clearly a signal of the aesthetic approach of the show. Doyle's passing of the visions to Cordelia is revealed in 'Parting Gifts' (1:10). The first Cordy vision is also rather brief and simple, but the style of presentation is already evolving. The smears of motion here are much more kinetic and vibrant. Each of these is a vision of something occurring in the present or near future. 'Belonging' (2:19) is the first instance of a vision revealing something that took place in the past: Cordy is stricken with the image of a woman in a library, and we learn in the episode that this woman was in this place five years before. Here a new main character, Fred, is introduced through a vision.

By 'That Vision Thing' (3:2), Cordelia is struggling with the burden of the visions, and even says she doesn't want them any more. The vision sequences in this episode show an increasingly elaborate design as Cordy experiences physical manifestations of the images in her head. The first begins just a few minutes into the episode, as Cordy is violently tossed about by images of Chinese characters, a coin, the shadow of a clawed hand and flashing. The beast in the vision leaves scars on Cordelia's body in the present space and time. The slashing is occurring both in the vision and in the real Now.

This is reminiscent of Paul Sharits' 1968 flicker film *T,O,U,C,H,I,N,G*, a work the filmmaker described as an 'uncutting and unscratching mandala'.[7] In this work, single-frame edits of positive images with varying dark- and light-coloured backgrounds are juxtaposed with negative images of the same shot. There are only a few actions seen, among them a man holding his tongue within the blades of some scissors and a female hand dragging her fingernails across his face. This film, like most flicker films, is extremely kinetic. The editorial style causes the image to pulse, literally pounding the audience's visual field as it leaps from the screen. The remarkable thing about the film is that the internal action is mimicked by its physical presence. The film derives its energy from the act of cutting, from the intervals of positive and negative material in conflict. But the most brilliant element of *T,O,U,C,H,I,N,G* is that the film's surface is scratched as the hand scratches the face in the image. Emulsion is scraped back from the surface to create those marks on the film as well as *in* the film. The manifestation of this violent act is like the rips in Cordelia's flesh being inflicted by the vision.

In 'Offspring' (3:7), there are several excellent examples of cinematic experimentation. Darla, now pregnant, attacks Cordy in a wildly kinetic sequence of vampire trauma and vision combined. At the moment of the bite, we move from a wide-angle shot to a close-up of Cordelia's face. Then a vision strikes. We see vibrantly coloured scenes of smeared motion alternating between posterized and normal visual effects, flash-forwards and flashbacks, Cordy's neck with the bite, repeating scenes of children in an arcade, and light flares. Cordelia then pushes Darla away. The entire sequence lasts only about twenty seconds, but the feeling it creates through the use of slow motion and repetition makes it seem to go on much longer. This sequence is reminiscent of the paintings of Francis Bacon as its streaks of light and movement and variations in hue press the viewer into a space of anxiety and terror. Several minutes later, Cordelia experiences another vision, but it is interpreted in the narrative as more of a dream. She sees images somewhat similar to those from the previous vision, but they are presented in an unusual manner. This sequence is dark, grainy and very contrasty compared to the rest of the episode. This look is created through a lab process called bleach bi-pass, which leaves more silver deposits on the film stock than normal. This produces an unusual visual display, wherein the blacks are greatly enhanced and the colours are desaturated.[8] The scene is imbued with a creepy uncertainty, an otherworldly ambience, and imagery that looks as though it were printed on a lush, velvety surface. We do not know whether this is a visionary moment or a daydream, and the shift in formal design elements here enhances the surreal feeling.

The experimentation apparent in the series continues into the fourth season. In 'Ground State' (4:2), the viewer is rushed forth into an extreme close-up of Cordelia's eye. Her new status as a Higher Power is illustrated by this image of an expanding world, a scene that telescopes out through cityscapes in a move reminiscent of the 1977 film *Powers of Ten* by Charles and Ray Eames. This film begins with a man sleeping on a picnic blanket. The film follows 'a journey of 38 powers of ten', so that we travel from the hand to the far reaches of space, to a point 'ten million light years out' before the operation is reversed. We travel back to the hand and into it, to a subatomic level, finally stopping at the point where a single proton fills the screen.[9] At the end of 'Ground State', the camera zooms out from the hotel to cityscapes, then back to Cordelia in a cinematic gesture that suggests the value of shifting frames of reference. Here we see the world of the story as viewers and as well as the visual comprehension of a Higher Power simultaneously. The viewer may be reminded of Angel's declaration that the smallest act of kindness is the greatest thing in the world.

The final season of *Angel* is more like a traditional narrative than the previous four. Attention is given to slow motion as an element of the storytelling, and this is intriguing in the context of the episodes. Time in suspension calls attention to itself, and the viewer is held in a place where a more thorough investigation of the information is possible. Now the visual subtext becomes text. The subliminal quality of the design is replaced with a sense of simultaneity. The viewer is engaged at an experiential level, moving at different mental and emotional speeds, which are harmonious with or contrapuntal to the characters and events. In 'Shells' (5:16), we learn that Illyria can alter the experience of time and move within other dimensions, and we begin to see the repercussions of this. The memorable fight scene in which Angel, Spike, Gunn, Wesley and 'tactical' guys with weapons meet Illyria in the lab is a pivot point for this material. She tosses Angel through the window and he falls several storeys down to the street, but she is able to leave the lab, get out of the building and go on her way before Angel lands on the ground. We are suspended in time just like the characters. When they discuss the events afterwards, Gunn says it was as if she was 'moving really fast', and Wesley responds with 'or we were moving very slow'.

In 'Time Bomb' (5:19), this investigation continues, with Illyria speaking of this 'aberration in the timeline' represented through repeated scenes that may have tiny variations in action. In this episode we see Spike suspended in mid-air as his body very slowly responds to a punch from Illyria. The homage to martial arts films here is obvious, but this kind of suspension is much more than that. There is a doubling of the experience of time here. Illyria continues to be in the present and exhibits what we would call normal motion. Yet in the same scene, Spike drifts languidly across the room. This creates a feeling of uncertainty and anticipation in the viewer, as well as acting as a form of storyline development that explores the simultaneity of motion and time between characters.

In 'Power Play' (5:21), it is revealed that Cordelia's mysterious visit to Angel earlier in the season culminated in the transference of the visions to him. This is given as an explanation for Angel's strange behaviour. When Wes asks, incredulous, 'Cordelia gave you her visions?', Angel replies simply, 'One shot deal.' This is not the gift of visions exactly, but the gift of the ultimate vision. No more are necessary, as the Apocalypse is underway. The vision Angel receives fuels his response to the rising battle. The time expansion in this sequence is immense; we see images of the coming evil and the things it creates and destroys as fragments of the past, present and future intertwine. The vision begins with Angel waking suddenly from sleep, gasping from the force of the experience. The cue of the white flash of light signals the onslaught of visual information that starts with the sign of the Circle of the Black Thorn on a wooden table. The members' hands are seen around the edges of the tabletop as a rapid zoom-out pulls us away from this moment. The image shifts to a negative representation of the symbol of the Circle, then the white flash again, and then an image of fire. From here we see a kind of disembodied scary face as a frightening mask appears out of blackness. The face turns towards the fire that is entering the scene as a superimposition before dominating the frame as the face dissolves. Fire continues, then the masked face returns. The camera rises to match the movement of a hooded figure who raises a stick and strikes a bound man on the ground. White flashes follow, then a negative image of the masked face followed by the positive image of the same, then another white flash. The negative image appears again, immediately replaced by a shot of a woman lying on a floor. Fresh scratches cross her entire face. Another white flash gives way to a scene of several people lying dead on a floor. More white follows, then a shot of a man in a suit lying on the floor, blood covering the papers scattered by his side. There is a small camera movement here, and we see that there are more blood-soaked documents around him. A negative image of a wall streaked with blood follows, and this part pulses as the negative is replaced by the positive image of the same, then again the negative. White flashes separate this from the final bits of the vision, as we see Angel walking away from us, into the fire. The camera zooms into this scene, until the frame is filled with fire. A final white flash ends the sequence. The sequence only lasts a few seconds onscreen, but it uncovers several layers of plot twists and character development. This, the final vision experienced on *Angel*, makes use of all the techniques seen in the formal invention of the show's previous five years.

Angel is a visual masterwork of television programming. The action-movie sensibility in play at the end of the series when Angel says he wants to slay the dragon is a fitting end to five years of risk taking in prime time and this fine example of cinematic invention owes much to the avant-garde of the twentieth century. A reverence for the show is in order, as there are so few examples of actual cinematic invention and genre expansion in television and *Angel* – without a doubt – was able to accomplish both.

NOTES

1 Jennifer Bothamley, *Dictionary of Theories* (London: Gale Research, 1993), p. 409.
2 William Wees, *Light Moving in Time: Studies in the Visual Aesthetics of Avant-Garde Film* (Berkeley and Los Angeles: University of California Press, 1992), pp. 32–4.
3 Natalia Nussinova, 'The Soviet Union and the Russian Émigrés', in G. Nowell-Smith (ed.), *The Oxford History of World Cinema* (Oxford: Oxford University Press, 1996), p. 167.
4 Lincoln F. Johnson, *Film: Space, Time, Light and Sound* (New York: Holt, Rinehart and Winston, 1974), p. 114.
5 Suranjan Ganguly, 'All That is Light: Brakhage at 60', *Sight and Sound*, 21: 10 (1993), p. 21.
6 Wees, *Light Moving in Time*, pp. 146–8.
7 Wheeler Winston Dixon, *The Exploding Eye: A Re-visionary History of 1960s American Experimental Cinema* (New York: State University of New York Press, 1997), p. 150.
8 Zoran Perisic, *Visual Effects Cinematography* (Boston: Focal Press, 2000), p. 125.
9 Lucia Eames, *The Powers of Ten Flipbook* (Venice, CA: W. H. Freeman and Company, 1997), p. 1.

4

A Sense of the Ending: Schrodinger's Angel

ROZ KAVENEY

J oss Whedon has often stated that each year of *Buffy the Vampire Slayer* was planned to end in such a way that, were the show not renewed, the finale would act as an apt summation of the series so far. This was obviously truer of some years than others – generally speaking, the odd-numbered years were far more clearly possible endings than the even ones, offering definitive closure of a phase in Buffy's career rather than a slingshot into another phase. Both Season Five and Season Seven were particularly planned as artistically satisfying conclusions, albeit with very different messages – Season Five arguing that Buffy's situation can only be relieved by her heroic death, Season Seven allowing her to share, and thus entirely alleviate, slayerhood. Being the Chosen One is a fatal burden; being one of the Chosen Several Thousand is something a young woman might live with.

It has never been the case that endings in *Angel* were so clear-cut and each year culminated in a slingshot ending, an attention-grabber that kept viewers interested by allowing them to speculate on where things were going. Season One ended with the revelation that Angel might, at some stage, expect redemption and rehumanization – the Shanshu of the souled vampire – as the reward for his labours, and with the resurrection of his vampiric sire and lover, Darla, by the law firm of Wolfram & Hart and its demonic masters ('To Shanshu in LA', 1:22). Season Two ended with Cordelia's renunciation of love, glamour and freedom from mortal pain for the sake of her duty; with the arrival of the unknown quantity, Fred; with the information that the Wolf, the Ram and the Hart have power in many dimensions; and, at a moment of happiness, with the revelation of Buffy's death ('There's No Place Like Plrtz Glrb', 2:22).

Season Three ended with Connor's betrayal and imprisonment of Angel and Cordelia's ascension to become a Higher Being ('Tomorrow', 3:22). Season Four, at a point when the show was struggling for renewal, culminated in a major plot twist: Angel's decision, in order to save Connor's sanity and Cordelia's comatose life, to accept a deal whereby he took over Wolfram & Hart's LA office and wiped his friends' memories of Connor and much of their lives for the previous year and a half ('Home', 4:22).

It will be noticed at once that each of these slingshots was to some extent misleading. Darla had been raised as a human with a capacity for being redeemed – by a further irony, her eventual redemption was as a vampire. Angel's concern with the Shanshu got briefly in the way of the daily grind of his mission. Buffy's death was impermanent. Cordelia's self-sacrifice was betrayed by the Powers That Be. Angel's removal of Connor from the fight, his saving of Cordelia and even the memory wipe were temporary phenomena, while the deal with Wolfram & Hart turned out to be precisely the temptation and trap it seemed; sometimes the expectation of further revelations is itself deceitful.

In the light of all of this, how we assess 'Not Fade Away' (5:22), the finale of *Angel's* fifth and final season depends radically on whether this finale is in fact the end. Joss Whedon has stated, repeatedly, that this ending was in most respects what it would have been had the show been renewed for a sixth season. Further, Whedon – and also writers David Fury and Jeff Bell – have indicated, both generally and in detail, the theme and some of the plot arcs of a sixth season that would have followed this finale.[1] With vague talk of some future project that would unite at least a few members of the *Angel* cast – at the time of writing, James Marsters (Spike) has indicated, interviewed on the Australian television show *Rove Live* in early July, that talk of four television movies is more than a rumour – the status of 'Not Fade Away' as definitive concluding statement is uncertain. If, as seems moderately likely, it is in fact the last of *Angel*, it has to be treated one way; and if the future projects come to fruition, another. It is, as my subtitle states, the creation of Schrodinger's *Angel*, who at this point in the game is neither undead nor dead. Whedon had the option of a more definitive statement, but preferred this. 'Did I make it so it could lead into an exciting sixth season? I did', he said to *AngelNews*. 'But it's still a final statement if that's what it needs to be.'

Let us assume, for the sake of argument, that there will be no canonical addition to *Buffy* and *Angel* set at a date later than the battle against overwhelming odds in an alley behind the Hyperion Hotel, a spot which previously saw the final death of Darla, the birth of Connor and the rising of the Beast. In this case, the charge of Angel, Spike, Illyria and the already mortally wounded Gunn is a suicidal death charge, a recognition that, in a world ruled by untrustworthy Powers and the Senior Partners, the path of the hero is to go down fighting.

It can be argued, not least by Jennifer Stoy, that this ending contradicts much of what *Angel* has always stood for.[2] A death charge that will inevitably leave parts of LA despoiled by demons and dragons is, in this view, a piece of self-indulgent existentialist nonsense in which Angel chooses defiance over practical solutions, chooses to affront the Senior Partners by wiping out their immediate support network – the Circle of the Black Thorn – at the cost of never being able to do anything else good again and, incidentally, signing away his Shanshu and murdering the heroic Drogyn in order to do so. Remarks by Whedon and Fury that, had Season Six happened, it would have been a *Mad Max*-like tale of coping with the aftermath of apocalypse strengthen this argument.

In this reading, the ending of 'Not Fade Away' is an example of what can be called 'Superhero Exceptionalism', the idea that superheroes are exempt from normal considerations and entitled to ignore consequences. Part of the ongoing polemical debate within comics has always been precisely this question – Spider-Man learned at an early stage that 'with great power comes great responsibility', but other super-heroes, from the Hulk to Batman, have lived constantly in far greyer areas. As a self-confessed comics geek, one of whose post-*Angel* gigs has been taking over scripting 'The Astonishing X-Men', Joss Whedon will be as obsessed with this debate as any other comics creator or fan.

This view is not without merit; the considerations that have to be weighed against it have, in part, to do with the way that Season Five in general, and its last two episodes in particular, either completes various long-running story and character arcs or, if some form of the show continues later, at least moves them into a radically new phase. This is particularly true of those arcs that deal with Angel and with characters that are in some sense versions of Angel.

The show *Angel* has always been about earning redemption one day at a time, by slow increments and by helping individuals in trouble case by case, precisely the opposite of attempting redemption by a single gratuitous heroic act of defiance. It is particularly significant, then, that – sent off by Angel to have one last perfect day – Gunn goes to see Anne at her refuge for the homeless and helps her lift charitable donations onto a truck. Anne, it is worth remembering, has a long history as a minor character in this universe – vampire wannabe, slave in an industrial hell, reborn activist tricked by Wolfram & Hart and menaced by zombie cops. Repeatedly saved from supernatural jeopardy, she has become a constant example of both doing mundane good one day at a time and of the point that to save someone is to save the good works they might subsequently do. To bring her back, three years after we last saw her, is clearly intended to establish a plot point: we are deliberately reminded of the core mission of Angel Investigations.

It is particularly appropriate that it is Gunn who goes to her, the one of the core team most obviously compromised and for a while corrupted by involvement with Wolfram & Hart. As the musical themes associated with him on his first appearance in Season One indicate – they are variations on Angel's own themes – he is also the one most like Angel in some ways. One of the major arcs of Season Five is Gunn's progressive corruption and then recuperation. He allows Wolfram & Hart to install legal knowledge in his brain and almost at once becomes capable of legal chicanery ('Conviction', 5:1); he is also the member of the Angel Investigations team chosen to have direct communication with the Senior Partners through their Conduit in the White Room ('Home'). He is tricked into signing the customs form for the sarcophagus that will destroy Fred and does so as the price of regaining his legal expertise when it begins to slip away ('Smile Time', 5:14). During Fred's painful death Gunn confronts the Conduit, which has taken his own face, and is rebuffed when he asks for Fred's life:

> Gunn: I didn't come for a favour. We can make a deal.
> Gunn 2: [*disdainfully*] Deals are for the devil.
> Gunn: You want someone else? A life for hers. You'll get it. You can have mine.
> Gunn 2: I already do.
>
> ('A Hole in the World', 5:15)

Forced to admit his complicity in Fred's death, Gunn is stabbed by Wesley and rejected by Angel; ironically, only Harmony shows any compassion for him. This is the most abject point he reaches; thereafter he sacrifices himself ('Shells', 5:16). Rescued from hell by Illyria, he is the first to confront Angel over his seeming decision to become entirely complicit with the Senior Partners ('Time Bomb', 5:19). His reversion to the side of good is signalled in part by a return to his personal style and original image – he reshaves his head and adopts a less formal mode of dress. Gunn's path demonstrates that good intentions are not enough, or more precisely that good intentions can easily be corrupted by vices as apparently trivial as vanity in his competence. His conversation with Anne indicates the importance of the mission for its own sake:

> Gunn: What if I told you it doesn't help? What would you
>   do if you found out none of it matters, that it's all
>   controlled by forces more powerful and uncaring
>   than we can conceive and they will never let it get
>   better down here? What would you do?
> Anne: I'd get this truck packed before the new stuff gets
>   here. You wanna give me a hand?

We last see him mortally wounded and determined to go
down fighting:

> Gunn: Okay … you take the 30,000 on the left …
> Illyria: You're fading. You'll last ten minutes at best.
> Gunn: Let's make 'em memorable.

Of *Angel*'s main cast, Gunn was often the one least well used,
partly because of uncertainties of tone on the part of the white
writers about the handling of black street dialogue; Season
Five gave him an arc that was an admirable counterpart to the
more wobbly handling of more central characters.

The major arc of the fifth season is, of course, that of its central character. The other core characters have accepted the
deal with Wolfram & Hart from a combination of idealism
and conceit, believing that they can make a difference from
the inside and delighted by the shiny new toys they are
offered: knowledge for Wesley, a laboratory for Fred, a sense
of self-worth for Gunn, limitless showbiz power for Lorne.
Angel knows from the beginning that he has taken the deal
primarily in order to save Connor and Cordelia and that he
has betrayed his friends by altering their memories. He has
reason to suspect that he has been tricked by his worst enemies and no way, because of the memory wipe, of fully
discussing this with his friends. The restoration of Wesley's
memories – which include the extent of his failed attempts to
redeem Lilah – are part of what breaks him; Angel helps
destroy his closest friend.

Angel's constant sense of his bad faith is reinforced by various things that happen to him in the course of the season.
Earlier errors on his part – his obsession with being a champion, or a lone wolf avenger, or a good provider – have been

similarly demonstrated to him over an episode or an arc. In the course of Season Five, he is magically compelled to have sex with the Senior Partners' minion ('Life of the Party', 5:5), confronted with the apparent meaninglessness of another hero's struggles ('The Cautionary Tale of Numero Cinco', 5:6), poisoned by a demon parasite into endless hallucinations of his own worthlessness ('Soul Purpose', 5:10) and finally literally reduced to the status of a puppet ('Smile Time', 5:14). He is specifically told that he has made the wrong choice, both by his dead love Cordelia, now an angelic messenger of the Powers ('You're Welcome', 5:12), and by Buffy's comic sidekick Andrew ('Damage', 5:11). Angel has to have fallen a long way for the reformed murderer Andrew to be entitled to tell him that he has been corrupted – and Andrew's judgment is confirmed by Giles in a phone call when Angel asks for help from Willow with Fred's final illness ('A Hole in the World').

And yet the choice Angel made in 'Home' is not straightforwardly condemned either. When we meet Connor again, he is sane and untroubled, and manages to remain so even after discovering his superpowers and regaining his memories ('Origin', 5:18). In the final episode, it is with his son that Angel spends his last perfect hours and, during Angel's fight with the Senior Partners' supercharged minion Hamilton, Connor appears and buys Angel a precious few minutes to find a way of defeating Hamilton.

Part of Angel's trouble is that he refuses to listen to the person who most frequently tells him the truth in the course of this season: Spike, who reverts to his *Buffy* Seasons Two to Four status as the trickster teller of uncomfortable truths. As we see in a sequence of flashbacks, Spike has good reason to distrust Angel, who was always the alpha male of their little vampire family and who seduced the neophyte vampire William into the ways of atrocity. Spike points out to him that while it was Drusilla that turned him, it was Angelus who made him a monster. The homoeroticism that many fans have always seen in the relationship – and written reams of 'slash' erotic fan-fiction about – is at the very least closely related to this power dynamic between them; when Spike finally says

"Cause Angel and me have never been intimate – except that one ...', many fans purred with pleasure ('Power Play', 5:21).

Spike has, after all, always been the most obvious of Angel's shadow doubles. They share their original names – Angel's Liam is the Irish form of Spike's William – and to some extent exchanged natures on becoming vampires; the drunken wastrel Liam became the moody aesthete of death Angelus, whereas the poet William became Spike, who would rather have the instant gratification of a brawl than the drawn-out refined pleasures of sadism. Both are at their most petulant when dealing with their rivalry over Buffy: to pick but one example, Spike has the Buffybot programmed with the belief that Angel 'has stupid hair' ('Intervention', B5:18). One of the completed arcs of Season Five is the process whereby they accept that they are, and always have been, the best of friends, in spite of apparent bitter enmity and mutual betrayal, just as Angelus said they would be on their first meeting.

Spike has acquired the authority needed to tell Angel the bitter truth. He chose to have a soul and chose to save the world at the cost of his own destruction. When they fight for the right to be champion, Spike beats him, simply because he is less conflicted ('Destiny', 5:8). Though Spike's decision, once he is solid, to replace Angel as the lone vigilante of LA's night streets is manipulated by Lindsey it is nonetheless valid, as is his later decision to rejoin the group to save Fred and then to help control Illyria ('Soul Purpose', 'A Hole in the World'). After a last resurgence of the old jealousy over Buffy in a weak comedic episode, the two vampires finally accept the immaturity of their bickering ('The Girl in Question', 5:20). Like everyone else, Spike is fooled by Angel's pretence of having been corrupted but he does not believe that Angel has become Angelus – Spike would know that, he says. Once Angel has revealed his strategy and asked his friends to assist him in the destruction of the Black Thorn, Spike is the first to volunteer ('Power Play'). He never loses the chippiness that comes from suspecting he is a better man than Angel, but he decides to die, a loyal lieutenant at his side. There is a generosity to this on the part of both which is deeply attractive.

This season is endlessly stuffed, as befits what was always perhaps a final season, with flashbacks and ironic continuity references.[3] For example, in the simultaneous assassinations that are Angel's scheme in 'Not Fade Away', Angel trusts Spike to save a newborn from the Fell Brethren. Back in Shanghai, Angel chose to save a baby rather than stay with Darla, who condemned his decision to protect its parents with an unfavourable comparison with the detested Spike's murder of a slayer ('Darla', 2:7). This back reference helps point to an important issue: the assassination of the Black Thorn is not merely a nihilistic act of defiance but a way of continuing the mission. The rescued baby stands for all the specific victims that the killing saves, and all the potential that such victims embody.

The decision to raise Spike from the dead[4] and introduce him to *Angel*, a show where he had only ever previously appeared as a villain of the week ('In the Dark', 1:3) or in flashbacks ('Darla'), was originally made, not for artistic reasons, but because the Warner Brothers network insisted on the addition of this popular character as one of a number of preconditions for commissioning a fifth season. It was not a universally popular decision; admirers of *Angel* were not necessarily admirers of the later seasons of *Buffy* in which Spike became so important. In conjunction with a general background of cuts in the show's budget, the necessity of providing James Marsters with an appropriate salary meant that other characters had to be written out or forgotten.

Nonetheless, by season end, artistic reasons for it had been found – one of the most touching moments of 'Not Fade Away' comes with a classic Whedon bait-and-switch, where Spike's perfect day is spent in a bar where we are led to believe he is going to brawl, only to discover that he is reading William's dreadful love poetry and improvising a new poem about the mother he turned and then dusted. This scene closes Spike's personal arc very neatly – should this episode be the last we ever see of the character – by integrating the warrior and the poet, the prickly rough with the sensitive twit he has done so much to repress.

One of the show's themes has always been that self-reinvention is both necessary and morally dangerous. Lindsey, the closest thing Season Five has to a season-long onscreen villain, has always been another of Angel's shadows, as poor boy made good by doing bad. We first meet him as a self-possessed lawyer ('City Of', 1:1) and only gradually realize his complexity and vulnerability. He feints at redemption only to take an improved deal from evil and be maimed by Angel ('Blind Date', 1:21; 'To Shanshu in LA'). The loss of his hand re-invents him as a liminal being, since part of him is alive and part dead, and this does not cease to be the case when he is given new hands, first plastic and then real. His feeling for Darla is in part genuine love and in part a struggle to possess something which is Angel's. When, after losing her, he attacks Angel brutally, he does so in old clothes and a truck that make explicit what we always suspected – that under the smooth surface of the LA lawyer is a working-class kid with a chip ('Epiphany', 2:16).

As with Spike, Lindsey's doubling with Angel has a strong and occasionally explicit element of homoeroticism: Darla says to him at one point 'It's not me you want to screw – it's him', and the line is entirely knowing. Lindsey's apparent redemption comes in part from a moral qualm – he is upset to discover that his new hand has been taken from someone he once knew – and in part from an innate rebelliousness. His pride is affronted by the Senior Partners' deceit in the matter of the hand and by the competitive games he is forced to play with Lilah Morgan ('Dead End', 2:18). It was redemption without all that much in the way of repentance, penance or even a firm purpose of amendment; it was by some criteria no redemption at all.

One of the reasons for the startling revelation that Lindsey is the secret manipulator behind Spike's resurrection and Eve's betrayal is, of course, that Lindsey has this complicated back-story of rivalry with Angel ('Destiny', 5:7). Another is that Christian Kane who plays him was a popular favourite and not a star, having largely abandoned acting for a while to pursue his musical career. Certainly the reappearance of an iconic figure from the show's past was an economic, and possibly a cheap, way of broad-brushing in a nemesis. For a while at least, it is unclear whether Lindsey is good or evil – his structural status as the season's Little Bad does not automatically determine which side he is on – though his attempts to kill Angel offer a clue. Perhaps he is responsible for Spike's resurrection to ensure that, should he kill Angel, there will still be a vampire with a soul around to fulfil the Shanshu prophecy. His attempt on Angel's life after the apparent resurrection of Cordelia – and his attempt to have Spike pre-empt any message she brings from the Powers by telling Spike she is still evil – clearly indicates that he is not, as hinted, working for Good. At the same time, his abduction by the Senior Partners to be tortured in a suburban Hell indicates that he is at most freelancing for Evil rather than a wholly owned subsidiary.

Lindsey's role is ambiguous to the end, partly because he gets loaded with expository material and partly because the writers never, I suggest, sat down clearly to work out what his motivation is, or why it is necessary that Angel commission his execution by Lorne. In 'Power Play', it becomes apparent that Lindsey is very well-informed indeed about the Circle of the Black Thorn and how one goes about joining it – his actions throughout the season make most sense on the assumption that this was his intention. One of the requirements appears to be that one kill someone close to one to demonstrate ruthlessness; Angel fulfils this by conning the Circle into believing he was responsible for Fred's death/ transformation into Illyria. To kill a straightforward enemy would not seem to complete this requirement – but, as has been demonstrated above, Angel is a deal more than that to Lindsey. The implication, not fully developed, is that Lindsey was trying to buy his way into the Circle by killing Angel, and that Angel qualified as a sacrifice because of Lindsey's quasi-erotic obsession. Accordingly, the last interview between him and Angel in which, on the surface of things, Angel recruits him both as a lieutenant in the assassination of the Circle and as a successor in the struggle should things go wrong, crystallizes Angel's decision to have him killed not because of anything Lindsey says, but because of what he does not.

In this reading, Angel's slip of the tongue reference to the erotic subtext between them is more than a sop to the fans:

Lindsey: You want me, I'm on your team.
Angel: I want you, Lindsey. [*beat*] I'm thinking about rephrasing that.
Lindsey: I'd be more comfortable.

This conversation can be read as Angel knowingly giving Lindsey an opportunity to come clean about what he planned and why Angel's death would have been a sacrifice for him. Significantly neither Lindsey nor his lover Eve tell each other the truth during their last encounter. She fails to admit to him that she had magically-induced sex with Angel and allows him to believe that she is the one thing in his life Angel never touched; and he never explains to the woman who gave up immortality for him why this should matter. In Lindsey's head, the huge drama is between him and Angel, which is why Angel commissions Lorne, a being Lindsey sees as his inferior, to kill Lindsey once he has served his turn; Lindsey's last words are of his affront that it should be Lorne who kills him, and not Angel.

There is a darkly humorous ruthless justice to the Angel who arranges this and accepts that the price of it is that Lorne will walk away from him and the struggle thereafter; losing Lorne's support is part of the butcher's bill he is prepared to pay. One of the structural reasons for the arrival on the scene of Illyria – 'the immaculate embodiment of rule' – is that she has been both monarch and general and can tell Angel things about being a leader that, at this point, he needs to know. Back in Season Two, a temporarily morally dark Angel talked of 'waging the war' as opposed to what Wesley and the others were still doing – 'fighting the good fight'. Now Illyria tells him through the mouth of the dead Fred that he must accept the logic of his situation again: 'So much power here, and you quibble over its price. Your conscience binds you. If you want to win a war, you must serve no master but your ambition ...

A true ruler is as moral as a hurricane ... Empty but for the force of his gale.' ('Time Bomb', 5:19)

It is precisely because Illyria is not a vampire that she is a worthwhile mirror of Angel's vampire nature, of the thing he has at the same time to accept and overcome. 'You're not looking at your friend; you're looking at the thing that killed him' (Giles in 'The Harvest', B1:2) is even truer of Illyria than it was of, say, Harmony; Illyria is a long dead god/demon that inhabits the corpse of Fred and devoured her soul in the fires of her re-creation. Yet, as with many vampires, it is not as simple as that; even before the restoration of Fred's memories of her penultimate year and a half of life she is totally Illyria, yet increasingly conjoined or contaminated with elements of Fred. If Illyria were wholly and solely the creature she claims, and believes herself, to be, she would not impersonate Fred for the dead woman's parents, or offer to give Wesley a final perfect day. Both *Buffy* and *Angel* have always been shows about redemption; the reason why Wesley refuses Illyria's offer and then accepts it when mortally wounded is not that he dies having finally chosen illusion over reality, but that her offer is an outward sign of genuine inward change. In an interview at the Hyperion convention, Amy Acker said that Joss Whedon redirected the scene having realized that it was not about Wesley's love for Illyria or Fred, but about Illyria's love for Wesley.

It is clear that Angel listens to Illyria, but that he does not do precisely what she says. He is, in the last two episodes, prepared to sacrifice people he likes and admires, such as Drogyn. However, his ruthlessness is the servant of his mission, not of his ego: he specifically renounces hope by signing away the Shanshu in order to preserve his cover with the Circle of the Black Thorn. He forgives Harmony for her betrayal, he judges her according to her nature, both as a vampire and as a selfish child, rather than for the personal betrayal, and implicitly accepts her argument that someone who was never trusted cannot have betrayed – she even explains, when he says he never trusted her because she doesn't have a soul, 'I would have if you had confidence in me'. Angel's decision to spare her to pursue what might be her redemption is based partly on recognition of the lost humanity they have in common, and on a ruler's sense of justice.

In *Angel*, the character who has most consistently acted as Angel's shadow and surrogate is Wesley, whose story has throughout been that of 'The Man who Learns Better'. Remembered by Angel and the audience as the largely useless fop of *Buffy* Season Three, the ex-Watcher has re-invented himself as a leather-clad rogue demon-hunter without having changed his essence. The ways in which he changes are many and varied: to pick but one, he consistently chooses Angel over earlier loyalties to the Watchers' Council, even when what appears to be his father arrives claiming to be its emissary ('Lineage', 5:7). Wesley is a character whose essence is to lose and yet lose so honourably as to be admirable. He is the 'loyal servant' who betrays Angel by kidnapping his son, but does it to save him from the prophesied guilt of killing him – and in the long run, Angel has to kill Connor so that he can be reborn as the sane heroic youth of Season Five. Wesley sells his own soul to Wolfram & Hart in a vain attempt to save that of Lilah, whom he no longer loves; he finally wins Fred, only to lose her to Illyria; and it is his death that finally redeems Illyria by teaching her the meaning of human grief. Wesley's death is both the price of Angel's victory and a demonstration that the mission is about self-sacrifice.[5]

In conclusion, then, we have to judge Season Five in general, and its finale in particular by the fact that they always had to serve two purposes: they had to provide both a series finale for five years of the show and lead logically to a sixth year should one be commissioned, and to further Buffyverse material should it ever be called for. These are not entirely compatible aims – the fact that the season and 'Not Fade Away' work for both as well as they do needs to be weighed against their partial failure at either.

Further, there were other issues. The network's demand that the show move away from strong plot arcs was less honoured than it might have been, but always created problems in a show which had moved into strong arc in its second season. The early part of the season does tend to deal in 'problems of the week', even if some of those problems, notably the fate of those earlier champions, the masked wrestlers, offer a strong symbolic resonance that implies an arc ('The Cautionary Tale of Numero Cinco', 5:6). The handling of Lindsey in this season is weakened by this avoidance of overt arc – he drifts around the background manipulating Spike by pretending to be the long-dead Doyle (another example of his liminal status) and his real motives remain largely obscure.

When Cordelia appears for a single episode, we hear her overt message to Angel, but not the secret one we are told about later; this feels like improvised retrofitting, even if it is not. The occasional appearance of what we later learn to be the Black Thorn's insignia – on the armoured cyborgs of the supposed Roger Wyndam-Pryce, for example – is not enough to prepare us for the eventual long-delayed appearance of the season's Big Bad, nor are the occasional appearances of beings we later learn to be among its members: Sebassis, Veil, Senator Brucker and so on.

In the end, though, Season Five is what *Angel* has always been about. It is the story of a man whose innate nature is to be a lonely, morally equivocal brooder, whose loyalty to his friends enables him to learn from them. It is the story of a man who learns moral lessons that always prove to be provisional; it is his preparedness to go on learning that counts. Angel is in this respect a wise fool, which is why he is so often clownlike; he is a saviour in constant need of his own redemption. He also has constantly to accept the paradoxes of his own nature – in the fight with the Senior Partners' emissary Hamilton, he wins partly because he accepts the freely proffered help of his son, and partly because he drains Hamilton's strength by biting him – he is both man and monstrous creature of the night.

If the last moments of the show take place in darkness and rain, this is not just noir gesturing – it is because Angel has always inhabited the moral borderland of great cities. If an entirely hostile reading of his final decision is possible, it is because Angel has always been morally ambiguous. And if the last episode of the television show, which is in the end all about him, is titled in a reference to one of the most amoral of rock bands, it is because part of the point of the show has always been to teach us sympathy for the devil.

Dedicated to the memory of Selena Ulrich.

NOTES

1 Joss Whedon has stated that a sixth season would have dealt with the chaos after the system is smashed, *Angel News*, 18 May 2004, cited at http://www.whedonesque.com; David Fury that it would have been their attempt to re-invent the series as *The Road Warrior/(Mad Max)*, 'Sixth Sense', interview by Tara Dilullo, *DreamWatch*, 118 (2004), p. 32; Jeffrey Bell has mentioned that it would have continued the arc of Illyria's acceptance of her now double nature as Illyria/Fred, *Official Angel Magazine*, 4 (2004), cited at http://www.whedonesque.com.
2 In conversation.
3 Perhaps the most obscure of these comes during Angel's halluci-nations in 'Soul Purpose' (5:10) where Fred removes his soul from his chest in the shape of a goldfish in a dirty bowl. Back in Season Two of Buffy, in 'Passion' (B2:17), Angelus tormented Willow by killing her goldfish. The soul is the thing that stops Angel being the Angelus that does such things, and is so repre-sented as the least of his victims. Angel's soul when restored, in 'Becoming Pt. 2' (B2:22), and when removed in *Angel*'s fourth season, is held in a globe that shines brightly; Angel is worried that his pragmatic compromise with evil has soiled him irre-deemably – Fred talks of simply flushing fish and water away.
4 After his heroic self-sacrifice in 'Chosen' (B7:22)
5 However, remarks by Alexis Denisof in interview that he likes the character of Wesley so much that he would always be pre-pared to play him again may indicate that this self-sacrificing death, like Spike's, may not be all it seems, 'Parting Gifts: Inter-view with Alexis Denisof', *Official Angel Magazine*, 13 (2004), pp. 10–16.

PART TWO:

*'The Big Wacky
Variety Show We Call
Los Angeles':*
The City of Angel

5

Los Angelus: The City of Angel

BENJAMIN JACOB

'Los Angeles' are the first words spoken in the first episode of *Angel*. The first images to appear in the opening credits are of the Los Angeles skyline and empty downtown streets – not the series' eponymous hero. Montage shots of LA's freeways and skyscrapers intersperse each episode and the LA skyline appears on the packaging of accompanying videos, books and DVDs. The extent to which LA embraces *Angel* is also present in episode titles – consider 'City Of' (1:1) and 'To Shanshu in LA' (1:22) – and even the soundtrack: the ballad of emotional alienation written by David Greenwalt and sung by Lindsey ('Dead End', 2:18) and later, Eve ('A Hole in the World', 5:15), is entitled 'LA'. Indeed, hardly an episode passes without a character commenting on the nature of the city. Recall the opening shots of the second series in which Lorne breaks off his self-aware rendition of Gloria Gaynor's 'I Will Survive' to deliver the following observation:

> In this city you better learn to get along 'cause LA's got it all:
> the glamour and the grit, the big breaks and the heartaches,
> the sweet young lovers and the nasty, ugly, hairy fiends that
> suck out your brain through your face. It's all part of the big
> wacky variety show we call Los Angeles [...] And let's
> admit it folks, isn't that why we love her?
>
> ('Judgement', 2:1)

LA's integral role in the series has been noted by previous critics. Karen Sayer has observed that LA, being a real city, dark, urban and seedy, stands in contrast to the suburban, white, middle-class and imaginary Sunnydale, setting for *Buffy the Vampire Slayer*.[1] But … why LA? Why not an imaginary American metropolis? Or, if real, why not San Francisco, Chicago, New Orleans or New York? What purpose does LA serve within the series? Given the obvious centrality of this *particular* city to the series these questions seem central to understanding *Angel*.

So what does LA have that other American cities do not? And in what way might these properties be relevant to 'reading' the series? Firstly, LA is more than just the home of 'big breaks and heartaches'. It is the one city in the United States with an immediate connection between place and protagonist. That is, of course, the names: Angelus and Los Angeles; Angel and the City of Angels. Some might argue that this echo alone was enough to lead the series' creators to choose LA as its setting. Perhaps, in name alone, Los Angeles was a suitable 'home' for Angel/Angelus. As we will see, this name association is far more than a nice touch; it indicates a deeper relationship between Angel and the city – an important point to which I will return. For now, however, despite their almost identical names, it would be wrong to call the city of *Angel* anyone's 'home' – let alone Angel's. *Angel*'s LA – what I call 'Los Angelus' – is a place where the glittering skyscrapers of late twentieth-century wealth meet darkness, alienation and threat.

This world is established in the opening title sequence. First, behind the title 'Angel', we see a slow tracking aerial shot of LA's skyline. It is night and the lights of the skyscrapers burn like stars. Shot two: night-time. The bright lights have gone. A lone woman stands on the curb of a downtown street. A few cars pass by. In series three onwards this image, which sets female vulnerability against a mise-enscène of nocturnal urban threat, dissolves into another which reinforces the same themes. Shot three shows a bridge, again at night, artificially lit, deserted except for a single, anonymous woman walking. In most episodes, these frames – followed by rapidly dissolving images of lone figures, anguished faces, shots of LA exclusively as a place of deep shadows, silhouettes and artificial lighting – introduce Los Angelus to the viewer. Their message is clear: beneath the glitz and starry lights, *Angel's* LA is a place of pain and anonymity, alienation, broken dreams and an almost omniscient darkness. This Los Angeles is the 'other' side of the stereotypical city of sunshine, Beach Boys and Walt Disney – or, in an ironic twist, the only time LA appears *as* a place of sun, sea and the Beach Boys, is when it has come under the spell of an evil entity ('The Magic Bullet', 4:19). More usual is the LA that Connor encounters in 'A New World' (3:20): a hellish maze of sleazy rooming houses, hostile strangers, drug addicts, dealers and violence.

Indeed, all the series' settings – hotels, motels, brothels, hospitals, casinos, warehouses, sewers, fairgrounds – unless they become a final resting place, are locations of transition. No one belongs in Los Angelus; there is no home, there is no safe family. Initially, Gunn is literally homeless; Cordelia moved to LA to (unsuccessfully) fulfil her dream of stardom; neither truly human nor vampire, Angel murdered his family and drifted across just about every continent before ending (or pausing) in LA; the Englishman Wesley had recently been fired from the Council and thus effectively disowned by both his literal and metaphorical 'family' (Wesley's father also belongs to the Council); Fred is a long way from her Texan family; Lorne is in self-imposed exile from his 'home' dimension; and, in Season Five, the presence of Spike adds another geographically displaced English 'man'. Around these characters, in bars and light-slashed clubs, those who have come to Los Angelus either to find something or escape something, search for – as one demon says – 'a connection' ('Lonely Heart', 1:2). In *Angel's* city their chances of finding a safe connection among its (sometimes literally) faceless hordes is poor. As Roz Kaveney says, 'People come to [*Angel's*] LA to accept exile'.[2] Perhaps in some cases less to 'accept' exile than to endure and overcome it, but, either way they certainly do not come to Los Angelus to find a home.

As already noted, Karen Sayer and others have called the city of *Angel* 'real'. Let's be clear: *Angel*'s LA is not 'real'. Many people are happily at home in 'real' LA, there are no portals to other dimensions and demons don't gather in karaoke bars. That said (and with no disrespect to Los Angelians everywhere) of all the cities in America, LA is arguably the one where the fabric of reality has worn thinnest. After all, LA – the 'real' geographical LA – has long figured as 'unreal' and 'ideal'. Indeed, it is nearly impossible to talk, in simple terms, of a 'real' LA. If there is a 'real' LA it segues almost effortlessly and perhaps disquietingly into an imagined 'unreal' version of itself. After all, as Lorne says, Los Angeles is a 'big wacky variety show'. The process started in the early twentieth century, when real estate and leisure companies began marketing LA as the city of the American Dream.[3] And with such a heavenly name, what other major American city could contend? So LA's more-than-real/unreal status began ... and continues. In today's 'real' LA you can see R2D2's foot prints cast in cement, and mute, life-sized cartoon characters walking beneath the California sun. You can ride through film sets and at Universal Studios be attacked by the shark from *Jaws*. In addition, according to urban geographers, many people who live in the city's sprawl get no closer to downtown LA than does the rest of the world, whose knowledge of it is filtered through television and cinema screens.[4]

LA therefore, perhaps more than any other American city, is in the unique position of being simultaneously real and fantasy. Surely this is an appropriate property for the setting of a series which questions a single reality and introduces (with as much plausibility as possible) mythical creatures to the streets of a geographically 'real' place. That said, no matter how 'unreal' it may be, Los Angelus – just like other fictionalized portrayals of LA – cannot but help engage with the other side of the ideal, i.e. the less salubrious 'reality' of Los Angeles.

Urban geographers have long recognized that Los Angeles is unique. To describe 'real' LA they use terms such as 'monstro-City' and 'Citadel-LA'.[5] They debate whether LA is indeed the American Dream fulfilled or, as two experts write,

the 'dystopian nightmare of "Hell Town" grown to gargan-
tuan proportions'.[6] Today's Los Angeles is the largest
industrial metropolis in America. With a population of 15 million to date, it hovers in sixth or seventh place among the
world's 'megacities'.[7] These figures rest uneasily alongside its
history of racial violence: as early as 1871 there was a Chinese
massacre; in 1942 more than 30,000 Japanese Americans from
the area were interred in concentration camps; 1943 saw the
'Zoot Suit' riots and more recently there were the race riots of
1965 and 1992.[8] Thus, 'real' LA as much as *Angel*'s LA plays
host to deep and often violent divisions. 'Real' LA may be
home to the stars, but, as we have already seen echoed in the
series, it is also the 'homeless capital' of America and 'America's leading Third World city'.[9] LA may be synonymous with
the American Dream but during the Californian Gold Rush it
was dubbed 'Hell Town' due to its excessive daily murder
count.[10] Frequently equating LA with hell (for example in
'Reprise' (2:15), when LA is revealed to be 'The Home Office'
of the demonic Wolfram & Hart), *Angel* never lets us forget
this city's less celebrated past.

'Monster city', 'Gargantua', 'nightmare': 'real' Los Angeles,
let alone that portrayed in *Angel*, is an urban American levia-
than. As those title shots illustrate, Los Angelus, like Los
Angeles, is a place where wealth exists alongside deprivation.
In this way, when the series' creators populate Beverly Hills
and Westwood with demons, they are taking 'real' LA's monstrosity and darkness to a literal level. Thus, apparent amid
the inhabitants of Los Angelus, the presence of its humans,
pure-blood and half-breed demons, is a reference to the racial
issues within LA's past and present.[11] Finally, as Boyd Tonkin
reminds us, unlike those of most other US cities, and courtesy
of the San Andreas Fault, the inhabitants of 'real' LA live in
constant fear of, as Fred says ('Players,' 4:16) 'the earth that
opens up and swallows you whole'. In other words, apo-
calyptic destruction.[12] This precarious geographical balance
also finds its echo in *Angel*'s constantly looming apocalypses.
With these themes in mind – race, monstrosity, violence, a
hellish past, a unique blend of reality and fantasy and loom-

ing destructive forces – could any other city in the States be more suited to Angel's world?

Of course, *Angel* is not alone in finding LA an appropriate backdrop to its themes or in depicting a nightmarish side to this city of dreams. Almost identical preoccupations and settings to those of *Angel* appear in American noir.[13] Indeed, *Angel*'s adoption of noir accompanies the series' embrace of the city: after all, 'American' noir was originally a 'Los Angelian' genre that represented Los Angeles steeped in literal and metaphorical darkness.

Angel's creators are aware of the 'noir' legacy into which they are tapping and to which they contribute. In 'Judgement' (2:1) reference is made to Cordelia watching a 'noir festival' on TV. In 'Dear Boy' (2:5) Wesley compares Angel to that archetypal noir hero Philip Marlowe. We shouldn't forget that noir originated in the hard-boiled crime writing of Raymond Chandler and his private eye protagonist, Philip Marlowe, of which more is said below. 'Are You Now, or Have You Ever Been' (2:2) provides further proof of *Angel*'s self-aware adoption of LA's noir tradition. Most of this episode is told in flashback to the events of 1952: one of the years in which Chandler's Marlowe would have been gumshoeing around LA.[14] Although present in every frame of this particular episode, evidence of *Angel*'s assimilation of film noir visual style can be found throughout the series: scenes are steeped in shadow; faces are half-lit, figures silhouetted; visual symbols of entrapment – images of barred windows, banisters and iron railings – abound; and motifs of the night and the city are continually interwoven.

Rather than concentrating on *Angel*'s 'neo-noir' style (other essays in this collection do so at more length), I want to look at Angel as the noir detective hero. This leads us towards what LA represents within the series. Thus, consider this definition of noir from the writers of *Film Noir: An Encyclopedic Reference to the American Style*:

> Film noir evoke[s] the dark side of the American persona. The central figures in these films, caught in their double binds, filled with existential bitterness, drowning outside

the social mainstream, are America's stylized vision of itself, a true cultural reflection of the mental dysfunction of a nation in uncertain transition.[15]

These writers are referring to classic noir films such as *The Big Sleep* (Howard Hawks, 1946) and characters like Marlowe. Yet, in terms of noir, Angel himself emerges as the perfectly imperfect noir protagonist: he is flawed (he cannot enter daylight and is rendered more or less sterile by the curse of perfect happiness). Haunted by a dark past, trapped by remorse, he is alienated from both vampires and humans. Furthermore, he is a vampire with a soul, who – like the archetypal noir detective, Marlowe – is a private eye helping the helpless survive in a nocturnal city; who, like Marlowe, freely crosses between the city's underbelly and its skyscrapers; and finally, who, again like Marlowe, isn't averse to taking the law into his own hands and fulfilling his role as hero, questor and champion.

Heroes and champions may seem to oppose classic noir's gritty realism. However, many critics have traced chivalric themes through works such as *The Big Sleep*. Furthermore, studies have shown that existing within Chandler's noir shamus is a 'gumshoe Galahad', a heroic knight with a strong sense of the chivalric code of honour, *comitatus*.[16]

Angel's association with Marlowe is not all that connects him to an older chivalric tradition. In 'Sanctuary' (1:19), Faith refers to Angel as Buffy's 'brave knight'. In 'Untouched' (2:4) Cordelia describes Angel to a client as, 'He's old-fashioned: *old* fashioned, like the age of chivalry. He sees you pretty much as the damsel in distress.' In 'Judgement' (2:1) Angel engages in a medieval joust at the intersection of Fourth and Spring. And these are just a few examples. More could be said of Angel's 'Round Table' of fellow champions, the Gothic façade of Angel's first office, the Hyperion Hotel's castle-like halls, towers, ramparts and arches, not to mention the various damsels in distress, swords and battle axes, wizards and warriors, magic and monsters of Los Angelus. Certainly, if the chivalric tradition informs 'noir' and Marlowe, then *Angel* renders this theme more explicit. Yet, what does this influence have to do with Los Angelus?

In medieval quest narratives, the fates of questor and world, character and place, are intertwined. Consider the story of the Fisher King. As Jessie Weston's *From Ritual to Romance* shows, many different versions of the myth exist. However, a summary of the plot would go something like this: the Fisher King, ruler of a land, is wounded. The wound renders the king sterile. The kingdom's fate is linked to the king's and so the land too becomes sterile and begins to die. In some versions of this myth it is the king himself, in others a courageous knight, who embarks on a quest. After overcoming various tests, the champion reaches the life-giving Grail. The Grail heals the wounded king and by healing the king, returns life to the dying land.[17]

Now reconsider the name connection: Angelus and Los Angeles; the City of Angels and the city of *Angel*. In the manner of the medieval quest, we find character and place entangled and not in name alone: the dark, monstrous side of Los Angeles is Angelus; the City of Angels is Angel, providing hope to the helpless. Of course, American 'noir' and *Angel* don't depict a kingdom so much as the moral and spiritual wasteland of the modern city. Yet, in both, LA appears as a mise-en-scène which acts as a potent, symbolic sounding-board to plot and the condition of its protagonists. Consequently, the rapidly spliced shots of the city that are interspersed in each episode change to reflect Angel's demise. When world-threatening danger or evil Angelus are ascendant in the story, the accompanying images of LA show it bathed in darkness. In contrast, when Angel's quest appears to be succeeding, those city shots – urban sprawl, highways and palm trees – are bathed in daylight (the aforementioned opening shots of 'The Magic Bullet', (4:19) are an ironic exception). The dream episode, 'Awakening' (4:10) neatly plays out this metaphor: evil blacks out LA's sun, but by the time Angel fulfils his quest and consummates his love for Cordelia, the sun has returned.

It is not only these characters – Marlowe and Angel, their chivalric qualities and the fate they share with their world – which emerge from much older narratives. The depictions of the city as a place of threat and alienation do so as well. In fact, give or take a couple of decades, Angelus/Angel's life-span corresponds to that of the modern metropolis. And almost as long as the metropolis has existed so has its other side, the dark city: a place of regression and darkness as counterpoint to the city's promise of progress and civilization.

The English poet, William Blake (1757–1827), was among the first to evoke the dark industrial landscape of the modern metropolis. In Blake's case, this city was London. In the early to mid nineteenth century, Charles Dickens (1812–70) was another whose writing lingered on the crime, poverty and alienation of that supposedly prosperous Western capital. Once established, the dark city continued to evolve as a motif. Russian novelist Fyodor Dostoevsky's (1821–81) nightmare city reflected his characters' troubled souls, and his French contemporary, Charles Baudelaire (1821–67) portrayed the monstrous side, the flawed modernity, of Paris. Of all the poets in history it is surely significant that, as well as quoting lines from his poem 'Le Vampire' (1855), in 'She' (1:13) Angel names and describes Baudelaire, one of the most influential poets of the dark and 'unreal' metropolis.

Alongside Baudelaire, an equally pertinent name for Angel to evoke would be that of the American-born poet, T. S. Eliot (1888–1965). Like many modernist artists at the beginning of the twentieth century, Eliot adopted and altered the image of the city. In the words of Eliot's most famous poem, 'The Waste Land' (1922),[18] the city has become not simply 'dark' but also a sterile, 'Unreal City' (ll. 60, 207, 376), through which the living dead walk in circles (ll. 40–70). In contrast to the Dickensian city, when encountering 'The Waste Land', we notice that certainties such as fantasy and reality, character and place, are rendered indistinct. 'In the modern urban novel', confirms Malcolm Bradbury in his study on modernism, 'the buildings, noises, sights and smells of the city are all part of the single, racing, modern consciousness'.[19] The 'real' city – in the sense of the 'external' city – is no more. This is an 'unreal city', indistinguishable from the narrator's self. Recalling the medieval quest narrative, this fusing of character and place sounds familiar. A closer look at Eliot's poem confirms this connection.

'The Waste Land' is made up of a cacophony of voices and fragments of literature – Baudelaire, Shakespeare, Greek and Roman mythology, Biblical references and Dante's 'Inferno', to name just a few – all juxtaposed into a ragged, enigmatic text. Throughout this poem is a desperate sense of gathering this chaos into some kind of permanent order, something which will prevent the further falling apart of the interlinked self and city; indeed, one voice refers to the poem itself as 'fragments shored against my ruin' (l. 430). References to one particular narrative give 'The Waste Land' a hint of structure and note of hope. The narrative Eliot uses is that of the medieval quest, specifically, the Fisher King.[20]

James Naremore's study, *More Than Night: Film Noir in its Contexts*, illustrates how 'noir' adopted various themes, including its concept of modern culture as a moral and spiritual wasteland, from modernism.[21] Both 'genres' are primarily urban arts that depict a darker side to the West's ethos of progress and hope. In *Angel* the evil and the dead drift through LA, a city as unreal, dark, alienated and sterile as Eliot's modernist London. We also find in Los Angelus the private eyes, seedy bars, motels, secrets and car journeys of 'noir', as well as the demons, supernatural forces and medieval weapons of the chivalric romance.

Chivalry, quests, the living dead, dark and unreal cities, Blake, Dickens, Baudelaire, modernism, 'noir': *Angel* is one of the most recent descendants of a centuries-long legacy. In the light of this tradition Los Angelus can be seen as more than just the series' setting and it is more than – indeed never simply was – 'real' LA.

Darkness, literal and metaphorical, is central to all these narratives. Casting back to the tradition of the medieval quest, in many we also find the figure of the Redeemer. In *Angel*, this figure is the eponymous hero. He is the noir shamus, the good cowboy, the chivalric champion who, like the Fisher King, is flawed and in need of the healing Grail. Angel's penance, his quest for redemption, which, the promise goes, may ultimately be rewarded with the return of his mortality, is his Grail. Not only his, but that of Los Angelus. It too is a place of urban alienation and chaotic fragments of LA's historical and geographical past – including reference to LA's Wild West origins (Angel is called a 'vampire in a white hat' in 'War Zone', 1:20), the ghosts of 'Hell Town', social divisions and the threat of apocalypse – just as much as LA's unique media legacy. As examples of the last, consider not only *Angel*'s references to 'noir', but also how the law firm Wolfram & Hart provides a demonic reflection of the 1980s television series, *LA Law*. In addition, *Angel* embraces aspects of buddy movies, martial arts movies, soap operas, sitcoms, period drama, urban myths, sport commentaries and all manner of Hollywood productions with shards of ancient mythologies, chivalric romance, Dante's 'Inferno' and Baudelaire. It could be said that *Angel*'s is a postmodern cannibalizing of past styles. I argue, however, that Los Angelus is not a postmodern play of superficiality, but a work which gathers these, often specifically and necessarily Los Angelian, narrative fragments to its cause in a way that recalls Eliot's 'The Waste Land'. That too was dark and made up of relics of the past transformed into something rich and strange, 'shored up against' its own ruin and awaiting redemption.

In conclusion, we find the question 'why Los Angeles?' leads us to the unique 'real' city, its geography and media and social history. In terms of the role Los Angelus plays, we are led in two directions. Firstly, like the kingdom of chivalric romances and the dark city of 'noir' and earlier literature, Los Angelus is a reflection of the protagonist and the protagonist is a reflection of the setting. Within the narrative their fates are intertwined. Second, like the 'dark city' of modernism and 'noir', Los Angelus tacitly presents a challenge to the American Dream. In *Angel*'s vision of the world, just as Angelus lies behind and within Angel, LA, to which 'people are drawn [...] People and other things' ('City Of', 1:1) is a city of vampires more than angels, which despite (or indeed because of) the lure of its glittering skyscrapers is a place of darkness in sunny California.

NOTES

1 Karen Sayer, '"It Wasn't our World Anymore. They Made it Theirs": Reading Space and Place', in Roz Kaveney (ed.), *Reading the Vampire Slayer: An Unofficial Critical Companion to Buffy and Angel* (London and New York: I.B.Tauris and Palgrave, 2001), p. 102.

2 Roz Kaveney, '"She Saved the World. A Lot": An Introduction to the Themes and structures of *Buffy* and *Angel*', in Kaveney (ed.), *Reading the Vampire Slayer*, p. 31.

3 Edward W. Soja and Allen J. Scott, 'Introduction to Los Angeles: City and Region', in Allen J. Scott and Edward W. Soja (eds), *The City: Los Angeles and Urban Theory at the End of the Twentieth Century* (Berkeley: University of California Press, 1998), p. 8. See also Richard S. Weinstein, 'The First American City', in Soja and Scott (eds), *The City*, pp. 22–6.

4 Edward W. Soja, *Thirdspace: Journeys to Los Angeles and Other Real-and-Imagined Places* (Oxford: Blackwell Publishers, 1999), p. 297.

5 Soja, *Thirdspace*, pp. 298 and 310.

6 Soja and Scott, 'Introduction', pp. 1–2.

7 Ibid., p. 1.

8 Ibid., p. 9.

9 Jennifer Wolch, 'From Global to Local; the Rise of Homelessness in Los Angeles During the 1980s', in Soja and Scott (eds), *The City*, p. 390; Soja and Scott, 'Introduction', p. 14.

10 Ibid., p. 20 fn. 3.

11 See also Brian Wall and Michael Zyrd, 'Vampire Dialectics: Knowledge, Institutions, Labour', in Kaveney (ed.), *Reading the Vampire Slayer*, p. 66.

12 Boyd Tonkin, 'Entropy as Demon: Buffy in Southern California', in Kaveney (ed.), *Reading the Vampire Slayer*, pp. 40–3.

13 See also ibid., pp. 39 and 47 and Sayer, '"It Wasn't our World Anymore"', p. 103.

14 Chandler's Marlowe books appeared between 1939 and 1958.

15 Alain Silver and Elizabeth Ward (eds), *Film Noir: An Encyclopedic Reference Guide to the American Style* (Woodstock, NY: Overlook Press, 1992), p. 6.

16 Charles J. Rzepka, '"I'm in the Business Too": Gothic Chivalry, Private Eyes, and Proxy Sex and Violence in Chandler's "The Big Sleep"', *Modern Fiction Studies*, 46: 3 (2000), pp. 695–723.

17 Jessie L Weston, *From Ritual to Romance* (Gloucester, MA: Cambridge University Press, 1983). The legend of King Arthur is one popular version of this narrative.

18 T. S. Eliot, 'The Waste Land', in *Collected Poems 1909–1962* (London and Boston: Faber & Faber, 1963).

19 Malcolm Bradbury, 'The Cities of Modernism', in Malcolm Bradbury and James MacFarlane (eds), *Modernism* (Harmondsworth: Penguin Books, 1990), p. 99.

20 Editor's note: for a discussion of T. S. Eliot and 'The Waste Land' in relation to *Buffy the Vampire Slayer*, see Rhonda V. Wilcox, 'T. S. Eliot Comes to Television: *Buffy's "Restless"'*, *Slayage: The Online International Journal of Buffy Studies*, 7 (2003), at www.slayage.tv/essays/slayage7/Wilcox.htm.

21 James Naremore, *More Than Night: Film Noir in its Contexts* (Berkeley: University of California Press, 1998), pp. 35–45.

6

Outing Lorne:
Performance for the Performers

STAN BEELER

LA is the most futuristic city in the world. People come here because they have a dream: thousands arrive here every year flawed and penniless and morph into beautiful and successful.[1]

In Season Two of *Angel* a new character took his place among the shifting group of friends, employees/employers that make up the ensemble cast of the series. Initially known only as 'The Host', Lorne, or Krevlornswath of the Deathwok Clan, is owner/operator of the demon-friendly karaoke bar Caritas. Green-skinned (Lorne Green), horned and with a sartorial sense reminiscent of the zenith of the disco era, Lorne becomes increasingly important to the plot arc of *Angel* throughout Season Two. His dialogue and actions are motivated by a laissez-faire sense of morality that firmly locates the series in Los Angeles, a place where people (and demons) go to re-create themselves. Lorne is presented as an individual who was uncomfortable in his home dimension of Pylea and, therefore, perceives Los Angeles as a place where his heretofore unappreciated talents can become his defining characteristics.

LORNE IS CAMP!

Lorne is a metaphorical representative of the entertainment industry, which is the soul of Los Angeles. His first speech, appearing before the credits, is the first scene of Season Two of *Angel*. Lorne appears on stage, microphone in hand, resplendent in a white jacket that sets off his green skin, ruby red horns and soulful red eyes. He pauses dramatically for a few seconds, there is a rather ominous burst of music as he leans into the frame which is then undermined by him raising the mike and starting to sing in a very un-demonic voice. He is being set up as a typical Angel demon, and we are surprised, as he croons a few bars of Gloria Gaynor's disco anthem 'I Will Survive', which then segues smoothly into the following:

> Oh, you know what I'm talking about. In this city you better learn to get along, 'cause LA's got it all: the glamour and the grit, the big breaks and the heartaches, the sweet young lovers and the nasty, ugly, hairy fiends that suck out your brain through your face. It's all part of the big wacky variety show we call Los Angeles. You never know what's coming next. And let's admit it folks, isn't that why we love her?
>
> ('Judgement', 2:1)

The juxtaposition of the music, Lorne's clothing style and the mise-en-scène of the club combine to position the new character clearly in the tradition of Camp. This digression from the general film-noir ambience of the series opens up a whole new methodology for its continuing focus on the LA-specific theme of performance. 'Camp favors "exaggeration, artifice, and extremity." It exists in tension with popular culture', but 'outside the cultural mainstream' and is 'affiliated with homosexual culture'.[2] It is a strategy for allowing the representation of the marginal to appear in mainstream forms of discourse; forms which would not normally tolerate the representation of gay men without recourse to camp humour. The elements of 'exaggeration, artifice, and extremity' that are so important to the camp mode of expression are integral to Lorne as a camp figure representing the quintessential LA performer. Exaggeration is present not only in Lorne's over-the-top physical appearance, but also in his club. In contrast to the dingy bars, dark alleys, warehouses and basement apartments that define the visual space of the series, Caritas is well lit, decorated in bright primary colours and invites its patrons to reveal their innermost feelings to a sympathetic audience. Caritas is decorated with an intensely camp sensibility; the mise-en-scène is littered with objects more appropriate to Club 54 than a karaoke bar – including a fully functioning disco ball.

Lorne is a specific example of a general metatextual concern with the performing arts that recurs in this series, and his camp sensibility is completely in keeping with this tendency. As Susan Sontag indicates in her seminal article 'Notes on Camp', '[t]o perceive Camp in objects and persons is to understand Being-as-Playing-A-Role. It is the farthest extension, in sensibility, of the metaphor of life as theatre.'[3] From Cordelia's obsession with her acting career to delicate commentary on classical art forms like the ballet ('Waiting in the Wings', 3:13), *Angel* the series is often about performers and performances; it is often camp in a less stylized manner than Lorne's over-the-top representation of the entertainment business. This alternate form of engagement with the theme of life-as-theatre is apparent in the first few minutes of Season Two. After Lorne's initial appearance in 'Judgement' the action then moves, by means of a jump cut, to Cordelia in a tearful break up with a man unfamiliar to the series fan. It is soon revealed that this is an acting class and Cordelia has been ad-libbing and confusing her partner. Because of the jump cut, the audience does not, at first, understand that this is fiction-within-fiction and we wonder what romantic adventures Cordelia has been up to during the hiatus. This false perception is almost immediately undercut as Cordelia slaps her partner, and he rushes off stage to see if the blow is in the script. The camera draws back from the intimate two-shot and reveals the stage, acting coach and the other students. Charisma Carpenter's comic timing is impeccable, and this scene provides a clear thematic link to Lorne's opening monologue.

COME TO LA AND BE A STAR

Lorne's history, which is slowly revealed over the course of Season Two, is particularly appropriate to the camp conception of life as performance. In the environment of Caritas, Lorne is witty, smooth and quick, full of ironic asides to his 'enlightened' audience: the ultimate hip, big-city host. He is the embodiment of the urban dweller's contempt for anything outside the familiar metropolitan setting. The underlying reasons for this attitude are rooted in the disparity between Lorne's home and his chosen environment; we gradually become aware that his current existence is based upon his maintenance of a performance. Lorne's true origins are revealed in 'Belonging' (2:19) as his past comes back to haunt him in the form of a demon that crosses over from his home dimension. This occurs in the middle of a performance of Stevie Wonder's 'Superstition': the lyrics providing a foreshadowing of subsequent events.

For the first eighteen episodes of Season Two Lorne is known simply as 'The Host': unifying name and job description in one functional soubriquet. This changes in 'Belonging', as contact with an interdimensional traveller, Lorne's cousin Landoc, reveals his formal name, Krevlornswath of the Deathwok Clan, as well as the fact that he prefers to be called Lorne. Angel immediately reveals the intertextual reference to *Bonanza*'s star Lorne Green, but the rest of his crew are too young to remember the series: 'Fifteen years on the air not mean anything to anyone here? Now I really feel old.' This television industry in-joke is completely in keeping with Lorne's function as a representative of the performance spirit of LA. Moreover, it is in harmony with the thematic structure of this episode. 'Belonging' opens with Angel, Wesley, Gunn and Cordelia in an upscale restaurant celebrating Cordelia's new job in a suntan lotion commercial. Later, when Angel goes to visit her on the set, he is appalled by the abuse she suffers at the hands of the director. She is treated like a piece of meat, and Angel's protective instinct prompts him to threaten violence. Although Cordelia is initially angry with Angel for jeopardizing her career, she later admits that the experience was humiliating: 'All I wanted to do was act, for them to like me because I was good. I never wanted to feel like this.' Angel expresses his confusion to Wesley and Gunn: 'Acting's her dream job? People like that? That's the world she wants to live in? I don't get it! … And the way he [the director] talks to her, it's like she's a commodity, like she's a slave or something!'

The hero's dismay with the ugly truths of backstage politics are in sharp contrast to his attraction to the artificial reality of the sunny, palm bedecked beach scene which is the setting for Cordelia's suntan lotion commercial. Reluctant creature of the night that he is, Angel has a moment of pure bliss when he stands on the beach and turns his face to the 'sun' without bursting into flames. The series has a complex message concerning performance and performers; although life as a performer is sometimes hard, the resulting art is often of great value.

One of Cordelia's main functions in the series is to provide comic relief through her attempts to break into the entertainment industry.[4] She is represented as a would-be actress who has come to LA only to be constantly disappointed in her aspirations; Lorne serves an opposite function. His accidental journey to LA allows him to escape an unpleasant past, and he is happy with the moderate success of his 'show business' career. While Cordelia thinks fondly of her small-town origins and her former life as a big fish in a small pond, Lorne is dismayed to be reminded of his home. The story of his unhappy life of unfulfilled expectations in his home dimension is recounted by Landoc. Lorne is told that his mother 'rips your images into tiny pieces and feeds them to the swine, butchers the pigs and has their remains scattered for the dogs' ('Belonging'). All this because Lorne has refused the way of the warrior, thereby bringing great shame on the family. Lorne describes his home as 'black and white with no grey'. The reason that he brings shame on his family is that he uses his talent for empathy to see other moral points of view. This makes him more or less useless as a warrior champion, but is a great asset in the morally ambiguous world of LA's entertainment industry where even swinish directors can make a beautiful scene.

After 'Belonging' the balance of Season Two takes place in Pylea, Lorne's home dimension. As one might expect, Lorne suffers humiliation, abuse and, less predictably, even temporary dismemberment. On the other hand, Cordelia has a wonderful time, as a fairy-tale princess who may be 'forced' to mate with a handsome hero. The trip to Pylea provides the audience with deeper insight into the character of Lorne as an individual as well as an understanding of an entertainment industry archetype: the performer who is completely comfortable in his or her created persona. Lorne's dismemberment is a graphic enactment of the feeling of disintegration when a performer is forced to give up a new and better life and return to an awkward childhood.

LORNE IS OUT

In keeping with the contrast between Lorne's origins and his current metropolitan lifestyle, the representation of Lorne's sexual orientation is indeterminate. His discourse reflects many of the epicene clichés of high camp; his references to other males border on sexual harassment. There is a running gag in which Lorne refers to Angel by a series of pet names throughout several of the episodes. In 'Waiting in the Wings' Lorne calls Angel 'crumb-cake', 'cornmuffin', 'strudel' and 'cinnamonbuns' all within the space of a three-minute conversation. It is undeniable that Lorne's taste in music and his singing style fit societal expectations for homosexual entertainers. Nevertheless, Lorne's sexuality is never made explicit. This allows the writers to develop the metaphorical structure of Lorne as a small-town misfit who shines in the big city on several different levels. And, of course, it is part of one strategy of camp to use excessive, flamboyant indicators of homosexuality without open statements of sexual preference in order to allow the representation of marginal sexuality in mainstream media. As Sam Able indicates: 'Precision is essential to camp, for in order to execute a critique of social norms, the camp artist must achieve simultaneously an embodiment of the target and a parody of it, living in the object and turning it upside-down at once.'[5] *Angel*, like *Buffy the Vampire Slayer* before it, walks a thin line between classification as a teen show – with all the concomitant censorship restrictions that would entail – and adult programming. Nevertheless, it does not take a particularly subtle mind to distinguish the theme of male homosexuality that enters into the series in Season Two. For example, the first task that Angel, Cordelia, and Wesley take on in 'Judgement' is the disruption of a ritual sacrifice of humans by a horned demon hiding behind a mirrored wall in an upscale LA gym club. When the investigators return to their temporary headquarters in Cordelia's apartment Angel is obsessed with the idea of joining a gym. Cordelia at first tries to dissuade him by pointing out that as an immortal he has no need of physical exercise, and when this argument fails, she points out that he would have to shower with a lot of men. Angel considers this and quickly drops the idea.

We may discover the logic behind Lorne's representation as flamboyant, campy demon rather than a human homosexual in Caroline Joan Picart's analysis of the function of the monster in comedy:

> [...] monsters are the liminal point of *not only what* we are *not*, but also what we *are*; they reveal and conceal not only what we *fear*, but also what we *hope for*; and allow us imaginatively to excavate the depths of not only who we *could be* in relation to nature and divinity, but also who we are in relation to the daemons [sic] that lurk within.[6]

Angel's equivocal relationship with Lorne may on one level be related to his inability to reconcile his own internal gay 'demon' with his straight human soul. Although Angel is never presented as openly homophobic, he is consistently represented as extremely uncomfortable with the idea that he is attractive to gay men. Caritas, in its metaphorical function as a gay club, is therefore, a place that gives rise to expressions of considerable discomfort in Angel. There is a connection between Angel's karaoke performance and his negative reaction to all things homosexual. When the situation forces him to actually go onstage and expose his 'spirit' to Lorne through song, he chooses Barry Manilow's 'Mandy'. Lorne asks him why he chose this particular tune and Angel confesses it is the only song to which he knows the words and besides, 'I think it's kinda pretty' ('Judgement'). Manilow's popularity among gay audiences is legendary and Angel's choice of the tune for performance in Caritas immediately places him within the camp framework of the club. In 'Belonging' Lorne suggests that he and Angel could attend an Elton John concert together and 'sit in the back'. Lorne's admiration for Elton John – the king (or perhaps queen) of camp music performance – is as obvious as Angel's suspicion that he has just been asked out on a date by another male.

AMATEURS' NIGHT

Lorne's spiritual function, aiding the karaoke performers to access their 'true destiny', is clearly related to the concept of karaoke as an opportunity for amateurs to express themselves artistically. The quality of the performance does not matter since the focus is not upon pleasing the audience; the primary function of karaoke is to provide the performer with a rewarding experience. Lorne, as the central figure of the camp sensibility of the series, is a natural choice for the association with karaoke. As indicated by Jane Feuer, the amateur performance is central to the concept of camp.[7] Sam Abel reiterates this point in his essay on the camp cartoons of Chuck Jones.[8] Lorne is the perfect camp audience, searching for the emotional heart of even the most appalling rendition of a pop tune and turning the experience into a form of therapy that is essential to the general structure of this series. The introduction of Lorne and his campy karaoke bar signifies the introduction of a new direction in the use of demons as a metaphorical strategy in *Angel*. In the first season, 'Hero' (1:9) uses the theme of racial purity in demons to reference themes of persecution and Nazism, so the idea of a sympathetic yet persecuted Other has already been established. However, as indicated above, Lorne is a key to interpreting the fine moral distinctions peculiar to the entertainment industry.

Lorne and his club serve as a centrepiece for a study in moral distinctions in 'That Old Gang of Mine' (3:3). Gunn's demon-killing 'crew' from the ghetto acquire a new member from Miami, Gio, who convinces them to give up all contact with non-human allies and start killing all demons: both malignant and benign. This comes to a head in Caritas when Gio and Gunn's 'old gang' break in and hold all the patrons hostage. The human patrons, members of Angel Investigations, are given the choice of killing Angel or dying with the demons in a massacre. It is important to note that the terminology used by the 'crew' is directed equally at sexual deviance and race. The scene can be read both ways. For example Gio accuses Gunn of having sexual desires for his own sister and uses the phrase 'A monster-lover ain't no better than a monster' to describe Gunn ('That Old Gang of Mine'). The phrase 'monster-lover' has sexual connotations but also reflects racist terminology. The bonding between the pairs of demon patrons in the club, although subtle, appears to be generally male to male; Fred and Cordelia have – at least for this evening – some of the visual signifiers of a couple as well. In order to remove the spell on Caritas that prevents the demons from protecting themselves Cordelia makes a bargain involving Angel having sexual relations with three sisters. In this episode Caritas is used to focus on the persecution of sexual minorities and it finishes in a triumph of the oppressed. The plot of 'That Old Gang of Mine' brings to mind the 1969 riots in New York that were sparked by police harassment of the staff and patrons of the Stonewall Inn, a gay club on Christopher Street. The police raided the Stonewall Inn and lined up all 200 patrons and staff and made everyone show identification. In the end only the staff and a few transsexuals and transvestites were selected and arrested. This outraged the gay community and sparked riots that affirmed the political strength of gay people in the United States. Although a focal point for the events in this episode, Lorne's function is symbolic rather than active. He shows resolute courage in the face of persecution, but it is up to a quiet demon sitting in the corner to complete the cycle by literally biting Gio's head off.

IT'S GOOD TO BE ON TOP?

In 'The House Always Wins' (4:3) Lorne is again represented as a victim of unscrupulous humans who use his talent to steal the luck of Las Vegas club patrons. Lorne's campy karaoke act has made a move to big-time performances in Las Vegas' Tropicana Club. When Lorne carries his microphone around the crowd to allow his audience to sing a few lines of 'Lady Marmalade' he is forced to betray their fate to his captors. Those who are destined for 'luck' are singled out and sucked dry of their promising future. In this episode we see that performance – even very bad performance – can reveal the depths of a character.

The move from Los Angeles to Las Vegas for this episode is to be expected, considering the relationship of the entertainment industry in the two cities. Las Vegas casinos are a centre for live performances by the stars of the LA film and broadcast industries. Lorne's stage show is reminiscent of the camp excellence of Liberace *sans* piano. The scenes of the Tropicana Club and the Las Vegas Strip at night are Caritas writ large: bright colours abound. In this episode Lorne's special relationship to performance and performers is entwined with the moral dilemma of gambling. The mechanism for the removal of an individual's luck is a special roulette table that steals the destiny of all who are selected to play. We have, therefore, a model of the Las Vegas entertainer's bargain with the devil; the entertainer draws in the crowd and stands by while the gambling ruins their lives. This principle is, of course, applicable to the general situation of performers and therefore a subject of interest for the series as well as an appropriate vehicle for Lorne. 'The House Always Wins' makes it clear that entertainment has moral ramifications, and no matter how hard they try to ignore this fact, entertainers must live with the consequences of their work. There is very little difference between the moral resonance of a shill for a gambling house and a cigarette company or a firm that uses child labour to keep production costs down.

The fifth and last season of *Angel* represents a new facet of LA life for the characters of Angel Investigations. Angel's deal with the Senior Partners of Wolfram & Hart entails a move from the marginal detective lifestyle appropriate to the film noir homage of the earlier seasons to an office tower at the corporate heart of Los Angeles. Considering the importance of the entertainment industry to the economy of the city, it is not surprising that Lorne takes on the role of producer and impresario. This aspect of Lorne's development as a character and symbol is natural given the concern for all aspects of the entertainment industry that is so important to the structure of the series.

'The Life of the Party' (5:5), opens with a low-angle shot of Lorne stalking the halls of Wolfram & Hart, cellphone in hand, dropping names of famous performers – both the quick and the dead – making film deals and arranging futures, a lackey behind him taking notes and catching the cellphone as Lorne enters his office. Like Caritas, which appeared to have elements of a karaoke bar and a gay dance club, Lorne's office also appears to serve dual functions: including the desk appropriate to an office environment and the brightly lit mirror and make-up table suitable to a star performer's dressing room. Camp ambiguity abounds, and Lorne is completely at home in this mixture.

The plot of this episode revolves around the annual Wolfram & Hart Hallowe'en party. Lorne has the responsibility of arranging things, and he is finding it difficult since his boss, Angel, is clearly uncomfortable with the moral ambiguity necessary to make up a guest list of Wolfram & Hart clients. In order to deal with the increasing level of his responsibilities Lorne has had his need to sleep removed. The obvious metaphorical referant is the use of stimulants – perhaps cocaine or amphetamines – to enhance the abilities of an overworked entertainment executive. In the real world this often results in the symptoms of a bipolar personality; extreme highs alternating with depressed or angry periods. In the magical world of *Angel*, Lorne physically splits into two entities: one who spends the entire party keeping things running smoothly and another – bearing a startling resemblance to the Incredible Hulk – who lurks in the toilets murdering guests. Although the threat posed by the angry monstrous version of Lorne is real to the guests, the apparently normal Lorne is dangerous to his friends and co-workers, for he has acquired a new power as an effect of the split. Lorne's suggestions now have the force of command and when he idly instructs Wesley and Fred to 'go get drunk', they are instantly inebriated although they have not been drinking. The metaphorical import of this new situation is related to Lorne's increased potency in the entertainment world. He has been transformed from a small-time performer in a karaoke bar to a powerful media executive with a drug problem whose whims have a devastating effect on those around him. The resolution of this dangerous situation is, as one might suspect, the return of sleep and the reintegration of the two aspects of Lorne's character.

CONCLUSION

In this brief look at the function of Lorne in the series it has become clear that the character serves as the microcosm to the macrocosm of the Los Angeles entertainment industry. He provides a platform to represent the moral ambiguities inherent in a series that 'challenges the distinctions between good and evil in a godless world where there is only choice'.[9] Lorne's whole being is predicated upon a rejection of the simple binary logic of hero versus monster. According to Tanya Krzywinska, 'characters [in *Angel*] do not always neatly align as good or bad, and both humans and demons are potential avatars of evil'.[10] In Lorne's case this, at times equivocal, but generally positive, balance is accomplished through his special connection to entertainment and entertainers and his character highlights a love/hate relationship with Los Angeles as a centre of the existential world of performance.

NOTES

1 Shirin Karimi and Jane Bussman, 'How Not To Have a Shit Life: A Los Angeles Guide', *The Face* (April 2004), p. 98.

2 Karen Pike, 'Bitextual Pleasures: Camp, Parody, and the Fantastic Film', *Literature and Film Quarterly*, 29: 1 (2001), p. 2.

3 Susan Sontag, 'Notes on Camp', in Susan Sontag, *Against Interpretation* (Toronto: Doubleday, 1986), p. 280.

4 Editor's note: for a more detailed discussion of Cordelia Chase and her relationship to the entertainment industry, see Janet K. Halfyard, 'The Greatest Love of All: Cordelia's Journey of Self-discovery', paper presented at the *Slayage* Conference on *Buffy the Vampire Slayer*, Nashville, TN, 28–30 May 2004, at http://www.slayage.tv/SCBTVS-Archive.htm.

5 Sam Abel, 'The Rabbit in Drag: Camp and Gender Construction in the American Animated Cartoon', *Journal of Popular Culture*, 29: 3 (1995), p. 184.

6 Caroline Joan Picart, 'Humor and Horror in Science Fiction and Comedic Frankensteinian Films', *Scope: An Online Journal of Film Studies* (May 2004), at http://www.nottingham.ac.uk/film/journal/articles/humour-and-horror.html.

7 Jane Feuer, *Seeing Through the Eighties: Television and Reaganism* (London, NC: Duke University Press, 1995), pp. 135–6.

8 Abel, 'The Rabbit in Drag', p. 183.

9 Stacey Abbott, 'Walking the Fine Line Between Angel and Angelus', *Slayage: The Online International Journal of Buffy Studies*, 9 (2003), at http://www.slayage.tv/essays/slayage9/Abbott.htm.

10 Tanya Krzywinska, 'Hubble Bubble, Herbs and Grimoires: Magic Manichaeanism, and Witchcraft in *Buffy*', in Rhonda V. Wilcox and David Lavery (eds), *Fighting the Forces: What's at Stake in Buffy the Vampire Slayer* (Lanham, MD: Rowman & Littlefield, 2002), p. 183.

7

'LA's Got it All':
Hybridity and Otherness in
Angel's Postmodern City[1]

SARA UPSTONE

F rom its pilot episode, dialogue and images situate
location as central to *Angel*'s identity. In Seasons One
to Three, images of LA continually return: as location, aerial map, backdrop to opening credits and, perhaps
most memorably, as the heavily lit skyline at night that opens
episodes and – particularly in Season One – flashes as inter-
stitial in-between scenes. Such concentration is more than
simply playing on the concept of a 'City of Angels'. Viewed by
theorists such as Edward Soja as the ultimate postmodern city,
a space that can encompass everything –'is everywhere' – LA
is a model of possibilities that sits well with *Angel*'s fantastic
foundations.[2] Yet the fact that it is at the same time cast by
social commentators as a space of great social division, forever
haunted by the events of Watts and Rodney King, provides an
alternative view, resonant with the representations of alienation and difference also so much a part of *Angel*. Exploring
Angel's interaction with such concerns, a show emerges that
captures simultaneously the city's vibrancy and darkness, its
fantasy and its realism – as Lorne acknowledges an 'all' that is
both 'glamour' and 'nasty […] hairy fiends' ('Judgement', 2:1)
– a city at once of hybridity, and of Otherness.

Much may be garnered about *Angel*'s relationship to such
tensions by examining particularities of representation.

Discussing his vision, David Greenwalt reveals a desire to move away from the fantasy world of *Buffy the Vampire Slayer* (*BtVS*), to a more realist construction: 'this *Angel* show, it will be older, it will be urban and gritty, it will take place in big bad Los Angeles, not this mythical Santa Barbara-like town of Sunnydale where it's sunny and bright but terrible things happen'.[3]

Diverging not just from *BtVS*, but also from the world of privilege captured in series such as *Beverly Hills 90210* and *The O.C.*, *Angel* focuses on a world less-documented in teen and popular television: the dark underside of the wealthy West-side suburbs and glitzy entertainment industries, not the glamour of LA, but its dirty, violent, and divided urbanity. In these terms, LA is a postmodern city not because of a celebratory, vibrant spirit, but because of a chaotic and destructive reality.

I would suggest that, cast in such terms, *Angel* creates a city of the Other. Usefully employed by both feminist and post-colonial theory, the Other comes to stand for the socially or politically disenfranchised. It is therefore particularly useful to describe a city seen to embody difference in its very con-struction, as 'the traditional role of Los Angeles both in urban theory and in the popular imagination was to be the "other"',[4] where marginalization is not a simple matter of racial, sexual or class-based discrimination, but is instead part of 'a city inhabited by millions of marginalized people'.[5]

As a vampire isolated from the daytime world and its inhabitants, Angel embodies this idea. His monstrous status resonates with monster theory, where:

> The monster is difference made flesh, come to dwell among us. In its function as dialectical Other or third-term supple-ment, the monster is an incorporation of the Outside, the Beyond [...] Any kind of alterity can be inscribed across (constructed through) the monstrous body, but for the most part monstrous difference tends to be cultural, political, racial, economic, sexual.[6]

Angel represents the general figure of difference within the city: his alienation from society stands as metaphor for the multiple forms of marginality existing within an urban context; his experience resonates with the city's own diverse Otherness, which itself reinforces the profundity of Angel's experience. In this way, the relationship between Angel's difference and LA might be usefully described as forming a positive feedback loop, in which the presence of each element causes increased production of the other. Representing LA facilitates a pronounced intensification in the sense of Otherness in *Angel*, drawing on the city's history to foreground issues of marginality and alienation. Conversely, Angel's own Otherness is itself an impetus for focusing on the Otherness of the city – rather than, say, its entertainment connections – as an embodiment of this central aspect of the vampire's character. LA and Angel's marginality are caught in a reciprocal partnership, entwined intimately so that attention to one only heightens the focus on the other, acting to re-affirm the place of both at the centre of the show.

Read in these terms, elements reinforcing Otherness must be seen as supporting coterminously both Angel's character development and the representation of LA. The show's very style, its dominant night-time location, reflects not only Angel's photophobia, but also stresses LA's darkness: that Angel is just one of many isolated figures dwelling in its shadows. Its leitmotif of Angel walking into the darkness emphasizes not only his own exclusion, but provides the context within which the city is viewed: narrow alleyways suggesting constrained experience, smoke highlighting the presence of the unseen, and tunnels offering indication of a parallel existence: a city underneath a city as metaphor for the underworld within which many of its inhabitants – human as well as inhuman – exist. This is the world of Anne, transposed from her original appearance in *BtVS* to a shelter where she describes a reality of 'worse things' than vampires: 'a fourteen-year-old girl sitting in her own blood after a rough trick and dozens of people just walking right by' ('Blood Money', 2:12), and of the homeless figures carefully placed within street scenes. It is this city that 'became the homeless capital of the United States in the 1980s' – the world of burnt

out cars, derelict housing and littered streets, the flipside of
the affluent suburbs of 'The Bachelor Party' (1:7) and Hollywood mansions.[7] The gated nature of these mansions,
represented prominently as early as 'City Of' (1:1), and the
show's frequent focus on wire fences, physically indicates the
multiple divisions – gender, race, sexual and class – preoccu-
pying LA life. What emerges is a representation that resonates
strongly with Mike Davis' now-famous 'Fortress LA', where
you are subject to surveillance and containment: 'newly gated
communities [...] based on the fundamental agreement of the
residents that what is urban about a city should be left in front
of the gates', a population 'imagining a demonising and
demonised Other that needs to be set apart'.[8]

Angel refuses to deny this 'in front of the gates' reality,
where victims are from the 'low-rent neighbourhood' ('Somnambulist', 1:11) and vampire nests form in 'low-income
housing' ('Provider', 3:12). Two characters in particular –
Gunn and Lorne – reinforce this representation by presenting,
in detail, specific forms of Otherness. Lorne's first appearance
centres around strategic choices clearly representing him not
only as demon Other, reinforcing Angel's position, but also as
sexual Other: flamboyant dress, physical mannerisms, the use
of 'I Will Survive' as his opening performance ('Judgement').
Situating Caritas in downtown LA displaces Lorne from the
'activist homosexual population' of West Hollywood, into a
locale where antipathy towards demon status may be read
metaphorically as hostility towards homosexual identity.[9] Yet
as a haven within harsh urbanity, Caritas captures simultaneously the power of West Hollywood's community. Read as a
site where 'the most dazzling cabarets have always been a
sideshow to the upheavals of history', Lorne's psychic abilities mirror this as his entertainments capture the city's current
traumas.[10]

Similarly, Gunn's location represents the urban ghettoiza-
tion of African Americans. Like Lorne, distinctive identity
marks his difference: street clothing and a dialect peppered
with frequent uses of language such as 'y'all' and 'brothers'.
Gunn's initial underground home with his 'crew' indicates an

actual unseen world denied by the LA administration, as illustrated by his exclusion from the support of official law-enforcement and the city's opportunities. Gunn's attack on Cordelia as a 'skinny white beauty queen' who doesn't 'have a clue why I do the things I do' ('First Impressions', 2:3) reveals a gritty, real world of difference initially beyond the realms of the former Sunnydale girl's reality. Outside the city proper, Gunn exists in a world of local allegiances, where the neighbourhood is everything, informing local criminals: 'you wanna jack beamers in Brentwood, be my guest, but leave the neighbourhood cars alone' ('First Impressions'). Here, the distinction is no longer between the lawful and the lawless, but those who have and those who have not: those inside the system, and those on its margins. In 'The Thin Dead Line' (2:14) the connection between this marginality and the specifics of LA are explicit, where police brutality is combined with the filming of its violence, and Gunn announces: 'Cops see me with this [video camera], there ain't no way we can Rodney King 'em'.

This overarching presence of Otherness, tied inherently to LA, produces episodes in which it is the most prominent theme. One particularly notable example is 'Are You Now, or Have You Ever Been' (2:2), interesting in that its concern with Otherness is not motivated by development of particular characters, but rather by multiple registers of marginality and difference. The episode is conspicuous in bearing little relation to wider story arcs; though it introduces the Hyperion Hotel as Angel Investigations' new headquarters, achieving this through an account set in the 1950s seems unnecessary apart from desire to reflect on LA's history of social exclusion. In the present, the hotel is a deserted building surrounded by barbed wire. In its 1950s past, a black family are told there are 'no vacancies', reflecting exclusion of African Americans from public establishments; an openly homosexual couple wander through the lobby, and the McCarthy communism trials are on television. A paranoia demon involves the hotel inhabitants in a hysteria that mirrors the fears of communism surrounding LA's entertainment community. Yet, ending in

Angel's lynching for being a 'freak' after his attempts to help a woman who is 'passing' as white, it also reflects white supremacist violence against black individuals, capturing the connection between anti-communism and racist policing.[11] Following from comments that 'the King beating bore the familiar markings of the 1950s and 1960s', such an episode is transformed from a disconnected, seemingly incongruous reflection on the history of LA, to a direct comment on the perpetuation of past prejudices and their relevance to recent events.[12]

Angel has not limited its construction of Otherness to class and race but extends its concerns to issues of gender. In 'Billy' (3:6), for example, Cordelia and Lilah unite in gendered Otherness against a man who would 'beat you down 'til you stay down 'cause he doesn't even think of you as alive', and Fred faces Wesley's own patriarchal power: a 'good man' in whom, nevertheless, an innate prejudice, 'was forced to the surface'. Such concern undermines any association of *Angel* with one particular form of social exclusion: instead it is evidence of a complex web of dehumanization of all who are viewed as different. Wider story arcs have to some extent reinforced this relationship; the destruction of the city in Season Four culminating in its burning, in particular, resonates not only with the 1992 riots, but also with a history of representations of LA that see the city 'die by fire' as a result of its tensions.[13]

In Season Three, however, Otherness begins to be interrogated seriously by an alternative reading of urban society. As Gunn rejects his African-American community in 'That Old Gang of Mine' (3:3) in favour of the 'mission', Wesley asserts that 'I can't have any one member of this team compromising the safety of the group'. Reinforced by Lorne's departure from Caritas and habitation of the hotel ('Dad', 3:10), what thus emerges is a cross-cultural team where individual identities become increasingly merged to serve the needs of the community. Such a position may be termed not Otherness, but hybridity: what postcolonial theorist Homi Bhabha has referred to as a position that 'resists the binary opposition of racial and cultural groups' in favour of, on one hand, the recognition of shared values and, on the other, productive tensions that cause groups to re-evaluate their own positions.[14] In Season Three, such difference-within-commonality is maintained by subtle, problematic readings: the fact that Gunn continues to face his background in episodes such as 'Double or Nothing' (3:18), and does not easily reject his 'crew', asserting his continued difference from Angel as just 'the way it is' ('That Old Gang of Mine'). This may be seen as the realization of a desire imbedded even in earlier constructions of Otherness: the distinction between *BtVS*'s individualistic 'I'm the slayer' and *Angel*'s communal 'we can help' ('Lonely Heart', 1:2), Doyle's sacrifice in the name of hybrid identity in 'Hero' (1:9), and Caritas' status as an inclusive space that obliterates difference and conflict through its protected status, mimicking West Hollywood's representation of itself 'as the melting pot of […] national and international cultures'.[15]

In a city where 'everybody who differed from the white conservative model was excluded' this hybrid alliance in many ways provides a more apt model than *Angel*'s initial focus on Otherness. Indeed, while realizing LA's harsh social reality is of great significance, it has been noted recently that this image of the city has in fact condemned its marginalized inhabitants to an increasingly ghettoized existence. Media representation is seen to mirror real-world discrimination, where post-1992: 'From the European press, the news on LA is consistently about disintegration and civil collapse, with imagery as familiar as a hip-hop video: a bleached ghetto street, burnt-out store fronts, perhaps a chain-link fence prominent' as the Davis image of 'Fortress LA' 'seems impossible to shake'.[16] Stagnating in such images only plays into negative constructions of the city, ultimately further marginalizing its Others. Containing, by the show's finale, two vampires, a working-class African American, an ambiguously sexed demon, an English immigrant and a human–demon hybrid – each being asked to contribute their own unique skills and abilities – *Angel* encapsulates a coalition of celebrated difference, an answer to David Theo Goldberg's cry for a city that must be seen as 'uncontainable, unrestrictable, as the refusal to be divided'.[17] If we accept the reading of 1992 as the action of a 'rainbow coalition', protests that encompass race, class and – interestingly bringing the Otherness of Lorne and Gunn together once again – sexuality, where the homo-sexual community actively supported class- and race-motivated protests, then *Angel's* hybrid fusion captures LA's existing, postmodern reality.[18] Perhaps more powerfully, accepting the dark vision *Angel* began with as reflecting more intractable division behind such events, the show has now progressed to provide an alternative urban model.

Such a shift, however, is not without its problems. As destruction means the city vanishes in Season Four, so the relationship between the city and a reinforcement of issues of Otherness is profoundly marked by absence. As Angel's feed-back loop is disrupted by removal of the city, his own Otherness no longer has a location from which to develop. For while the burning of the city itself has cultural relevance, the socially aware episodes of Seasons One to Three them-selves disappear in Season Four, replaced in the Jasmine and Beast plots by longer uninterrupted story arcs more fitting of *BtVS*, and approaching the 'BYO: bring your own' policy that Joss Whedon applied to the earlier series specifically to pre-vent 'issue' episodes.[19] Here it must be remembered that hybridity is not a removal of difference, it relies on a moment where 'cultural differences "contingently" and conflictually touch', where individual perspectives merge to create new meanings.[20] If the figures in this coalition subsume their individual identities – if there is no longer the 'pull of divided loyalties' ('That Old Gang of Mine') – they no longer continue to serve as useful models: either for a critique of their own marginalization, or of LA's general marginalization of difference.

Bearing this problem in mind, Season Five must be approached with trepidation. Following from Season Four, it sets up a position in which, subsumed into Wolfram & Hart's corporate vision, each main character loses further their dis-tinctive difference. The flamboyance and sexual ambiguity defining Lorne's initial appearances never returns, Gunn is subjected to a startling erasure of his black identity – losing both his dialect and distinctive street style – and Angel himself loses the explicit Otherness marking his original character. In 'In the Dark' (1:3) Angel makes his case for defending those in the darkness, outside the reach of conventional services: 'Daytime people have help. The whole world is designed for them, so much so that they have no idea what goes on around them after dark. They don't see the weak ones lost in the night or the things that prey on them. And if I join them, maybe I'd stop seeing too.' Posturing behind Wolfram & Hart's specially treated glass, Angel becomes exactly what he feared: a figure of the day, with no access to those truly on the city's borders. No longer showing his vampire face in battle, his persona now echoes Buffy's position of representing moderate difference within the system, rather than the absolute outsider he once represented.

Yet the motivation behind such construction in the final season reveals itself as very different from Season Four's removal of difference. As viewers are no longer expected to identify with the central characters, but are asked instead to lament their descent into the corporate world, foregrounding the disappearance of Otherness in the final season serves as part of a self-conscious critique; lost identities intended to be noticed and heighten the show's social commentary, rather than continued distancing from urban reality. For example, Gunn's acceptance of having his brain filled with knowledge to become a lawyer appears as an offensive acceptance of the suggestion that working-class African-American individuals would be unable to function in such roles without mystical intervention. Seeing the Conduit to begin with as a black panther indicating his proud African-American identity, Gunn sees by the end of the season simply his corporate, individualist self, only to be informed that its form is 'determined by the viewer' ('A Hole in the World', 5:15), indicating his rejection of difference. When the consequence of this action is Fred's death, it alerts the viewer to the need to identify against Gunn's current identity, in favour of his original character.

This is borne out in his transformation as the season draws to a close. Facing the reality of his behaviour, Gunn poignantly reveals the desire to transcend stereotype, explaining his actions as a result of being unable to lose 'everything that made me different, special. I couldn't go back to being just the muscle' ('Shells', 5:16); he is caught in self-hatred reminiscent of that illuminated in Frantz Fanon's seminal *Black Skin, White Masks*.[21] Gunn recognizes he has lost his cultural identity, that 'I was weak. I wanted to be somebody that I wasn't. 'Cause I don't know where I fit. 'Cause I never did' ('Shells'), a return to his earlier meditations on identity in Season Three. Returning to his street clothes for the rest of the season, he appears to resolve such issues through a return to his Otherness, and to his black, working-class marginal identity as a sense of strength, rather than disability, becoming the voice of the Other once again in 'Time Bomb' (5:19) against Angel's directive to 'serve our clients'.[22]

Similarly, Angel's increasing dissatisfaction with Wolfram & Hart as the season continues suggests explicit desire to resume a marginal position. As his proclamation that you 'can't sweat the small stuff' ('Power Play', 5:21) is revealed in the same episode as cover for infiltration of the Black Thorn, we learn this is exactly what Angel has been doing all along: sweating the 'small stuff' that are the marginalized victims he originally came to LA to protect. The city returns as well. In 'You're Welcome' (5:12) the aerial image of the city reappears, at the same time that Cordelia materializes to inform Angel 'you forgot who you are', the city and identity once again indissolubly linked in an episode that – featuring a flashback to Doyle's original advertisement for Angel Investigations – returns the show to its original concerns. By the end of the season, opponents are no longer divorced from the city; instead, in a senator whose staff 'prey on the homeless' ('Power Play'), the direct social relevance of earlier seasons resurfaces. Similarly, challenging the institutions supporting Wolfram & Hart suggests desire to recognize the 'interesting correspondence between great concentrations of corporate power and large concentrations of an amalgamated "other"':

infiltrating the neo-colonial corporate power networks that maintain the exploitation of LA's poor and that were the villains of *Angel*'s very first episode.[23] Against the corporate meetings of the first half of the season, in 'Shells' each figure appears alone, isolated in grief for Fred, no longer a united coalition. And, in *Angel*'s final episode, Spike returns to his poetry, Gunn to Anne and his own neighbourhood, Wesley to his role of Watcher in his position as Illyria's caretaker, Lorne to cabaret performance: each figure returning to his identity and to an acknowledgment that hybridity only functions effectively within an awareness of difference.

What emerges in the very final scene of *Angel* is recognition of this contrapuntal reality: Angel as Other, emerging in the alley alone, again framed by barbed wire, only to then be joined gradually by his team members, who form a coalition of difference and hybrid potential. To never resolve such tension is not necessarily problematic; rather it represents a fitting conclusion mirroring the dilemma real-world Others of LA must face: how to maintain unique individuality, yet at the same time build a united city that allows for the celebration of difference in *all* its forms. The fusion of Angel Investigations thus offers the opportunity to represent a critique of those who cast LA as beyond redemption, 'the countervailing force which created much interethnic solidarity [...] usually unnoticed by the common depiction of the 1992 events', but also the trauma of attempting to negotiate positions of identity and belonging.[24] Being both inside and outside the city, hovering on its margins, reflects the tension in such a location. Returning to the city in response to Angel's call, 'let's go to work' ('Not Fade Away', 5:22) – fighting evil where they began – *Angel* at its end, and therefore as a whole, returns ultimately to a very complex postmodern urban reality: an onslaught of monsters that must continually be faced, challenged at the same time by both the individual's unique strengths, and the community's cross-cultural resilience.

NOTES

1   'Judgement' (2:1): subsequent season references within text.
2   Edward Soja, *Postmodern Geographies* (London: Verso, 1989), p. 222.
3   David Greenwalt, BBC Online, n.d., at http://www.bbc.co.uk/cult/buffy/angel/interviews/greenwalt/page4.shtml.
4   Roger Keil, *Los Angeles: Globalization, Urbanization and Social Struggles* (Chichester: John Wiley and Sons, 1998), p. xiv.
5   Ibid., p. xxvi.
6   Jeffrey Jerome Cohen, *Monster Theory* (Minneapolis and London: University of Minnesota Press, 1996), p. 7.
7   Jennifer Wolch, 'From Global to Local: The Rise of Homelessness in Los Angeles During the 1980s', in Allen J. Scott and Edward W. Soja (eds), *The City: Los Angeles and Urban Theory at the End of the Twentieth Century* (Berkeley: University of California Press, 1996), p. 390.
8   Keil, *Los Angeles*, p. xxxiv.
9   Ibid., p. 177.
10 Ibid., p. 179.
11 See Martin J. Schiesl, 'Behind the Badge: The Police and Social Discontent in Los Angeles since 1950', in Norman M. Klein and Martin J. Schiesl (eds), *Twentieth-Century Los Angeles: Power, Promotion, and Social Conflict* (Claremont, VA: Regina, 1990), p. 153.
12 Keil, *Los Angeles*, p. xxiv.
13 Norman M. Klein, *The History of Forgetting: Los Angeles and the Erasure of Memory* (London and New York: Verso, 1997), p. 73.
14 Homi Bhabha, *The Location of Culture* (London and New York: Routledge, 1994), p. 207.
15 Keil, *Los Angeles*, p. 180.
16 Klein, *The History of Forgetting*, pp. 114, 237.
17 David Theo Goldberg, 'The New Segregation', in David Bell and Azzedine Haddour (eds), *City Visions* (Harlow: Longman, 2000), p. 199.
18 See Marc Cooper and Greg Goldin, 'Some People Don't Count', in Don Hazen (ed.), *Inside the LA Riots: What Really Happened – and Why it Will Happen Again* (United States: Institute of Alternative Journalism, 1992), p. 46.
19 See Roz Kaveney, '"She Saved the World. A Lot": An Introduction to the Themes and Structures of *Buffy* and *Angel*', in Roz Kaveney (ed.), *Reading the Vampire Slayer: An Unofficial and Critical Companion to Buffy and Angel* (London and New York: I.B. Tauris, 2001) pp. 1–36; and Rhonda Wilcox and David Lavery,

'Introduction', in Rhonda Wilcox and David Lavery (eds), *Fighting the Forces: What's at Stake in Buffy the Vampire Slayer* (Lanham, MD: Rowman & Littlefield, 2002), p. xix.

20 Bhabha, *The Location of Culture*, p. 207.

21 Frantz Fanon, *Black Skin, White Masks* (New York: Grove Weidenfeld, 1967).

22 Of course, Angel's statement is part of his subterfuge: see below.

23 Saskia Sassen, 'Analytic Borderlands: Race, Gender and Representation in the New City', in Anthony King (ed.), *Re-Presenting the City: Ethnicity, Capital and Culture in the Twenty-First-Century Metropolis* (Hampshire: Macmillan, 1996), p. 188.

24 Keil, *Los Angeles*, p. 207.

PART THREE:

'Hell Incorporated':
Wolfram & Hart's
Big Bad

8

Gender Politics in Angel: *Traditional vs. Non-Traditional Corporate Climates*

JANINE R. HARRISON

Lilah to Holtz: I said I'm a lawyer. I don't care about the law.
('Lullaby', 3:9)

Kate to Angel: This job is making me crazy.
('The Thin Dead Line', 2:14)

Cordelia to Harmony: I am happier now than I was then.
('Disharmony', 2:17)

Angel: Who's helping me here?
Fred to Angel: I am!   ('Fredless', 3:5)

W hat do Wolfram & Hart attorney Lilah Morgan, Los Angeles Police Department (LAPD) Detective Kate Lockley, budding actor Cordelia (Cordy) Chase, and former physics graduate student Winifred (Fred) Burkle have in common? Each is endowed with a strong constitution, intelligence and beauty. Yet two of these *Angel* characters lose their sense of self within the course of five seasons, while the remaining duo find their life's path and become increasingly empowered. Although multiple factors contribute to the characters' outcomes, gender politics of the corporate climates to which they become accustomed serve as a determining factor in their fates.

Robert P. McNamara discusses 'socialization', a lifelong process by which people learn to conform to the roles, values and norms of their society. He cites three stages: primary, secondary and adult. In the adult stage, occupational roles are learned. When a person becomes immersed in a workplace culture, McNamara maintains, '[...] an individual's worldview, attitudes toward others, and general well-being are influenced'. [1] This holds true for Lilah, Kate, Cordelia and Fred. While Lilah and Kate are employed in the traditional, patriarchal corporate climates of law/law enforcement, Cordelia and Fred work in the non-traditional, androgynous climate of Angel Investigations. By analysing external factors that may affect each character, overall environments of their workplaces and, more specifically, verbal and non-verbal communication styles, the importance of career choice to each woman's future will be illustrated.

TRADITIONAL CORPORATE CLIMATES

Attorney Lilah Morgan serves as an employee of the multidimensional evil law firm, Wolfram & Hart (W&H), during the first four seasons of *Angel*. While much can be gathered concerning Lilah's work life, little exists regarding her personal one. Only one external factor mentioned may affect her character. To Angel, in the context of her motivation for working at W&H, she reveals that her mother no longer recognizes her but has 'the best room in the clinic' ('Sleep Tight', 3:16). Money to support her mother proves a factor in her employment.

No other mention is made of family or friends; Lilah is alone. Whether she was equally isolated prior to W&H remains unknown; however, she definitely is isolated throughout the series, probably because of the demands of W&H. The firm permeates *every* aspect of employees' personal lives. Prior to Lilah's physical-turned-affectionate, albeit unhealthy, relationship with Wesley, she is uninvolved. Gavin remarks, 'From what I hear, bumping uglies with an old man who body-jumped into a vampire is the closest thing you've had to a meaningful relationship in years' ('Quickening', 3:8). Even her relations with Wesley contain ulterior motives. She tries to elicit information from him concerning Angel's whereabouts ('Deep Down', 4:1). Soon after, she sets him up to allow her firm access to Lorne, to drain a vision from his mind ('Slouching Toward Bethlehem', 4:4). Never does Lilah experience romance untainted by her employment. All told, Lilah's entire life is afflicted by the firm, which has a corporate culture so aggressive that it pervades employees' personal and even afterlives.

Indeed, Wolfram & Hart is the epitome of a competitive, cut-throat environment based upon a masculine management style. Even though the ideas of 'masculine' and 'feminine' change constantly, W&H has existed for millennia. It is safe to assume that the corporation is traditional. After all, ritual is part of the workplace culture as in the Senior Partners' seventy-five-year review. The patriarchy of the US workplace, then, has probably been passed down through generations of LA branch male employees. This is evident by their use of masculine methodologies. R. W. Connell asserts that the most dominant form of masculinity in Western society entails qualities such as aggressiveness and violent tendencies that are reflected in the workplace, the ethos of which is possessed by professional middle-class men.[2] This idea is reinforced by Judy Wajcman, who posits, 'Success means being lean, mean, aggressive, and competitive with tough, forceful leaders. Managerial work itself is conceptualized as involving constant action.' She states that organizations built using a masculine management style are erected upon the emotions of fear, anxiety and aggression. Wajcman writes, '[…] uncontrolled competition and aggression are seen as rational when in pursuit of organizational goals'.[3] W&H's corporate climate stinks of competition, violence and fear as its employees aggressively attempt to fulfil the firm's goals.

W&H is so competitive that its employees are often pitted against one another, sometimes resulting in counter-productivity. For instance, in Season Two the resurrected human Darla catches Lilah snooping in Lindsey's office after business hours. Lilah explains, 'I just like to keep abreast of his latest projects, and he's probably in my office right now trying to find out about mine. That's just how it works at our firm' ('Untouched', 2:4). Similarly, when Gavin shares his intent to embroil Angel in the red tape of the Hyperion Hotel's building-code violations, Lilah feels threatened and has her secretary call a forger so she can sabotage his plan by providing Angel with legitimate documentation ('Carpe Noctum', 3:4). Not only is W&H masculine in this sense, it also oscillates between the regular use of violence and fear.

On one hand, W&H employees threaten/use violence routinely. On the other hand, they live in fear of violence should they fail the firm. Numerous times Lilah uses threats. In 'Lullaby', a W&H translator comments that deciphering the Nyazian Scrolls 'should be fun'. Lilah replies, 'No. It shouldn't be fun. What it should be is done by morning or I'll have your family killed.' This same woman feels afraid when Nathan Reed, special representative to the Senior Partners, announces that the Special Projects Division, then co-directed by Lilah and Lindsey McDonald, will be re-evaluated. Lilah comments, 'They'll promote one and cut the other. Around here that's a literal cutting.' In preparation should she lose to Lindsey, she packs a gun and a bottle of pills in her purse, presumably to commit homicide/suicide during the meeting ('Dead End', 2:18). The mentality of threaten or be threatened, one of utter distrust, is in keeping with the masculine management style that defines W&H's corporate climate.

Lilah is the only female in W&H's LA branch who ascends the corporate ladder from attorney to an upper-level management position, vice-president of Special Projects. However, the climb is difficult. During the first several seasons, preferential treatment by higher-ups is shown to male counterparts Lindsey and Gavin. Even though Lilah and Lindsey appear to have comparable work histories, toward the Season One conclusion a very fatherly Holland Manners gives Lindsey a posh office and considerable raise for showing spirit by betraying the firm, whereas Lilah receives nothing for devout loyalty ('Blind Date', 1:21). Likewise, in the third season, newcomer

Gavin brags that special representative to the Senior Partners, Linwood Murrow, has given him – *not* her – his personal cell-phone number ('The Price', 3:19). Lilah's trek to upper management is more arduous than the males'. She admits this in 'Sleep Tight':

Angel: Don't you ever get tired of the whole femme fatale act?

Lilah: Look – I've been doing this a long damned time. I've had to be better, smarter, quicker than every man at Wolfram & Hart.

Angel: So, it's a feminist thing.

Lilah: No, it's a survival thing.

Lilah sacrifices considerably to excel. It is plausible that she even forfeits her womanhood. Wajcman argues, '[...] a marked gender imbalance persists at the apex of organizational career structures. [...] There is not much room at the top for women, and we shall see that successful women are not so much representatives of, as exiles from, their sex.'[4] Lilah is, for all intents and purposes, male. When Lindsey resigns during the meeting in which he is to be promoted to permanent division head, he tells Nathan Reed, 'Lilah is your guy' ('Dead End'). He chooses a male descriptor over 'woman', 'gal', or even 'girl'.

Lilah perceives herself similarly. When she and Lindsey recruit Faith to assassinate Angel, Lindsey discusses Faith's felony charge:

Lindsey: I think if a service is rendered, we can get you off.

Faith: You don't know how many men have promised me that.

Lilah: I'm sure you won't be disappointed in *our* performance.

Lilah sees herself as part of the 'company penis' capable of satisfying Faith ('Five by Five', 1:18).

Her verbal and non-verbal communication styles are masculine too. Linguistics professor Deborah Tannen defines 'linguistic style' as: '(1) a person's characteristic speaking pattern; (2) a set of culturally learned symbols by which we not only communicate but also interpret others' meanings and evaluate one another as people.'[5] Linguistic styles can be subcategorized by gender. Dr Senta Troemel-Ploetz discusses the traditionally dominant speech patterns of males versus the submissive patterns of females learned during socialization. Troemel defines dominant acts as: '[...] commands, orders, explanations, contradictions, doubts, advice, criticism, evaluations, definitions, punishment, attacks, challenges, accusations, reproaches [...]'. In contrast, submissive acts include: '[...] apologize, defend, ask for favours, beg, request permission, justify herself, agree, support, adjust, accommodate, and accept someone else's definition of the situation'.[6] Lilah's speech pattern involves dominant acts. She commands, orders and attacks her colleagues and subordinates and never apologizes nor accepts a peer's definition of a situation.

Lilah's non-verbal communication is equally as masculine. Authors Pat Heim and Susan K. Golant assert that powerful people, such as physicians and attorneys, employ the stone face as a means of signalling power. Women who ascend the corporate ladder tend to become less readable.[7] Of Lilah, Kate, Cordy and Fred, Lilah's face is the least scrutable. Her fashion sense is also masculine. George B. Sproles and Leslie Davis Burns believe that fabric forms a fashion code that can convey specific social meaning. They maintain, 'Fashion symbols can communicate impressions or illusions such as physical attractiveness, femininity and masculinity, power and dominance, and self-confidence and assurance.'[8] Lilah consistently wears suits, usually in the dark and/or muted colour schemes worn by businessmen. Her wardrobe also reinforces company loyalties. When colour is added to Lilah's clothing palette, it is usually red, often associated with hell. Her non-verbal communication emphasizes masculinity and the related qualities of power, dominance and self-assurance.

Season Four proves Lilah's undoing. To recap, Wesley terminates their relationship primarily because her loyalties are with W&H, not him. When the Beast destroys her firm, she has no place to turn to but Angel Investigations (AI), where a

Jasmine-controlled Cordelia murders her. She returns only once from hell, where she works because her W&H contract is eternal; when Wes attempts to destroy the document to give her peace, it mystically replicates instead.

In retrospect, when introduced in Season One, Lilah Morgan is a self-assured go-getter. But she is also a loner whose continual isolation and sacrifices to excel using a masculine management style in a man's world take their toll. By the end, she has surrendered possibilities of friendship and romance, even her own womanhood. Although she and her mother both gain 'best' rooms, the trade-off of isolation and eternal work for 'Hell, Incorporated' hardly seems worthwhile.

Meanwhile, LAPD Detective Kate Lockley, from the first two seasons of *Angel*, is an Award of Merit, Medal of Valour and Citizen's Auxiliary Achievement Award recipient ('Sense and Sensitivity', 1:6). In fact, like Lilah, her life *is* work. Kate follows her father into policing because as a child, after her mother dies, her father retreats into police work. While under a sensitivity spell, she tells him that it was, '[…] like you couldn't stand the sight of me. … But "big girls don't cry", right?' She continues, 'God, I wanted to drink with you. I wanted you to laugh with me the way you laugh with Jimmy or Frank […]'. This back-story illustrates that Kate was raised by an emotionally repressed male, preoccupied with the historically male occupation of policing. She grew up under this influence only to yearn for acceptance in a man's world to gain the love and approval never received as a child. This external factor directs her life.

The LAPD is portrayed typically, with tough, stoic personnel, characteristics considered masculine. In 'Sense and Sensitivity', though, when Kate's entire department is under a spell, both motivation and consequences for these traits are cited. During sensitivity training, for example, back-story is provided for fellow officer, Heath. He had no father but six older brothers, so he hid his emotions early. 'I learned to hit back pretty quick', he admits. Kate, similarly, had learned 'big girls don't cry'. The results of such emotional bottling are then shown when a traffic cop vents, 'I've got emotional whiplash from having to deal with people like you day in and day out! If anyone's the victim here, it's me! I've alienated my friends, my family – my own children are afraid of me – I can't even make love to my wife!' This officer sounds not only like Kate, who viewers learn is lonely in her debut, 'Lonely Heart' (1:2), but also the ever-isolated, repressed Lilah. Both law and law enforcement devalue open communication and co-operation.

Terence J. Fitzgerald maintains that women are relatively new to policing, since they were not fully integrated into the force until after the Second World War.[9] Kate, in turn, works diligently to be better than male co-workers. For an officer, this means 'bravery'. More than once, Kate pursues a suspect without using available back-up. In 'Somnambulist' (1:11), for instance, even though multiple squad cars are parked outside the building a suspect is in, Kate tells an officer, 'I'm going in!' and does so alone. Like Lilah, she must be better than men to receive even nearly equal treatment.

Kate has a masculine demeanour as evidenced by her speech and fashion style. She employs dominant speech-acts via terse sentences, particularly commands. She barks, 'Where?' to an officer ('Somnambulist') and orders another officer, 'Well, get statements!' ('The Prodigal', 1:15). Her fashion sense, as defined by Ruth P. Rubinstein, is categorized as 'nature' and 'practicality'. Kate wears dark and/or neutral colours; T-shirts; mannish dress shirts; vests or waist-length jackets with masculine accessories, such as her thick band, large-dial watch. According to Rubinstein, the social meaning of a 'nature' ensemble continues to be seen as an image of independence and self-reliance. A wardrobe classified as 'practicality', is '[...] attire that requires little upkeep and is durable and roomy [...] they suggest that pragmatism and efficiency may be essential elements of self-definition'.[10] Independence, self-reliance, pragmatism and efficiency are qualities associated with maleness. All in all, Kate appears a mannish figure, to the extent that her father questions her gender orientation. When Kate introduces him to Angel, he says that it is good to see her with a man because he was afraid she was 'leaning in the other direction altogether' ('Sense and Sensitivity').

While male tendencies serve her well in the department, female tendencies do not. When vampires kill her father, leaving Kate without closure, she becomes obsessed with otherworldly phenomena and revenge. Emotions over his death seize control and emotionalism is considered a female trait. Consequently, she is demoted to a smaller station ('Dear Boy', 2:5) and later faces a hearing. She tells Angel: 'They've just been looking for an excuse. You know this is about me. I'm a cop – that's all I've ever been – I can't take a suspension. I would just …'. Worse, she is fired. With no life outside policing, she overdoses; luckily, Angel rescues her ('Reprise', 2:15). Afterwards, she reveals, 'I feel like such an idiot. My whole life has been about being a cop. If I'm not a part of the force, it's like nothing I do means anything' ('Epiphany', 2:16). Kate, like Lilah, sacrifices femininity and her life for work in a traditional corporate climate. Since they *become* their workplace cultures, they feel utterly lost once work is removed.

NON-TRADITIONAL CORPORATE CLIMATE

Cordelia Chase grows up in Sunnydale as a superficial, rich girl nicknamed 'Queen C', with a high-school following of popular girls called the 'Cordettes'. She is determined to bat her eyelashes and fake-laugh her way into marriage with a prominent husband. However, her parents lose their wealth when caught for tax evasion, so Cordy seeks her fortune in LA. Instead of blooming as a starlet, she grows into a compassionate, capable woman. This is due to her and Angel's formation of Angel Investigations.

AI is a start-up company, but unlike the hierarchical organizations present in W&H and the LAPD, it contains a circular structure. Sally Helgesen discusses this approach: in a 'Web of Inclusion', leaders are at the centre instead of on top, which facilitates increased access and communication for employees.[11] Angel, usually boss, is at the centre of AI. The company atmosphere is casual and Angel, accessible professionally and personally, often listens to his colleagues and follows their advice. AI applies an androgynous management style, one employing a balance of masculine and feminine qualities. Even though Angel is male, he has previously worked with enabled females such as Buffy Summers and, confident himself, has no need for male superiority. While he tends toward solitary reflection and the traditionally masculine ideas of toughness, assertiveness and risk taking, Cordelia guides him in forming a corporate environment based in part on the feminine management concepts of communication and cooperation, which create 'family'. Doing so empowers her in turn.

Cordelia is the most psychosocially androgynous character discussed. She speaks directly and honestly, using orders, explanations, advice and challenges. Yet she also agrees, supports, adjusts and accommodates. This helps AI succeed. For instance, in 'I Fall to Pieces' (1:4), Angel admits, 'I'm not comfortable asking people for money.' Cordy replies, 'Then get over it! I mean that in a sensitive way.' She's practical; they need income. Angel responds to her wording, which perches between toughness (male) and caring (female). In another example, she chides him:

Cordy: You act like you don't have a pulse.
Angel: I don't.
Cordy: Well spend a little time listening to how the living
          interact.

('Sense and Sensitivity')

Strong advice from the heart frequently makes Angel analyse his behaviour; consequently, he becomes more involved with the AI staff. As each season passes, Cordy, too, becomes more compassionate.

Midway through Season One she shows significant growth. After her date abandons her during a vampire attack and Doyle saves her, she tells Angel, 'Rich and handsome isn't enough for me. Now I expect a guy to be all brave and interesting, and it's your fault – both of you' ('The Bachelor Party', 1:7). Later, in 'Expecting' (1:12), after being impregnated with demon spawn and saved by Angel and Wes, Cordy tells them, '[…] I learned that I have two people I trust absolutely with my life, and that part's new'. Furthermore, when both Doyle and Buffy die, she wants Angel to share his feelings. Denise Gurer maintains that females are socialized toward transformative leadership and inclusion particularly by their use of interpersonal communication skills.[12] In part because Cordy encourages open communication through her own honesty and urges sharing, these colleagues build trust and become 'family'.

The family does not just include Cordelia, Angel and Wesley but Gunn, Fred and Lorne as well. Season Three's 'Dad' (3:10), in fact, depicts the Fang Gang as an emergent family. When Connor is born, Angel initially considers himself to be solely responsible, disbelieving Cordy when she maintains he cannot raise Connor alone. However, when Fred learns that multiple parties plan to kidnap Connor, the Fang Gang work together to ensure his safety. Once they have, the Gang meet Angel at a hospital for Connor's first check-up. There, Cordy holds Connor; Gunn enters with a new stroller. Realizing that Cordy was right, Angel thanks them. The episode ends symbolically with Wes, Cordy, Angel with Connor, Fred and Gunn exiting side by side, appearing a proud family.

AI continually changes Cordelia for the better. In 'Disharmony', Cordy tells Harmony, 'I am happier now than I was then [in high school]. I had these air pockets inside of me and the work I'm doing – we're doing – it's like the pockets keep getting filled, and I'm becoming me …'. Her growth can also be seen in 'Billy' (3:6) as she compares herself to Lilah:

Cordy: … you are a vicious bitch.
Lilah: So? You know me.
Cordy: Please, I was you – with better shoes.

Cordy is always a powerful presence. At Sunnydale High, her face is intimidating while angered. Her clothes, latest trend, designer labels, speak to her high social status. However, as she grows on *Angel*, her facial expressions increase in warmth, and her clothing style relaxes to include T-shirts and sweatpants, as though as she has become comfortable with who she is.

Doyle, a founding AI member, gives Cordelia his visions from the Powers That Be (PTBs) before he dies. These undoubtedly help her learn to empathize with the victims in her visions. In turn, she understands the importance of helping the helpless and the AI family ('Provider', 3:12). In Season Four, though, Cordelia is used to bring evil Jasmine into the world; this birth sends Cordy into a coma from which she never awakens. Only on a mystical level is Cordy able to pay one last visit to Angel during Season Five ('You're Welcome', 5:12). Their final conversation ends as follows:

Cordy: Don't make this hard, Angel. I'm just on a different road … and this is my off-ramp. The Powers that Be owed me one, and I didn't waste it. I got my guy back on track.

Angel: Cordy, there's just —

Cordy: We take what we can get, champ, and we do our best with it. I'll be seeing you. [*She walks away but then says*] Oh, what the hell. One for the road?

She runs into Angel's arms, where they kiss passionately. Her parting words are 'You're welcome.'

Moreover, unlike Lilah who dies alone, lost and committed to an eternity's work from hell, and unlike Kate, who loses her job and does not know what holds meaning anymore, Cordelia gains permission from the PTBs to return for one last selfless deed and to say goodbye to the man she loves. 'You're welcome' are her final words because she *knows* her worth. Cordy leaves life needed, loved and valued, instead of the 'vicious bitch' she could be in high school. Thriving in AI, a company she helped to form into a family through the androgynous management style of inclusion, communication and co-operation, makes this possible.

AI affects Fred Burkle similarly. Fred, a UCLA physics graduate student, is sucked into an alternate dimension, Pylea, and enslaved until the Fang Gang rescue her five years later ('There's No Place Like Plrtz Glrb', 2:22). In Pylea, Fred is crafty enough to escape enslavement and brave enough to save Wes and Gunn from an out-of-control Angel. Still, the most feminine of the characters, she sees herself as neither crafty nor brave and has been socialized into romantic notions and insecurities. In 'Through the Looking Glass' (2:21) Angel rescues her. Fred's response is, 'Handsome man saved me from the monsters.' After Pylea and too scared to leave the Hyperion Hotel, she scribbles madly on her walls, including a drawing of Angel akin to the romanticized image of the knight on the white horse who saves the damsel in distress. The episode, 'Fredless', however, serves as a turning point. Having acknowledged that she is not the girl who left her parents' home, she still feels inessential at AI. Only after proving to herself that she is useful to the Fang Gang is she able to paint over Angel on horseback, signifying her empowerment. From here onwards, Fred becomes an increasingly valued member of the team.

Fred's communication styles are feminine. She speaks with a sweet Southern drawl using a recursive (female) rather than linear (male) speech pattern and submissive acts. For instance, she is the first to defend someone, as when Wesley takes Angel's son – she insists there *must* be a good reason ('Forgiving', 3:17). Also, she is supportive. In Pylea, Angel says, 'You saw what I turned into.' Fred responds, 'We all have our demons' ('There's No Place like Plrtz Glrb'). Her non-verbal communication is just as girlish and wholesome. During Seasons Three and Four, her hair is often in a ponytail or pigtails. She dresses in floral, spaghetti-strap sundresses, baby doll and tiny T-shirts, jeans and jeans jackets. Essentially, Fred begins at AI the picture of traditional, on-a-pedestal femininity: sweet and innocent.

While retaining these qualities, she grows up. She transforms from downplaying her contributions to heading her own research and development lab at the Fang Gang-run Wolfram & Hart, where she wears mature apparel: blouses, skirts, heels and a lab coat. She progresses from 'puppy loving' Angel to maintaining a mature relationship with Wesley. Furthermore, instead of being careful, as she promises her parents upon leaving for LA, 'I'll even be dull, boring' ('A Hole in the World', 5:15), she takes risks, like facing evil Jasmine ('The Magic Bullet', 4:19). In fact, she becomes so essential that while she's dying, Angel, the Fang Gang and Spike have the majority of Wolfram & Hart's resources working to save her.

Near the time of Fred's death, Angel and company realize that it is impossible to compromise with evil. Running the W&H LA branch through a patriarchal system dilutes their purpose: to 'help the helpless'. Fred, just before dying, questions, 'Why did we go there? Why did we think we could beat it? It's evil, Wesley; it's bigger than anything' ('A Hole in the World'). They come to understand that good cannot truly be performed within a corrupt system. Thus, in the series' finale they take a stand against W&H, eliminating its Senior Partners, in an effort to hinder ongoing evil.

In retrospect, gender politics of masculine versus androgynous corporate climates bear upon the outcomes of the lives of Lilah, Kate, Cordelia and Fred. A masculine management style entails a rigid hierarchy and control over employees. Competition, fear, distrust and aggression/violence are used to accomplish institutional goals. Employees are treated not as whole persons but as workers who must conform to their employers' corporate cultures. Both Lilah and Kate choose to submit to the rules of men's worlds; consequently, they sacrifice much, including their sense of self. In contrast, an androgynous management style employs both male and female traits. While AI contains the appropriately tough, risk-taking environment necessary for fighting evil, it also uses a circular organization that emphasizes not only honest communication and co-operation but also views its members as family and holistically as individuals. Consequently, Cordelia and Fred are able to actualize their potential. In Season Four's 'Deep Down', Angel explains to Connor, 'We live as though the world were as it should be, to show it what it can be.' Angel Investigations' corporate culture is an example of what the world *can* be. Had Angel and the Fang Gang continued to run Wolfram & Hart, their example, already tarnishing, would eventually have become as corroded as that of the Senior Partners'.

NOTES

1 Dennis Jay Kenney and Robert P. McNamara, *Police and Policing: Contemporary Issues* (Connecticut: Praeger Publishers, 1999), pp. 1–2.

2 R. W. Connell, *Masculinities* (Cambridge: Polity Press, 1995), p. 49.

3 Judy Wajcman, *Managing Like a Man: Women and Men in Corporate Management* (Pennsylvania: Penn State University Press, 1998), pp. 61–2.

4 Ibid., p. 11

5 Deborah Tannen, 'The Power of Talk', at http://www.ils.unc.edu/inls180/Summer99/tannen.htm, p. 1.

6 Senta Troemel-Ploetz, 'Selling the Apolitical', in Charles R. Cooper and Susan Peck MacDonald (eds), *Writing the World: Reading and Writing about Issues of the Day* (Boston: Bedford/St Martin's, 2000), p. 68.

7 Pat Heim with Susan K. Golant, *Hardball for Women: Winning at the Game of Business* (Los Angeles: Plume, 1992), p. 160.

8 George B. Sproles and Leslie Davis Burns, *Changing Appearances: Understanding Dress in Contemporary Society* (New York: Fairchild Publications, 1994), p. 2.

9 Terence J. Fitzgerald (ed.), *Police in Society* (New York: H. W. Wilson, 2000), p. 16.

10 Ruth P. Rubinstein, *Dress Codes: Meanings and Messages in American Culture* (Boulder, CO: Westview Press, 1995), pp. 246–7.

11 Sally Helgesen, *The Web of Inclusion* (New York: Doubleday, 1995), p. 95.

12 Denise Gurer, 'The New Management', at http://www.cobol-report.com/columnists/denise/08202001.asp, p. 3.

9

The Rule of Prophecy:
Source of Law in the City of Angel

SHARON SUTHERLAND AND SARAH SWAN

From the evil lawyers of 'City Of' (1:1) to the battle with the minions of the Senior Partners in 'Not Fade Away' (5:22), law has been a central concern of the Angelverse. *Angel's* exploration of legal themes has deepened with each successive season: beginning with an extended riff on the tropes of traditional legal dramas and law enforcement shows, *Angel* goes on to probe sources of law and to question the defining moral and ethical frameworks for its characters. By its final episodes, *Angel's* most resonant themes relate to the interconnection of law and power, and the potential empowerment of choice in a world of seemingly immutable prophecies. This chapter explores *Angel's* development of these legal themes as they evolve over the full five-season story arc.

RIFFING ON THE LAW GENRE

Law Enforcement and the P.I.
Much as *Buffy the Vampire Slayer* developed its own unique voice by inverting expectation within familiar genres – the high-school teen drama and the horror show[1] – *Angel* mixes motifs and allusions from television's law enforcement and private investigation series with images and stereotypes from traditional 'lawyer' shows to create a framework of expectations within which the writers and actors can play out

alternative readings.[2] The genre-derived roots of the city of *Angel* are developed with particular care through the first season.

The very first episodes of *Angel* locate the series within a specific genre of law enforcement shows. Angel, as private investigator, is an outsider – a figure who cannot and does not act within the structure of traditional law enforcement. On television, private investigators often offer an alternative to the dominant system of justice. '[T]he private eye is a figure imbued with a level of scepticism about the efficacy and ethics of forces of law and order, and who provides a moral counterbalance to the corruption of the police, courts and lawyers.'[3] Films and television shows commonly portray private investigators as 'our only hope of some kind of protection against the forces of evil'.[4]

Angel fits neatly within this tradition: his relationship with Kate Lockley – a representative of the LAPD – provides ample instances of the differences in resources between official law enforcement agencies and private eyes. For example, in 'I Fall to Pieces' (1:4), Angel seeks Kate's assistance to watch over his client, the target of a stalker. Kate is able to 'put a uniform on her building', simply by requesting it. Likewise, Angel calls on Kate for background information on Dennis – Cordelia's ghost – when she first moves into her apartment in 'Rm w/a Vu' (1:5). The ease with which Kate calls upon an assistant to pull the old file underscores the difference in conventional resources and access to information between Angel Investigations and the LAPD. As the season progresses, however, we learn that the police are in fact the ones lacking the right kind of resources to protect the population from evil. In this case, it is not the moral corruption of the police that is the problem, but the supernatural nature of the threat that requires the services of a supernatural private detective.[5]

Supernatural threats cannot be contained by standard law enforcement techniques, nor controlled by the same laws that apply to our world.[6] Even Kate is forced to take 'extra-legal measures' in dealing with her father's vampiric killers ('The Prodigal', 1:15). This resort to vigilante justice defines the moment when Kate is forced to confront the impossibility of fighting these forces within the system, and the audience feels with her the impossibility of the police and the courts enforcing laws. Lindsey spells out the challenge to Kate when he tells her:

> [T]ake for example ... the creatures who murdered your father. They could never have been brought to any kind of traditional justice, even if they had survived. And personally, I feel you were totally justified in taking whatever ... extra-legal measures that you found necessary. .... There are beings, detective, beings that are not governed by the laws and strictures that we as humans have devised.
>
> ('Sanctuary', 1:19)

By the end of Season One, the message is clear: the 'rule of law' is irrelevant in the Angelverse. An alternative set of rules applies.

A Twist on the Lawyer Show

As well as private investigator imagery, the exploration of legal themes in *Angel* is also founded upon traditional 'lawyer show' motifs. The lawyer show, of course, builds on the inherent conflict and formal adversarial structure of the common legal tradition of zealous representation. One of the oft-cited reasons for the popularity of the lawyer show is precisely this structure, which allows for the presentation of difficult moral dilemmas in the context of clashes between right and wrong.[7] The nature of these moral dilemmas, however, has changed over time: while older lawyer shows, like *Perry Mason*, offer black-and-white answers about clearly defined notions of right and wrong, lawyers on more modern shows, like *The Practice*, struggle with much murkier ethical dilemmas. *Angel* has much greater affinity to the difficult moral choices seen in current lawyer shows in which the lawyer protagonists are asked to act in the face of a lack of clarity as to the morality and potential consequences of their actions. Instead, they must believe in the overall justice of the system and play their role to the best of their abilities. The characters in *Angel* act in a similar pursuit of justice, never certain that their good intentions might not have unintended consequences.

In addition to the moral greyness of the world of *Angel,* the show builds on two other very common elements of the lawyer show: (1) the hero as sole practitioner, law student or otherwise low-powered champion taking on an overwhelmingly stronger adversary through superior skill, determination or luck; and (2) corporate entity as villain. In the Angelverse, just as Angel clearly reflects aspects of the private detective, others step more squarely into the role of legal David against Wolfram & Hart's corporate Goliath at different times in the series. Wesley, in particular, signifies the low-powered gladiator for justice – most especially in Seasons One and Two. Wesley has the 'legal' expertise in this world – knowledge of ancient languages and other arcane subjects covered in his studies with the Watchers' Council. As we will discuss below, the failure of traditional law in *Angel* leads not just to the replacement of traditional law enforcement agencies with the highly specialized paranormal private investigation service, but also results in the development of a parallel system of rules – rules based on prophecy. In this world, the equivalent of legal skill is facility with the prophecies and ancient languages. As the lawyer translates legalese and interprets statutes, Wesley translates ancient scrolls and interprets prophecy. In his studious way, he engages the forces of evil – the corporate might of the 'full-service law firm' ('City Of', 1:1) – in a battle of wits analogous to the battles of overmatched lawyers in so many legal shows.

Wesley is not the only character to fill this role, however. During Wesley's exile from the team after stealing the baby Connor away, Fred replaces him as the team's 'legal' expert. We see her developing expertise under Wes' mentorage before his departure – notably in 'Offspring' (3:7), when she combines her pre-demon-fighting mathematical skills with her newly developing translation skills to calculate the date for the coming of the Troclon from the very obscure Nyazian Prophecies:

Oh, it's a simple equation, really. The ancient Roman calendar has 1,464 days in a four-year cycle. The Etruscan, Sumerian and Druidian each have their own cycles. You work forward from the presumed day of the prophecy under each calendar, factoring in our own 365-day calendar and accounting for a three-day discrepancy for every four years and ... Oh. – That can't be right. – Unless the world ended last March.

('Offspring')

In some ways, Gunn might seem a natural successor to Fred in Season Five when she reasserts her scientific expertise to run the Research and Development Department at Wolfram & Hart, and Gunn accepts his super-lawyer 'brain dump'. This surface appearance, however, is yet another twist on genre expectations. Gunn, as super-lawyer, remains the 'muscle' of the gang, despite his desire to be more: in the new world of the corporate firm, 'muscle' equals legal expertise, not brawn. Gunn continues to fight off the minor villains while Angel defeats the more imposing threats – sometimes adopting explicitly legal strategies himself.[8] Wes and Fred continue to operate in the worlds of arcane knowledge and to fit more accurately the traditional role of the lawyer hero.

The second element in the traditional lawyer show is the corporate entity as monolithic villain. This identification of evil with corporate America generally plays on a long tradition of depicting corporations as evil. Michael Asimow has written about the manner in which corporate law firms come to stand in for all corporate evil:

The anti-big business bias in the movies affects law firm portrayals in two ways. First, big law firms are themselves large profit-oriented business organizations. Like any other big business entity, big law firms are portrayed in film as greedy and dishonest; we would expect to see them cheating or squashing ordinary human beings or small businesses.

Second, big law firms exist primarily to represent big business. If big business is evil, its champions must be equally so. The filmmaker who wants to vilify big business needs a human face to serve as the focus for the audience's hatred. It is difficult to show the corporate structure from the inside, and far easier to pick on the lawyer who is fronting for the corporation.[9]

Wolfram & Hart fills the traditional role of evil corporate entity. *Angel*, however, plays with this tradition, literalizing – as *Buffy the Vampire Slayer* (*BtVS*) before it – traditional fears through the use of real demons. Whereas *BtVS* literalized fears about high-school life, *Angel* creates a law firm for the demonically evil. The contemporary idea of the evils of global corporations is taken to the extreme: Wolfram & Hart is not only global, but inter-dimensional, and the law firm's power to shelter demons from the normal workings of justice sets up the firm's responsibility for evil greater than any single client could perform.

A further element of the traditional lawyer genre is the courtroom scene where formalized battle takes place between opposing forces. The courtroom scene has been less and less frequent in recent years, however, as law shows have situated more and more legal work outside the courtroom and inside the boardroom, representing in the process the corporate core of modern law.[10] *Angel* in some respects follows this more modern tradition, in that courtroom scenes are very rare, despite the prevalence of real lawyers amongst the characters; but the function of the courtroom scene in traditional lawyer shows has always been one of structure for the playing out of conflict and for finality in the determination of right and wrong. In this regard, *Angel*'s actual courtroom scenes serve to undermine expectations: the conflict is never played out to conclusion in the courtroom. But battle is engaged in *Angel*: the arena is simply not the law court, but the darkened streets of LA where trial by battle provides structure for the war between good and evil, and finality is achieved through the physical defeat of enemies. For example, both 'Five by Five' (1:18) and 'Blind Date' (1:21) begin with Angel thwarting one of Lindsey's trials, and end with battles on the street. Also, as the episode titles of 'The Trial' (2:9) and 'Judgement' (2:1) suggest, the terminology of the courtroom is often employed in reference to more literal physical street battles.

This legal wrangling-turned-physical is one of many images of law and battle that we see on *Angel*. The pairing of law and battle can be seen as a variation on Wink's 'Myth of Redemptive Violence'. In this exploration of theologies, Wink describes a series of creation myths in which good and evil fight, and the champion of good overcomes evil through violence.[11] In myths of redemptive violence, creation arises from an act of violence and humanity is created from the blood of a murdered god. Humanity itself perpetuates evil and is, by its very nature, incapable of peaceful coexistence. In this worldview, evil is a fundamental element of creation, and is ineradicably part of the world. This perpetual conflict between good and evil is often played out in law shows through scenes of ritualized conflict. Lawyers as 'hired guns' are sent into legal battles where crushing the opponent and its lawyers is the ultimate goal.[12]

Clearly the worldview of redemptive violence resonates within the Angelverse, where time after time Angel confronts the question of whether or not a champion for good can conquer evil through redemptive violence, and concludes that evil can never be wholly eradicated but that good must continue to fight. It is Holland Manners who first tells Angel:

> Our firm has always been here. In one form or another. The Inquisition. The Khmer Rouge. We were there when the very first cave man clubbed his neighbour. See, we're in the hearts and minds of every single living being. And that – friend – is what's making things so difficult for you. See, the world doesn't work in spite of evil, Angel. It works with us. It works because of us.
>
> ('Reprise', 2:15)

By the end of Season Five, Angel has accepted that evil is an inherent element in the world, and the best that a champion for good can do is to fight on.

> *Angel:*   We're in a machine. That machine's gonna be here long after our bodies are dust. But the Senior Partners will always exist in one form or another because mankind is weak.

Lorne: Uh, do you want me to point my crossbow at him,
          'cause I think he's gonna start talking about ants
          again.
Angel: We are weak. The powerful control everything ...
          except our will to choose. Look, Lindsey's a
          pathetic halfwit, but he was right about one thing.
          Heroes don't accept the way the world is. The Sen-
          ior Partners may be eternal, but we can make their
          existence painful.

                                              ('Power Play', 5:21)

THE RULE OF PROPHECY

Having adopted a myth of redemptive violence as the core of
its structure, *Angel* creates around it a mythology for the
source of moral order to replace the traditional legal system
which is demonstrably insufficient. Through the seasons, an
alternative structure for moral order is developed: in the city
of *Angel*, rule of law is replaced by rule of prophecy. Ancient
scrolls and prophecies form the real statutory laws of this
world, while visions from the Powers That Be (PTBs) provide
interpretative guidance.

The first season is instrumental in drawing the audience
into this alternative framework of prophecy. As noted, the
ineffectiveness of the police and the courts to respond to the
evil of Wolfram & Hart and its clients is demonstrated. The
one guiding light appears to be the visions from the PTBs
which first Doyle and then Cordelia receive. The visions are
seemingly infallible, and clearly aimed at good in as much as
they lead to the possibility of saving an innocent. The visions
and Angel's visit to the Oracles (intermediaries to the PTBs)
prepare the ground for 'To Shanshu in LA' (1:22), which for-
mally announces the framework of rule by prophecy. In this
season finale, Wes is able to translate enough of the Prophecies of Aberjian to advise Angel that a vampire with a soul
has been foretold, and that, through sufficient redemptive
services for good, he may live again as a human. The Prophecies of Aberjian, then, are both a guide for Angel's choices in

this morally ambiguous world and a statement of his personal
destiny. The importance of this prophecy is underscored by
the efforts Wolfram & Hart undertake to separate Angel from
the connection the prophecy gives him to the PTBs. The firm
raises the demon, Vocah, who slaughters the Oracles – one of
Angel's points of access to the PTBs – and causes Cordelia to
experience excruciating non-stop visions, thus severing
Angel's alternate access. Vocah also steals the scroll itself and
seeks to kill Wesley, the one person able to assist Angel to an
understanding of the text. Clearly Wolfram & Hart believe the
prophecies are directly related to the connection between
Angel and the PTBs. In fact, Vocah says, '[Angel] is in possession of the prophecies. His connection to the Powers That Be
is complete.' This connection forms the framework for the
series: Angel strives to maintain his link to the PTBs, while a
series of intermediaries carry messages to Wolfram & Hart
from the Senior Partners. The battle that is played out in the
streets of LA is thus elevated to a battle between champions of
the higher powers of both good and evil.

Prophecies, however, are intrinsically slippery. Angel's
comment in 'To Shanshu in LA', 'Don't believe everything
you're foretold', may be the best advice we have for understanding this world. The Nyazian Prophecies – which are
linked to Connor's role in the series – are especially difficult.
For example, Team Angel struggles to understand the arrival
of Holtz as part of the confluence of events foretold in connection with Connor's birth:

Fred: Maybe he's part of what's supposed to rain down
          ruination upon mankind. The Nyazian Prophecies
          did say that the Troclon was going to be a conflu-
          ence of events.
Cordelia: And the sudden appearance of an eighteenth-
          century vampire hunter in the twenty-first century
          does seem pretty confluey.
Gunn: You think he's here for the baby?
Angel: I don't think he even knows about it.
Fred: He wouldn't have to. That's the tragic beauty of a
          cosmic convergence. I—I mean, he just plays his

own small part. He—he comes here looking for
Angel and Darla, and in the process ends up finding Angel's unborn child, who, as it turns out,
wasn't evil at all as we feared, but was actually
meant to be some sort of Messianic figure. But
Holtz kills it before it's even born and his vengeance somehow triggers the end of the world! Or
not! It could go either way.

('Lullaby', 3:9)

The danger of falsely interpreting prophecy is very real. We
see a poignant example of this when Wesley kidnaps Connor
in a misguided attempt to avert the prophecy that 'the father
will kill the son'. Sahjahn, a demon, later claims authorship of
that prophecy, boasting that he created a false prophecy to
prevent another prophecy – one interpreted to mean that Connor will kill Sahjahn – from happening. Yet, to make matters
even more confusing, this 'false' prophecy actually comes to
pass: in 'Home' (4:22) Angel kills Connor, thereby enabling
Connor to have the normal suburban life Angel was otherwise
unable to offer. The death of Connor at Angel's hands, however, does not remove the obligations of the third aspect of the
Nyazian Prophecies, which foretells that Connor will kill Sahjahn. Despite his removal from the battlefield, Connor still
must return to fulfil his destined role in the battle, demonstrating again the inexorable nature of prophecy in constituting the
constant framework of the world ('Origin', 5:18).

Certainly, we are led to believe that prophecies cannot be
avoided: destiny is destiny. At the same time we have learned
from *BtVS* that while free will and moral choice may not prevent the actualization of prophecy, they may affect the
outcome. 'Prophecy Girl' (B1:12) is the obvious reference
point in the Buffyverse for an understanding of the way free
choice can alter the seeming meaning of a prophecy. Buffy
chooses the time and place to face the Master who is prophesied to kill her. She does die as foretold, but because of her
exercise of choice, Xander is there to resuscitate her. In *Angel*,
the choice to fight on is similarly highlighted as key to the
ultimate result of the realization of prophecy.

The elevation of prophecy to the status of immutable con-
stitutional framework raises one of the most important
questions in *Angel:* to what extent do we decide our own destiny? The Aberjian Prophecy states that Angel has a starring
role in the apocalypse, but is not clear whether that role is on
the side of good or evil.[13] This suggests that free will has its
place in the Angelverse: the choice to fight matters in the end,
even if it cannot stop a prophesied event from occurring. The
redemptive value of choosing to fight is underscored by even
the most minor characters. For example, Angel's many
speeches in the final episodes about the choice to continue
fighting may be more eloquently summed up in Anne's brief
comment in 'Not Fade Away'. Gunn asks her what she would
do if she knew all her efforts to help the homeless were
doomed to fail. Anne responds simply: 'I'd get this truck
packed before the new stuff gets here.' In other words, one
freely chooses to fight for good, regardless of the odds.
Prophecy is the framework, but the results of prophesied
events are determined by the choices made by the partici-
pants and there is redemptive value in making the hard
choices and continuing the unwinnable battle.

The rule of prophecy, as established within the Angelverse,
can be seen as an affirmation of natural law over positive
law.[14] In this world, humans have access through their souls
to an understanding of morality that is superior to enacted
law or prophetic writings. Any being with a soul has the ability to tap into this knowledge of essential right and wrong.
The choice to act in accordance with this common human
understanding of good and evil is the factor that determines
moral worth, not adherence to written rules nor even adherence to prophecy. As we have seen, prophecy is immutable,
but so is morality: despite the greyness of many moral questions, *Angel* affirms that humans have access to an ability to
recognize good from evil and the freedom to choose between
them.

Throughout five seasons, *Angel* has constructed many of its
best effects on a reversal of expectations – notably in its
reversal of set pieces of the genre structures built into its frame-

work. Others have written about the use of tropes and structural elements from film noir, the Western and the super-hero tradition, amongst others. This chapter has set out to demonstrate that the traditional law show has also played a part in shaping the structures of the show and hence the expec-tations of the audience. Given this development of legal-show structures and the emphasis on legal themes and characters from the worlds of law and law enforcement, one of the most striking reversals of expectation may be the theme developed throughout that law, as it is traditionally defined and practised, is irrelevant to the Angelverse. The moral and ethical issues facing the characters are of mythic proportion and human sys-tems cannot suffice. Instead, governing frameworks of prophecy and destiny form the true background – despite the constant presence of the earthly legal apparatus. Setting the show within an actual law firm in the final season only served to underscore the fact that much more important issues were in play. Ultimately, *Angel* uses positivist legal structures and law show tropes as contrast for the fundamental natural law mes-sage that morality derives from the essential nature of humans and is a constant that can be located in individual conscience. In this world, the exercise of free choice to do what one's con-science dictates as right is heroic. Evil cannot be defeated, but individuals carry the potential to choose to do good. Within this worldview, the series finale closes on a note of extraordi-nary hope. Faced with unspeakable odds against their very survival and no chance of ultimate victory, Angel simply rallies his troops to continue the fight.

NOTES

1 *BtVS* fans will recollect that the first episode, 'Welcome to the Hellmouth' (B1:1), opens with a scene that suggests a young female student being led into peril in a dark high school by a coaxing male student. In a reversal of expectations that estab-lishes the pattern for the series, the young woman turns out to be Darla the vampire and the young man is killed.
2 Several authors have discussed *Angel's* film noir influences. See for example: Stacey Abbott, 'Walking the Fine Line between

Angel and Angelus', *Slayage: The Online International Journal of Buffy Studies*, 9 (2003), at http://www.slayage.tv/essays/slayage9/Abbott.htm; and Benjamin Jacob and Jennifer Stoy's chapters in this volume (Chapters 5 and 11 respectively). This chapter focuses instead on the complementary influences of television legal dramas (both lawyer shows and law enforcement series) as a point of departure for *Angel*'s exploration of legal themes.

3 Steve Greenfield, Guy Osborn and Peter Robson, *Film and the Law* (London: Cavendish, 2001) p. 169.

4 Ibid., p. 169.

5 Charles Gunn's early appearances as urban gang leader allow him to play a parallel role to that of Angel. Gunn shares Angel's status as a marginalized crimefighter: a black gang member targeting vampires who prowl in the seedier areas of Los Angeles where traditional police protection is minimal against even the most common forms of crimes.

6 Bruce McClelland observes similarly that in *BtVS*, the police are 'irrelevant' in the destruction of immortal criminals. Bruce McClelland, 'By Whose Authority? The Magical Tradition, Violence and the Legitimation of the Vampire Slayer', *Slayage*, 1 (2001), at http://www.slayage.tv/essays/slayage1/bmcclelland.htm.

7 Paul Bergman and Michael Asimow, *Reel Justice: The Courtroom Goes to the Movies* (Kansas City: Andrews and McMeel, 1996), p. xvii.

8 For example, in 'Just Rewards' (5:2), Angel tells a client: 'I just froze all your bank accounts, terminated your paper assets and turned your books over to a very motivated contact we have at the IRS. Five minutes from now, you'll have nothing but this house. Ten minutes from now, that'll go into foreclosure.'

9 Michael Asimow, 'Embodiment of Evil: Law Firms in the Movies', *UCLA Law Review*, 48 (2001), p. 1373.

10 John Brigham, 'Representing Lawyers: From Courtrooms to Boardrooms and TV Studios', *Syracuse Law Review*, 53 (2003), p. 1180.

11 Walter Wink, *Engaging the Powers* (Minneapolis: Fortress Press, 1993).

12 Douglas Noll, *Peacemaking: Practice at the Intersection of Law and Human Conflict* (Telford, PA: Cascadia Publishing House, 2003), p. 41.

13 This ambiguous role is described by Nathan in 'Blood Money' (2:12): 'The prophecies all agree that when the final battle is waged, he plays a key role. ... Which side he's on is the grey area, and we're going to continue making it as grey as possible.'

14 The exact meaning of the term 'natural law' is debated amongst scholars in law, philosophy, religious morality and politics. For that reason, the term is often ambiguous. For the purposes of this paper, we use natural law to mean 'a system of right or justice held to be common to all humans and derived from nature rather than from the rules of society, or positive law' (Encyclopedia Britannica Online, at http://www.britannica.com/eb/article?eu=56423&tocid=0&query=philosophy%20of%20law).

PART FOUR:

'Trapped in What
I Can Only Describe as a
Turgid Supernatural Soap
Opera':

Issues of Genre and
Masculinity in Angel

10

The Dark Avenger:
Angel and the Cinematic Superhero

JANET K. HALFYARD

From the very first moment that we meet him in episode one, Season One of *Buffy the Vampire Slayer*
(*BtVS*), the character of Angel is positioned in a way
that hints at his relationship with the canon of cinematic
superheroes. In this first appearance, when Buffy encounters
him in an alley on her way to the Bronze, in response to her
question 'Who are you?' he replies, enigmatically, 'let's just
say … I'm a friend', this exchange mirroring an almost identical one between Lois Lane and Superman in Richard Donner's
Superman (1978).

However, Angel is rarely allowed to be obviously superheroic in *BtVS*, for the simple reason that Buffy herself is –
and must be – the unchallenged superhero of that narrative:
like operas, superhero films are invariably named after their
title characters, including those where the narrative concerns
a collective rather than a sole agent, as in the case of the X-
Men. Buffy's positioning as eponymous superhero relegates
Angel to the role of sidekick, along with the other members of
her Scooby Gang and, at the same time, tends to conceal the
extent to which he is also superheroic. By giving him his own
character-identified series, Joss Whedon and David Greenwalt created an opportunity to explore Angel's character and
his superheroism in more depth.

Buffy has relatively few superheroic antecedents: before Buffy and her immediate predecessor, Xena, female super-heroes were few and far between and as Sherrie A. Inness has noted, characters such as Wonder Woman found it difficult to sustain their position as narrative agents, frequently falling back on the agency of men in order to solve their problems.[1] Angel, on the other hand, has some very clear superheroic predecessors who are regularly referenced within the first season of *Angel*, sometimes overtly and sometimes more cov-ertly, but nonetheless establishing his superheroic credentials at the outset of the series that saw him breaking away from Buffy and establishing an identity and mission largely inde-pendent of hers. This chapter explores the way that ideas taken from other superheroes, in particular Batman and Superman, are woven into Angel's identity in Season One, and explores the particular positioning of superheroes as vampires and vampires as superheroes on which Angel's character draws and to which he makes a significant contribution.

DEFINING THE SUPERHERO

Richard Reynolds provides a working definition of the comic-book superheroes that form the model for their cinematic counterparts.[2] In particular, he identifies a number of features common to the majority of comic-book superheroes, which in turn map quite easily onto both Buffy and Angel.

Firstly, it is usual for the superhero either to have a prob-lematic relationship with his or her father, or for parents to be missing or deceased. Anthony Bradney has identified a gen-eral theme of dysfunctional families in the Buffyverse: all of the principal characters have parents who are either problem-atic or absent.[3] Buffy is estranged from her father and loses her mother in Season Five, while Angel provides the most extreme example: as we learn in *Angel* Season Two, he had an antagonistic relationship with his father, and one of his first acts as a vampire was to murder his family.

The second common feature is that of the secret identity. Again, Buffy qualifies, although her status as slayer is probably the worst-kept secret in Sunnydale: by the time we reach 'The Prom' (B3:20), her entire school appears to know, and her identity was never a secret within the demon world. Similarly, while Angel's nature is well known to other vampires, demons and the Powers That Be, his identity as a vampire is a much better-kept secret in the human world than the slayer's, and the problems when it is discovered tend to be greater. With Buffy, everyone generally takes the slayer in their stride, but each time Angel's identity is revealed – for example, in 'Angel' (B1:7) when Buffy learns the truth, and in 'The Prodigal' (1:15), when Kate also does – the result is fear, alienation and a definite threat to Angel's continued existence.

A third defining criterion is that the superhero should possess either special powers, above and beyond the normal abilities of humans, or should make use of special gadgets and technology that serve the same purpose. Superman is the classic example of the former model, while Batman represents the latter. These were the original comic-book superheroes, first appearing in 1938 and 1939 respectively, and establishing these two main types of *modus operandi*. Like Buffy, Angel is clearly possessed of superpowers in the form of his preternatural strength and heightened senses, which allies him again with Superman; but in the pilot episode of *Angel*, he makes use of gadgets such as the double-staking wrist-operated mechanism with which he kills his first two vampires in the episode's teaser. Greenwalt and Whedon attribute this plot device to Batman and his famous use of gadgetry, outlining how this was designed to distance Angel's fighting style from Buffy's.[4] This is maintained in the assistance they get in later stages of their narratives: Willow's use of magic contrasts similarly with Fred's construction of gadgetry.

The last two of Reynolds' points are closely related.[5] On the one hand, the superhero stands for justice, upholding the rights of the innocent. However, in order to do this he must often place himself over and above the law as represented by politics, the legislature and the police, and therefore finds himself standing in opposition to these legitimate authorities, whose expedience, corruption or ineffectiveness forces the hero to act illegally in order to uphold natural justice. This is a feature of both Tim Burton's *Batman* (1989), and Sam Raimi's *Spider-Man* (2002), where the press questions the intentions of the superhero, suggesting that he may be as dangerous as the villains he apparently opposes. Although Angel has no contact with the press, the extent to which he is positioned in opposition to the law is made very clear, both in his uneasy relationship in *Angel* Season One with the legitimate forces of law enforcement represented by Kate – who clearly comes to suspect that he is as bad as the demons he fights – and in the nature of the principal enemies throughout subsequent seasons, the lawyers of Wolfram & Hart.

ANGEL AS SUPERHERO: BATMAN AND SUPERMAN REFERENCES IN ANGEL

Whereas in *BtVS*, the first episode works hard to establish Buffy as a normal girl leading an extraordinary life, the first episode of *Angel* works equally hard to establish Angel as a superhero in the classic mould. The most obvious model for Angel is Batman: both are associated with darkness, literal and metaphorical, and with an urban night-time environment rather than Superman's primary colours, daytime environment and sunny optimism. Both are, in effect, superhero detectives who solve and fight crime committed by creatures obviously and bizarrely Other: in the cinema, Superman's adversaries have always looked just like him and us. When in their 'superpowers mode', Angel and Batman, in fact, look less like us, Angel with his vampire face and Batman with his concealing mask. This lends them an Otherness that Superman largely avoids: his differences are rarely visible, whilst Angel's and Batman's are sometimes all too obvious. In addition, Angel and Batman are characters whose names associate them with winged creatures, although unlike Superman, neither can fly; and both have apparently named themselves, whereas Superman is named by Lois Lane in Donner's film.

In Burton's film, it is Bruce Wayne who first describes his alter ego as Batman in a conversation with Vicki Vale, and we must assume that it was Angel who shortened his vampire name to one associated with guardians and goodness rather than simply reverting to his human name, Liam.

There is also, in keeping with the knowledge of popular culture that many of the characters possess, an overt awareness of Angel's superheroic resemblance to Batman. Cordelia's reinvention of him as the Dark Avenger in 'Hero' (1:9) takes this to an extreme, while her comment in that episode that it would help business, and not really hurt him, if he would dress up in tights and a cape now and then is one of the relatively rare invocations of the high camp of Batman's 1960s television series. More usually, *Angel* makes reference to the Batman of Tim Burton's film, a process that begins in the opening moments of the first episode with Angel's use of gadgetry. In the same episode, Doyle's very first comment when we find him in Angel's apartment is that the place has a 'Batcave sort of an air to it', while Spike quips 'quickly, to the Angel-mobile', in his mockingly imagined dialogue in 'In the Dark' (1:3). Again in the first episode, when we see Angel step off the side of a building, Whedon comments that this is 'our Batman moment', and the shot is a direct allusion to the end of the opening scene of Burton's *Batman*, when Batman steps off the side of a building after his attack on a pair of muggers.[6]

Another feature of Burton's film is that in the opening scenes Batman is shown as being in a position of moral peril and being more a dangerous vigilante than a just warrior. He appears to be restraining himself from killing the mugger, and there is a definite ambiguity about whether Jack Napier falls or is dropped by Batman into the vat of chemicals that causes his physical and psychological transformation into the Joker. Similarly, Doyle spells out the extent to which Angel is in moral peril, distancing himself from humanity to the extent that he will, ultimately, stop seeing people as people and start seeing them as food. Like Batman, Angel is in danger of becoming a straightforward killer, and their onscreen narratives both concern their quest to find a place within the world as a force for good. Where Batman eventually finds himself allied with the police, Angel, through Doyle and later Cordelia, allies himself with the Powers That Be, the visions acting as their equivalent of the police's Bat-signal.

The similarity of the moral dilemmas of Batman and Angel goes even deeper, however. Much of Burton's film emphasizes Batman's underlying connection to the Joker: like the Joker, Batman exists as a second personality emerging after the first was subjected to extreme trauma. In Batman's case, this was the young Bruce Wayne's witnessing his parents' murder rather than Jack/Joker's drop into a chemical vat, but the result is the creation of a persona as potentially dangerous as the Joker himself. Bruce Wayne may be sweet and harmless, but Batman is a stone's throw from psychosis, although it is unequivocally Batman, not Bruce, who is the superhero. Likewise, as Angel discovers in 'I Will Remember You' (1:8), without his vampire strength he is of no use to the Powers That Be. Angelus, like Batman, is the dangerous presence that lurks within, a threat that must be contained but without whom the hero loses his agency and cannot work for the greater good.[7]

An aspect of Angel's representation that links him to both Batman and Superman stems from the way that he is initially presented in the episode one teaser as a maudlin and rather idiotic drunk, as if he has suffered some kind of breakdown since leaving Buffy at the end of *BtVS* Season Three. In their commentary, Greenwalt and Whedon describe how Buffy was originally set up to look 'like a dope' but then turned out to be a hero. Angel, as they put it, looks incredibly heroic, and so they thought it would be fun to set him up as a dope and then let the audience discover that he is play-acting.[8] This is a similar conceit to that associated with the cinematic Clark Kent and Bruce Wayne.[9] In both films, the everyday persona of the superhero is vague and nerdish, masking the god-like Superman and the formidably focused and driven Batman. The fact that Angel's 'normal guy' persona is often played for comedy, both in the pilot and in later episodes, places him closer to Christopher Reeves' Clark Kent, but in general the Batman references are much clearer.

Nonetheless, Angel and Superman have a surprising amount in common, starting with their enigmatic introduction of themselves as 'a friend' and continuing on a number of levels. First, Batman is human but Angel and Superman are not, although they can both pass for one. Second, Batman can be killed like any normal human being: it is only his athleticism and his body-armour that make him seem invincible. Superman, however, is technically unkillable and Angel is theoretically immortal and cannot be killed in normal human ways, susceptible instead to wooden stakes, sunlight, crosses and holy water. Stacey Abbott has noted the way that, like silver and garlic in Stephen Norrington's *Blade* (1998), crosses and holy water essentially produce an allergic reaction in the vampires of the Buffyverse, comparable to Superman's vulnerability to Kryptonite, a substance to which he is also effectively allergic.[10]

However, one of the most striking parallels to Superman is found between the plots of *Superman II* (Richard Lester, 1980) and 'I Will Remember You'. In the film, Superman gives up his powers in order to be able to live a normal life with Lois, but takes them back when he discovers that he needs them in order to be able to defeat the Kryptonian renegades who are attempting to take over the world. He, therefore, must sacrifice his and Lois' personal happiness in order to be able to serve the greater good, but is left with the memory of their brief time together while Lois loses all memory of the fact that Clark is Superman. In 'I Will Remember You', Angel becomes human in a fight with a demon whose blood regenerates his mortality. He is therefore stripped of his superpowers but initially accepts this willingly, as it will allow him a normal life and a romantic future with Buffy without invoking his curse. However, just as Superman discovers that he needs his powers in order to be able to keep the world safe, so Angel realizes that he is useless to Buffy as a normal man. Not only can he not protect her but his vulnerability endangers her and, therefore, the world. He makes the same decision as Superman, to take up the burden of his powers again, lose the girl, and be the only one with any memory of what he has done. Like Lois, Buffy loses her memory of the brief time they had together, but Angel, like Superman, does not, although Angel is clearly more tormented by this than Superman. When Angel goes to the Oracles to ask them to take back his mortality so that he can be their warrior again, the female Oracle comments that this sacrifice indicates that he is not a lower being – by extension, even as a mortal, Angel is not a man but above man: a superman.

SUPERHEROES AS VAMPIRES, VAMPIRES AS SUPERHEROES

Similarities to Superman notwithstanding, Batman remains the more obvious model for Angel for another very good reason: there is some strong evidence that he is also a vampire. In Burton's film, Batman only ever appears at night, and even Bruce Wayne is never seen standing in direct sunlight: the few daytime scenes of the film are distinctly overcast and gloomy. In addition, the bat has always been one of Dracula's favourite transformational states, and Batman's distinctive cape simultaneously alludes to both the bat's wings and Dracula's own trademark, high-collared black cloak, found in practically every film that has featured him and, indeed, a feature of his appearance in Sunnydale ('Buffy versus Dracula', B5:1). Although Batman's vampiric coding is rarely noted by commentators, it is very much a feature of the early part of Burton's film, with half a dozen references to things such as drinking blood, gore, fangs and vampire bats occurring in the first few scenes. Batman, therefore, has been a vampiric superhero lurking in our midst since his inception in 1939, although Burton's film, fifty years later, contains some of the most overt acknowledgments of Batman's secret vampiric tendencies.

Where Donner's *Superman* and George Lucas' *Star Wars* (Luke Skywalker fulfils all of Reynolds' criteria for superheroism) inspired a host of films throughout the 1980s featuring sunnily optimistic cinematic heroes and superheroes, from the *Indiana Jones* trilogy (Steven Spielberg, 1981–9) to *The Last*

Starfighter (Nick Castle, 1984) and the *Back to the Future* series (Robert Zemeckis, 1985–90), Burton's film inspired a new interest in superhero narratives of a darker and more dystopic variety throughout the 1990s, such as *Darkman* (Sam Raimi, 1990) and *The Shadow* (Russell Mulcahy, 1994). This ultimately led to the last great superhero narrative of the twentieth century, *The Matrix* (Andy and Larry Wachowski, 1999), to which the emergence of another spate of movies featuring often deeply conflicted superheroes – including Spider-Man, the Hulk, Daredevil and the X-Men – may well owe its existence.

The 1990s also saw a return to some serious vampire films, quite different from the camp horror of Hammer's vampires in the 1960s and 1970s, in particular Coppola's *Bram Stoker's Dracula* (1992) and Neil Jordan's *Interview with the Vampire* (1994); in terms of the dark, Gothic brooding of these films, one senses Burton's *Batman* making itself felt here as well. This idea is perhaps best supported by the similarity of the music of these three films. Music does a great deal in determining the dramatic and narrative tone of a film, and Danny Elfman's score for *Batman* often seems more appropriate to a horror film than a superhero narrative, replacing the upbeat, major-key sounds of John Williams' scores for films – including *Superman*, *Star Wars*, and the *Indiana Jones* films – with minor-key, brooding music that placed great emphasis on melodies pitched very low in the orchestral texture, creating a sense of mystery, threat and foreboding. As I have discussed elsewhere, the *Batman* theme itself is alluded to in the music of both Coppola's *Dracula* and Jordan's *Interview*, and Elfman's music arguably had as profound an impact on the sound of both superhero and vampire movies as Burton's film had upon their narratives.[11]

The theme music of *Angel* also alludes to the *Batman* theme. Although not melodically identical, the two themes are still close enough for the similarity to be clearly audible, which is hardly surprising as Darling Violetta, the band who wrote the *Angel* theme, were given a brief that specifically asked them to write something along those lines. As Jymm Thomas recounts, 'our only instruction was to come up with something befitting a "dark superhero" along the lines of *Batman*'[12] and the theme they composed evokes the soundworld of Elfman's score at the same time subtly alluding to the theme tune of *BtVS* itself.[13]

Musically and narratively, there are also strong connections between the title characters of *Angel* and *Interview with the Vampire*. Both are eighteenth-century vampires; Louis is described in the film as 'the vampire with the human soul', a description that also fits Angel; and, as has been noted by several authors, both are tormented by the fact that they are vampires and wracked with remorse for the evil they have done in the past.[14] They are also quite specifically associated with the cello in the music written for them. The main title-music of *Interview* features a baroque viola da gamba, an instrument very similar to the cello in terms of appearance and timbre. The main title cue is a setting of words from a Requiem mass – '*Libera me a meo*', 'free me from myself' – with a child's voice alternating with the mournful tones of the viola da gamba, enhancing the sense of loss, longing and remorse that are Louis' main characteristics. The cello itself is used as the main melodic instrument in a theme entitled 'Born to Darkness' that accompanies Louis' voice-overs as he recounts the story of his life, connecting the cello with the idea of somewhat mournful reflection and remembering.

The theme of *Angel* features two main melodic instruments, the cello and the electric guitar, and Whedon describes the way that he himself reads this use, the music starting with 'the sad, poignant cello-world that then gets kinda rocking because Angel is there to protect people'.[15] However, Angel himself exists in the 'sad cello-world': in terms of the dualism of his character, the cello can equally be read as representing his troubled, reflective, remorseful human side, just as it does for Louis, and the guitar his all-action, aggressive and superheroic side.

The other cinematic figure to whom Angel is clearly connected is Blade, who similarly combines the attributes of both vampire and superhero. Blade shares with Batman and Angel three important themes in the nature of the central character and his mission. They all have 'normal' assistants who take part in the physical action to varying degrees, but who primarily act as a resource and support team for the hero and who take the place of the superhero's absent family. So, Bruce Wayne describes his butler, Alfred, as his family, Whistler acts as a father figure to Blade, and Angel realizes at the end of *Angel* Season One that he is not alone: Cordelia and Wesley are his family.

Secondly, they are all reluctant to let people get close to them: they have a tendency to hold even their surrogate families at emotional arm's length, and have problems forming emotional attachments and romantic relationships. Angel has his curse, which results in him losing his soul twice, once in *BtVS* Season Two, and again in *Angel* Season Four. Bruce/Batman appears to have no love-life and has immense difficulty telling Vicki how he feels about her;[16] the love-interest in *Blade* remains entirely latent, and the closest Blade and Karen come to a consummation is when she allows him to feed from her in order to regain his strength.

Finally, all three narratives are characterized by a scenario 'in which the hero [...] may be conflicted but the moral certainty of his mission helps him find a place in the world and overcome his internal conflict'.[17] Batman's conflict stems from the childhood trauma of watching his parents die, which appears to have created a schizophrenic split between the gentle, boyish Bruce and the grim, violent Batman, the pair acting as vulnerable child and protective adult, but simultaneously standing as a good/evil pairing, where the potential for evil in Batman is held in check by Bruce. The sense of the evil vampire held in check by the good man in both Angel and Blade connects them particularly strongly, as does the largely unconsummated nature of their romantic relationships and the fact that Angel, much like Blade, is saved when Buffy allows Angel to feed from her in the finale of *BtVS* Season Three.

As a vampire, Angel is positioned somewhere between Louis and Blade: he shares the qualities of superheroism and his mission with Blade, but in terms of his character he has more in common with Louis. In fact, he might be seen as the superhero that Louis could have become if he had not given in so entirely to despair and disillusionment with himself and his vampire state.

As *BtVS* has inspired a host of imitators in series including *Charmed*, *Dark Angel* and *Alias*, so *Angel* arguably has its own imitators in television series such as *Jake 2.0*, produced by *Angel*'s co-creator David Greenwalt, where the central character becomes a superhero after being taken over by an outside agent, Jake's nano-technology acting in place of *Angel*'s demon.[18] However, *Angel*'s main influence is seen more clearly in the cinema. Although Angel did not begin the 1990s reinvention of the superhero as a brooding, conflicted vampire, he is certainly the most fully developed and well rounded onscreen figure among characters such as Batman, Blade, Louis and Lestat, mainly because he is a television character rather than a filmic one. Blade, featuring in two films, has only four hours in which to establish his identity;[19] the cinematic Batman of the quartet of films made between 1989 and 1995, has around eight hours of time in our company, but is played by three different actors with a different director, Joel Schumacher, for the second two films, resulting in a shifting and re-establishing of Batman's identity. Angel, not including his three seasons on *BtVS*, has played out his narrative in over seventy hours of screentime and this has done much to bring new dimensions to the character of the vampire-as-superhero. Since *Blade*, but perhaps more particularly since *Angel*, vampire and superhero genres have found themselves combined in several other films, including Norrington's *The League of Extraordinary Gentlemen* (2003), *Underworld* (Len Wiseman, 2003) and *Van Helsing* (Stephen Sommers, 2004). While the most obvious cinematic precursors of these films are the dark, Gothic, dystopian superhero films that begin with *Batman*, continue with *Blade* and that find a new momentum after *The Matrix*, *Angel* is not a neutral presence in these developments. Angel, the vampire with a human soul, is a significant figure in the ongoing fascination with conflicted superheroes in a deeply troubled world.

NOTES

1 Sherrie A. Inness, *Tough Girls: Women Warriors and Wonder Women in Popular Culture* (Philadelphia: University of Pennsylvania Press, 1998), p. 88.

2 Richard Reynolds, *Superheroes: A Modern Mythology* (London: Batsford, 1992), pp. 12–16.

3 Anthony Bradney, 'Choosing Laws, Choosing Families: Images of Law, Love and Authority in *Buffy the Vampire Slayer*', *Web Journal of Current Legal Issues*, 2 (2003), at http://webjcli.ncl.ac.uk/2003/issue2/bradney2.html.

4 David Greenwalt and Joss Whedon, DVD commentary for 'City Of', *Angel Season One DVD Collection*, 20th Century Fox Home Entertainment (F1-DGB 22830DVD) Region 2.

5 There is, in fact, an additional category of the 'man-God', but Reynolds acknowledges that Superman is really the only superhero who truly fits this category.

6 Whedon, DVD commentary, 'City Of'.

7 Bruce/ Batman's position is less clear-cut than Angel/Angelus' Jekyll and Hyde situation. In the latter case, only one of the two personalities can exist at any one time, whereas Bruce and Batman not only take turns but on two or three occasions in Burton's film he is not obviously either Bruce or Batman, but a synthesis of the two. The Bruce/Batman relationship is truly symbiotic, whereas Angelus is more of a dangerous parasite, albeit a useful one.

8 Greenwalt and Whedon, DVD commentary, 'City Of'.

9 There was considerable controversy over Burton's casting of Michael Keaton, perceived as a lightweight comic actor, as Batman, but the contrast of Keaton's physical slightness and slightly quirky facial expressions provided a highly effective contrast between the Bruce Wayne persona and the grim, body-armoured Batman. See Janet K. Halfyard, *Danny Elfman's Batman: A Film Score Guide* (Lanham, MD: Scarecrow Press, 2004).

10 Stacey Abbott, 'A Little Less Ritual and a Little More Fun: The Modern Vampire in *Buffy the Vampire Slayer*', *Slayage: The Online International Journal of Buffy Studies*, 3 (2001), at http://www.slayage.tv/essays/slayage3/sabbott.htm.

11 Halfyard, *Danny Elfman's* Batman.

12 Anon.,'Behind the Scenes Featuring Darling Violetta: Creator and Performer of the *Angel* Theme', *City of Angel* (October 2000), at http://www.cityofangel.com/behindTheScenes/bts/musicDV1.html.

13 See Janet K. Halfyard, 'Love, Death, Curses and Reverses (in F Minor): Music, Gender and Identity in *Buffy the Vampire Slayer* and *Angel*', *Slayage*, 4 (2001), at http://www.slayage.tv/essays/slayage4/halfyard.htm.

14 See, for example Gina Wisker, 'Vampires and School Girls: High School Jinks on the Hellmouth', *Slayage*, 2 (2001), at http://www.slayage.tv/essays/slayage2/wisker.htm; Naomi Alderman and Annette Seidel-Arpaci, 'Imaginary Para-sites of the Soul: Vampires and Representations of "Blackness" and "Jewishness" in the *Buffy/Angel*verse', *Slayage*, 10 (2003) at http://www.slayage.tv/essays/slayage10/Alderman_&_Seidel-Arpaci.htm.

15 Whedon, DVD commentary, 'City Of'.

16 In the shooting script, Bruce is a notorious playboy, but all reference to this was excised from Burton's final cut.

17 Stacey Abbott, 'Walking the Fine Line between Angel and Angelus', *Slayage*, 9 (2003), at http://www.slayage.tv/essays/slayage9/Abbott.htm.

18 It is interesting to note that the abilities of the female characters in these series are innate; in the male characters, they are invasively acquired.

19 Editor's note: at the time of writing *Blade: Trinity* (David S. Goyer, 2004) and *Batman Begins* (Christopher Nolan, 2005) had yet to be released in the UK and therefore have not been included in these calculations.

11

'And Her Tears Flowed Like Wine': Wesley/Lilah and the Complicated(?) Role of the Female Agent on Angel

JENNIFER STOY

From its inception, *Angel* has been a noir series, borrowing everything from the visual aesthetic (a Los Angeles wreathed in shadow and occasionally pouring rain out of nowhere) to the stock characters (detective Angel, limey Wesley Wyndam-Pryce, girl Friday Cordelia Chase, femme fatale Lilah Morgan, right down to Lorne the friendly bar-keeping snitch) to familiar storylines. Throughout the run of the series, *Angel* has borrowed from the trope of Los Angeles noir for better and worse, juxtaposing the corrupt and ambiguous moral underworld with Joss Whedon's traditionally superheroic ethic and, as the series has progressed, the superhero ethos has triumphed over the noir ethos. However, in the Wesley and Lilah storyline of Seasons Three and Four, the writers, directors and actors of *Angel* have not only shown their great love of Los Angeles noir, they have demonstrated how the series succeeds artistically, aesthetically and ethically by relying on the world of noir – and how what I find to be Whedon's optimistic but naïve ethos cannot encompass its ambiguities and thus fails *Angel* as a series as compared to its parent series, *Buffy the Vampire Slayer*. The moral and romantic entanglement between Wesley and Lilah, ending as it does in a heartbreaking stalemate, is both satisfying and disappointing: satisfying because the moral difference between Wesley and Lilah, as well as Lilah Morgan's status as one of the few creative moralists in the shared *Buffy/Angel* universe, remains intact and beautifully rendered; disappointing because Lilah's punishment – damnation eternal at the hands of a truly unbreakable contract – seems uncharacteristically harsh for both Wesley and Lilah as characters, and for an ethical universe that allows love to equal redemption.

In short, what I will try to demonstrate in this in-depth analysis of the noir life and times of the Wesley/Lilah relationship is the incommensurability between the relationship's complicated, problematic and realistic take on corruption and redemption in *Angel*'s Los Angeles, and the pat moralism that surrounds the world around it. Thus, even as its representation provides a clever homage to several noir classics (most notably Howard Hawks' 1946 film, *The Big Sleep*) and fully embraces the world of noir hinted at throughout *Angel*, one must also note that its troubled place against the rest of the romantic liaisons on the series suggests that ultimately, while Joss Whedon might know how to portray a femme fatale, his sympathy towards her position and moral reasoning is as inflexible as his post-war forebears – a troublesome position for a 'feminist' television series maker.

'JUST LIKE BOGIE AND BACALL': THE CORE INTERTEXTUALITY OF WES/LILAH

As has been mentioned above, no one can accuse *Angel* of being unaware of its heavy debt to film noir; Cordelia humorously references it in 'Judgement' (2:1), saying they should, 'pay your stoolie a little visit. Make with the chin-music until he canaries …' and then sheepishly admitting 'I've been watching a little noir festival on Bravo'. However, the relationship between *Angel* and noir is raised to a high point with the introduction of the Wesley and Lilah romantic relationship, starting in 'A New World' (3:20) and ending in 'Home'

(4:22) after its first disastrous climax in 'Salvage' (4:13), where Wesley is obligated to behead Lilah's dead body and she returns the favour by giving him some tough pragmatic advice before the axe literally falls.

Of course, the character of Lilah Morgan, as played by Stephanie Romanov,[1] has always been physically a 'femme fatale' since her introduction in 'The Ring' (1:15) with her elegant appearance, long legs, red lips and double-crossing ways. As with most femmes fatale, she has many schemes and designs that are morally ambiguous at best and pure evil at worst, and her interest in the hero(es) of the series marks his journey into a dark underworld. This is taken to extremes once Lilah becomes interested in dissolute and disillusioned former right-hand man Wesley Wyndam-Pryce. Her entrance into the bar in 'Tomorrow' (3:22) is a fairly direct visual allusion to Lauren Bacall's entrance into a very similar bar in *The Big Sleep*; Romanov and the production and costume designers conspire to create marked similarities. The hairstyle is almost exactly the same, the outfits similar and the accessories (in particular, a watch) remind us that this show loves to work with genre convention. Yet, besides being amused by the level of detail of the homage in 'Tomorrow', we must also question if a subtle update to Lilah's character is being written into the script. After all, Bacall's character in *The Big Sleep*, Vivian Rutledge, is *not* a textbook femme fatale; while she is involved with power and corrupt men, she is ultimately a sympathetic, non-criminal character whose nature complements Humphrey Bogart's Philip Marlowe to a nicety. While Alexis Denisof plays Wesley Wyndam-Pryce as Marlowe by way of Mike Hammer,[2] less interested in flirty banter and too emotionally despondent to respond (at least on first blush) to Romanov's Lilah as a sexual figure, there is a hint of sincerity in Lilah's demeanour and expressions in the scene that has rarely marked the character until now, as characterized by this exchange:

Lilah: Okay. – The impossible is here. But what does it mean? Is it the herald of a new age, better things to come or – the mass-destruction of everything we hold dear?

Wesley: Yes. Every child born carries into the world the possibility of salvation – or slaughter.

Lilah: And one born to two vampires carries it in spades. … [s]o, if the kid's the next Stalin, do you kill him? You can't! He's Angel's son. But on the other hand, if you just watch while he up and kills Angel or somebody else – that cute girl from Texas, say? – wow, times like this? Glad I don't have a conscience.

While prurient interest dominates the conversation – Lilah is violently and literally choked off when she asks, clearly fascinated and aroused, 'What was it like? When she cut you?' – the specific homage to *The Big Sleep* and Lauren Bacall adds another layer of intrigue to the scene. In and of herself, Lilah is interested in Wesley's opinion of Connor rather than going to Linwood, Gavin or Angel on the topic, because, of the show's characters, only Wesley has shown a complicated understanding of the danger a miracle child born of two vampires can be. The theme of their complicated, ambiguous understanding of the deeply unclear moral world in which they live – for instance, 'hero' Angel has recently punished Wesley's 'betrayal' by trying to smother him with a pillow ('Forgiving', 3:17), and has also handled Lilah's indirect intervention in the vamping of lover Darla by locking her and other lawyers in a basement to die ('Reunion', 2:10), while 'villain' Lilah has killed menace Billy Blim ('Billy', 3:6) – is one that dominates the relationship as well as the bulk of the series. Furthermore, despite their ambivalent moral placement in the *Angel* universe, Wesley and Lilah are by and large proven to be correct in their fears – Connor does become a homicidal maniac and Angel does have to fulfil the prophecy of 'the father will kill the son' that caused Wesley to attempt Connor's removal from Angel's life ('Home', 4:22) – and would appear to have a more realistic comprehension of the world around them than anyone else on the series, which fits with their roles but is not often appreciated by other characters or the audience.

However, our first hint that there is a substantial clash between the noir pragmatics of Wesley and Lilah and Mutant Enemy's heroic ethic for *Angel* the series comes in how their relatively correct assessments of the situations they're enmeshed in are handled during the arc and in the future. Despite superior acting and a more convincing storyline, the Wesley and Lilah relationship is dismissed as an obstacle between Wesley and his 'true love' Winifred Burkle, whose numerous dismissals of Wesley's uncertain and dark nature did not prevent Whedon, in *Angel* Season Five, from shoe-horning the relationship in during 'Smile Time', (5:14), one episode before Fred's tragic death in 'A Hole in the World' (5:15), in a stunning display of misunderstanding of both the Wesley character *and* the complex morality of *Angel*'s Los Angeles. The bad girl dies; the redeemed prodigal engages in chaste interaction with his dream girl (with whom he notably does not have sex) before her Little Nell-style death. Despite Fred's previous involvement in the cold-blooded vengeance killing of a former professor in 'Supersymmetry' (4:5) and obvious proof that Wesley's brand of justice is often murky (for example, his murder of his 'father' in 'Lineage', 5:7), Fred and Wesley's relationship is played as apparently satisfying, real and deep – even though Fred herself asks, 'would you have loved me?' rather than accepting Wesley's vows of true love in 'A Hole in the World'. It appears that in the fifth season, *Angel* returns to a formula that has served well for other romances on *Buffy the Vampire Slayer*, although not always as well in *Angel*. Loyalty to the small group of heroes, no matter what, is paramount, and love's depth is predicated upon moral rectitude. This somewhat naïve ethical formula – which works to much better effect on *Buffy the Vampire Slayer*, though fans of the Spike/Buffy relationship might debate that – perhaps explains why the Fred/Wesley line has never quite 'sold' itself to the fans, as the characters mutually whitewash their moral failings and foibles to play an all-too-trite 'Pyramus and Thisbe'.[3] As Slavoj Zizek says of *Shrek* (Andrew Adamson and Vicky Jenson, 2001): 'the true function of these displacements and subversions is precisely to make the traditional story relevant to our "postmodern" age – and thus to prevent us replacing it with a new one'.[4]

But what of Lilah and Wesley? Can we find a 'new' story in one so mired in the traditions of the noir genre, to say nothing of Whedon's ethical conventions? I suggest that in fact, while we might not find a new story, we find a compelling disruption to typical characterizations of the 'fallen woman' in Lilah Morgan's moral perambulations. Also, we discover in Wesley's acquiescence (and by proxy that of Mutant Enemy's) to the bleak ending of his romance and involvement with Lilah not only a lack of subversion, but a curious transference of moral authority and power in the storyline away from Wesley and his cookie-cutter ideals of good and evil even as he silently supports Angel's 'grey' decisions, onto Lilah's more informed and honest take on the universe – an effect that is perhaps the very opposite of what was intended with the end of the affair, where forgiveness and redemption lie with the damned woman, rather than the heroic vampire and his do-gooders.

'IT MEANS SOMETHING THAT YOU TRIED': THE UNLIKELY SOURCE OF REDEMPTION AND RENEWAL IN ANGEL SEASON FOUR

Violent, sexual and conniving, Lilah Morgan is an unlikely voice of ethical reason in the baroque and increasingly personalized world of good and evil, but in many ways she becomes a note of moderation in the insoluble paradoxes surrounding *Angel* and its thorny moral dilemmas. In part, this stems from the certainty of her status – Lilah never misses an opportunity to remind the viewer and the characters of her moral standing. 'I don't do errands unless they're *evil* errands', she chides Angel in 'Ground State' (4:2), and later reminds him, 'Evil, not stupid' in 'Home' (4:22). Yet this stated amorality works to Angel Investigations' benefit as often as to Wolfram & Hart's; Lilah tries to circumvent co-worker Gavin Park's scheme to drive Angel from his home legally as early as 'Carpe Noctum' (3:5), and her two onscreen murders, in 'Billy' and 'Deep Down' (4:1) respectively, have removed clear and present dangers not just to herself, but to the heroes of the show. Throughout the run of the series, Lilah has overstated her devotion to the cause of evil while functioning as a balancing agent who has a clear view of what's going on between the titanic forces at play in the Angelverse.

Nowhere is this more evident than in Lilah's two 'final' appearances – her ghost/hallucination in 'Salvage' and her revivified body offering Angel Investigations Wolfram & Hart's Los Angeles branch in 'Peace Out' (4:21) and 'Home'. Both appearances share a theme of forgiveness, redemption and renewal that, while being visually foreshadowed, are an unusual role for Lilah Morgan, evil femme fatale, to play. Firstly, there is Wesley's vision of Lilah in 'Salvage', where she wryly tells him that her death makes his life 'simpler [and] cleaner' and debates their relationship's nature: 'Oh, come on, Wes. You hated yourself for being with me. Or maybe you just hated yourself for loving being with me … hey, semantics.' There is no condemnation of Wesley in his construction of Lilah, despite his visible and vocalized guilt about his responsibility for her death; instead, the hallucination calmly and poignantly reminds Wesley of the nature of the universe the lovers have inhabited in a way that is believable enough that, until Wesley screams 'you didn't love me!' it is difficult to tell whether the Lilah speaking to him is a vampire or not, largely because the manner in which she appears to rise is consistent with vampire risings in the past.

Lilah's less-than-ragged ghost serves as a curious remembrance: rather than the sexually charged, manipulative Lilah that the viewer sees throughout the relationship, Wesley recollects her as a pragmatic and honest lover who can remind him that 'you knew how I felt' and that sorry 'isn't a word people like you and me have in our vocabulary', a Lilah hinted at rather than explicitly seen in their sexual relationship. We get exposed to her in 'Habeas Corpses' (4:8) when she silently allows Wesley to abandon her to the sewers in order to save Connor and fight the apocalypse, but not until

after her death do we gain anything resembling a full understanding of Lilah as a moral agent, nor do we fully
understand the depth of Wesley's attachment until 'Salvage'.
Once she is safely dead, Wesley admits, however obliquely,
that he has desired redemption for Lilah and enjoyed 'being
with [her]'; if this were, in fact, the end of Lilah as a character,
a case could be made that we have a textbook noir story with
a supernatural twist. Wesley manipulates Lilah's dead body
literally to tell him what he wants to hear: redemption,
forgiveness and, most importantly, absolution. Wesley hallu-
cinates a contrite but realistic Lilah, one who acknowledges
the fated end of the affair but without placing guilt. Wesley
gives Lilah a deep and compassionate comprehension of the
nature of things – that he searches for redemption, that both
Wesley and Lilah maintain equal measures of guilt and regret
in their affair and that, ultimately, Wesley cannot spare her
from the inexorable demands of a cruel world even as he
returns to his place – that is a pat resolution to Wesley's moral
journey of the past half-season. The prodigal son returns,
offering as proof the literally broken and bloodied body of his
greatest sin against the moral order of *Angel*'s universe. Lilah's
ghost safely rewrites her as capable of a great and perhaps
redeeming forgiveness, understanding the unspoken order of
things and ultimately silenced.

A predictable, poignant, but not particularly progressive *or*
feminist ending for Lilah the moral agent; however, all is
thrown into chaos and ambiguity, as Lilah herself prophesies
in 'Habeas Corpses', when she says, 'no matter how much
white you mix in, you're never going to have anything but
grey'. The end of Lilah Morgan the character – and the resolution of the Lilah/Wesley relationship – is the much less settled
and much more opaque 'Home', which features more than
one disturbing thematic trope as it 'resolves' these characters
and their heated relationship.

First of all, 'Peace Out'/'Home' add to a recurring Christo-
logical visual motif tied to Lilah: Wesley, Fred, Gunn and
Lorne discover Lilah (who is not-so-coincidentally dressed in
white) in the courtyard of the Hyperion Hotel. This is after

her side wound in 'Habeas Corpses' is revealed to be stig-
matic in 'Calvary' (4:12), when she admits to Wesley 'I can't
make it stop' as her bloodied hands fall outward from her
stomach. Of course, one also notes the death in the provoca-
tively named 'Calvary' is not Angel, Connor, nor any of the
potential saviours; it's Lilah who dies, having opened tantaliz-
ing hints to the resolution of the mystery of the apocalypse
but *not* provided any sort of salvation for the world or herself.
As we promptly find out in 'Home', Lilah, in fact, is not resurrected; she is revivified, 'still dead' but able to offer Angel and
his friends Wolfram & Hart's Los Angeles branch as a cynical
'reward' for defeating Jasmine and her apocalypse of love and
group-think, effectively 'ending world peace'. What does one
do with this frankly bizarre set of events tied to the Lilah
character? Angel agrees to take over Wolfram & Hart to save
his son Connor, with the fringe benefit of a Lilah-given amu-
let that Spike uses to save the world in the *Buffy the Vampire
Slayer* finale, 'Chosen' (B7:22). Lilah facilitates a deal that
gives everyone their heart's desire, with the notable exception
of Wesley: Fred gets the scientific dream lab, Gunn is
'improved' to become more than the muscle he fears he is,
Lorne gains control of the Entertainment Division and access
to every celebrity he's ever wanted to work with, and Angel is
allowed to save his son from death and give him an ideal suburban existence. Wesley, on the other hand, is given a
disappointing tour of the ancient prophecies wing, which
seems a regression for his current character. He opts out of his
tour by disabling the former Watcher, an echo of his former
self, and uses his new skills to find – or to be allowed to find –
where all the secrets of Wolfram & Hart lie, complete with
Lilah awaiting him with yet more unhappy truths. Unlike in
the comforting fairy tale of 'Salvage', Wesley cannot burn
Lilah's eternal contract, allowing her 'peace' and himself
moral justification. Lilah's existence lingers, like her irritated
beheading scar: perpetual evidence that Lilah cannot be quietly disposed of and sugar-coated, and that Wesley's failure
remains real and with consequences he cannot eulogize away.

Indeed, the fact that the Whedon-helmed Season Five does exactly that only exacerbates the mystery and the problematics of its moral structure: the characters, while admittedly under a spell that alters their memories of events connected to Connor, behave as though Lilah's end was that of 'Salvage'; tragic, pat and easily accepted as an unfortunate truth of the war between good and evil. Nothing indicates that any member of Angel Investigations, other than Angel, even remembers that it is Lilah's undead presence and her offer that put them in their dangerous position as new rulers of Wolfram & Hart; it seems that Wesley, certainly, does not recall that, rather than being quietly dead, Lilah is actively working or burning in hell. He never speaks of Lilah's current circumstance; instead, when discussing Lilah, Wesley speaks of her beheading to his father in 'Lineage' and her death to Cordelia in 'You're Welcome' (5:12). The difficult woman and her quite correct assessments of the ambiguity, ambivalence and true dangers of the world around Angel Investigations are silenced, and the show suffers for it.

But the curious developments of Season Five aside, the final conversation between Wesley and Lilah demonstrates that there is more to the detective/femme fatale dynamics, and the strict moral world of both noir and *Angel* than meets the eye. Taking place in Wolfram & Hart's file room, which is described as a place where all the truths, 'all that evil, great and small', is open and accessible to Wesley, there is an immediate comment on the failure of Wesley and Lilah romantically: Lilah can finally offer Wesley full knowledge and understanding of herself and the secrets she has been forced to keep, a final and powerful gift in a sequence of gifts she has given Wesley. Lilah is again placed in a position where she is more knowledgeable than Angel or any of his people, this time including Wesley and, significantly, rather than offer Wesley his heart's desire in the form of a 'bribe' (which fails in 'Supersymmetry'), she gives Wesley the most important gift: the ability to understand Wolfram & Hart and perhaps comprehend why the law firm would offer Angel its power. Lilah even characterizes herself as a knower, saying, 'who knows you better than me?' which Wesley, at last, admits is true, before throwing a spanner into the works; instead of selflessly and ruthlessly pursuing ideals, he has come to find and destroy Lilah's eternal contract. Wesley, at last, is displaying some of the romantic selfishness that recurrently marks the lover in the Buffyverse, and breaks from the noir protagonist's ultimate dismissal of the femme fatale that has marked the genre since Sam Spade told Bridget O'Shaughnessy 'I'm sending you over, sweetheart' (*The Maltese Falcon*, John Huston, 1941).

In a second twist, however, Wesley cannot do the impossible on the strength of his devotion or his desire to save Lilah. The contract burns but is unbroken, which is almost unheard of in a fictional situation like the one between Wesley and Lilah. No loophole is found, no last-minute miracle. Lilah stays contracted, and her reaction is the third surprise of the sequence. There are no bitter remonstrations, no open avowals of love or unending devotion. Instead, Lilah's reaction is, at least in tone, forgiveness: 'flames wouldn't be eternal if they actually consumed anything', she tells Wesley gently, 'but it means something that you tried'. Her enigmatic words, which mark the end of the affair as well as the Lilah character, are on the surface, straightforward, but the dynamic and the actual meaning are not. It appears that the femme fatale, rather than the detective, is the one controlling things at the last, and that the 'queen bitch' of Los Angeles, rather than 'champion' Angel (who is about to sacrifice his son and his friends' memories because Connor is apparently unsaveable as he is), is the one demonstrating the much-vaunted Whedon virtue of forgiveness. Lilah, rather than Wesley, is sending her lover over, having gained proof at last that he has recognized his investment in their affair; thus, he may be renewed with the rest of his friends by Angel's (dubiously) cleansing mind wipe and reality-alteration, having given all the gifts she can: the possibility of knowledge and the renewal that only Lilah's real forgiveness – not merely the empty words of a neutered ghost – can provide.

CONCLUSION

The vagaries of production being what they are, it is hard to
know if Mutant Enemy intended for the Lilah/Wesley arc to
end as it did, with Wesley being forgiven in a magnanimous
gesture by a Lilah who remains, still without comment, in
hell. Stephanie Romanov's omnipresence and energetic performance in 'Home' might suggest otherwise, but as it stands,
Lilah's near-final comment that it means *something* that Wesley tried to find her eternal peace is an apt commentary on the
storyline as a whole. On the surface, we have a straightforward tale of the detective and the femme fatale, straight
out of 1948, where – after the threat of the dangerous woman
is removed – the world returns to placid normality. Well-shot,
well-written, and well-acted, if nothing else, Lilah and Wesley
is a treat to watch; far more *Angel* 'in its stride' than the
strange tones and modulations of the fifth season.

On the critical analytical level, however, much like Lilah's
something, the arc is problematic and impossible to nail down.
Wesley and Lilah's cynical yet truthful knowledge of the
underworld about them is compelling; are we supposed to
hear in their barbed comments on Angel Investigations any
measure of truth? Or is there merely pity for the ostracized,
knowing their cynicism is personal and agenda-motivated?
Given Wesley's fifth season romance with Fred and the subsequent depth of his madness in 'Underneath' (5:17), 'Origin'
(5:18) and 'Time Bomb' (5:19), can we assume that Wesley
loved Lilah at all, or was their interaction mere distraction
from Wesley's real love, Fred? Is this a story of redemption
and forgiveness from the least likely of people, or a tying-up
of ends served best by turning Lilah into a stereotypical saint
of a woman, forgiving even though she's trapped in hell?
Much like *Angel*'s filmic predecessors, the questions are easier
to pose than to answer definitively. But ultimately, that such
questions can be asked and be found viable does point to the
fact that Lilah and Wesley were not just a reproduction of Sam
Spade and Bridget O'Shaughnessy, or even Vivian Rutledge
and Philip Marlowe; their storyline was a way to analyse

unanswered ethical and genre questions of both noir and *Angel* the series.

NOTES

1 Romanov, given her physical type, is vocally open about how Lilah is played as a femme fatale, even as recently as April 2004 in an article with *Horror-Web*, at http://www.horrorweb.com/hollywood/angel/stephanie.html.

2 This famous detective, created by Mickey Spillane, is noted for being more violent and boorish than the noir detectives immortalized by Bogart's version of Philip Marlowe. The first Hollywood Mike Hammer film, *Kiss Me Deadly* (Robert Aldrich, 1955), has sometimes been seen as a shift in the genre.

3 Perhaps most famously portrayed for the modern viewer in Shakespeare's *A Midsummer's Night's Dream*, Pyramus and Thisbe are tragic lovers separated by a wall, who are thwarted just before their love is made real, by Thisbe being eaten by a lion.

4 Slavoj Zizek, *Welcome to the Desert of the Real!* (London: Verso, 2002), p. 60.

12

From Rogue in the 'Hood to Suave in a Suit: Black Masculinity and the Transformation of Charles Gunn

MICHAELA D. E. MEYER

The Warner Brothers' (WB) creation of character Charles Gunn came at a fortuitous time. *Angel* premiered in the middle of the National Association for the Advancement of Colored People (NAACP)'s charges of 'whitewash', a social statement by the black community that despite their increasing demographics, television networks continue to represent a majority of white actors, stories and interests.[1] Few black actors appear in prime time, especially in continuous roles, and what limited screentime is given to black actors frequently reifies stereotypical assumptions of black cultural life. Gunn appeared as a guest star in Season One and by Season Two the WB had integrated his role into *Angel's* ensemble cast.

J. August Richards, the actor who portrays Gunn in the series, appeared in a variety of small television parts prior to landing his role on *Angel*, including guest roles on *JAG*, *Moesha*, *The West Wing*, *The Practice*, *Sliders*, *Clueless*, *Chicago Hope*, *Nash Bridges*, *Diagnosis Murder* and *The Cosby Show*.[2] In fact, his relegation to guest roles became a point of contention in his family. The young actor commented to the press that, 'When I first started I'd have two lines in a show and my fam-

ily would say "When do you get to say more?" If only they
knew how hard I had to work for those two lines.'[3] Richards'
struggles in the television business led to a test. He agreed to
allow a journalist from the *Los Angeles Times* to test the concept of 'whitewash' by secretly following around the young
black actor as he tried to break into the business; the journalist
followed his career for an entire year and, fortunately, Richards landed the role of Gunn on *Angel*.[4]

Many scholars are interested in the representation of race
in media.[5] Gunn's incorporation into an all-white cast brought
hope to audiences seeking alternative representations of black
men on television. Although this move proved politically
interesting, Gunn's representation is ultimately problematic.
Gunn comes from the street literally, is taken in by his white
counterparts and ultimately does what he can to 'whiten'
himself throughout the series. As Ginsberg argues, 'When
"race" is no longer visible, it is no longer intelligible: if
"white" can be "black," what is white? Race passing not only
creates [...] a *category crisis* but also destabilizes the grounds
of privilege founded on racial identity.'[6] In other words, Gunn
becomes 'white' as the series progresses, a representation that
functions as racial passing. Thus, Gunn's character is not a
step towards positive change in representing black men on
television.

'I DON'T NEED NO ADVICE FROM SOME
MIDDLE-CLASS WHITE DUDE THAT'S DEAD!'
NIHILISM, THE 'HOOD, AND THE
REPRESENTATION OF BLACK URBAN LIFE

More often than not, mediated representations of black men
depict an 'urban aesthetic, a nihilistic attitude, and an aggressive posturing'.[7] In the late 1980s and early 1990s, successful
films such as *Do the Right Thing* (Spike Lee, 1989) and *Boyz 'N
the Hood* (John Singleton, 1991) provided audiences with visual depictions of black urban life, highlighting the presence of
multi-layered racism.[8] Characters in these films adopted

specific stereotypical attributes of black life while, at the same time, attempting to level a critique at white dominance.[9] Gunn's identity at his introductory point in the series is specifically linked to the 'hood (short for neighbourhood): a word commonly associated with black urban communities. This identity category is exemplified through Gunn's fast-talking, cool-posturing attitude. Observing that black men utilize 'cool pose' in their everyday performance of self, Majors and Billson define cool pose as 'a ritualized form of masculinity that entails behaviors, scripts, physical posturing, impression management, and carefully crafted performances that deliver a single, critical message: pride, strength and control'.[10] Gunn's performance when he is introduced as a main character on the series adopts this overarching attitude. Gunn's management of his gang of vampire-hunters also demonstrates his ability to be in control of his own life, a trait most exemplified by his willingness to stake his sister when she becomes a vampire.

As a result, when Gunn is introduced to the other white characters on the show, his urbanized identity drives the interaction. In 'Judgement' (2:1), Wesley and Cordelia meet Gunn for the first time, and their stereotypes of black culture are communicated:

> *Gunn:*   My name is Gunn. Angel sent me.
> *Cordelia:* Please, come in. Come in. Wesley, you've heard Angel talk about Gun. He's a great guy with a really fly street tag.
> *Wesley:*   What's he fly?
> *Cordelia:* It's how they know you on the street, dorko. Gun. It really lets them know you mean business.

Cordelia assumes that 'Gunn' is 'Gun', confusing Charles' name with the weapon. This mistake reinforces black men's associations with crime and violence, particularly as she assumes that this name is 'a really fly street tag'. Wesley's cluelessness about this marker further codifies white confusion toward black identity. When Gunn utilizes a sarcastic tone to indicate that Gunn is in fact his name, not a street tag, Cordelia is rightly embarrassed. The exchange serves to inform the viewer that white culture cannot truly understand the black urban experience. This representation is further reinforced through the clothing worn by each character – Gunn wears mismatched clothes topped by a bright orange zip-up sweatshirt with a hood, while Cordelia and Wesley are wearing colour coordinated outfits with sharp lines. In essence, Gunn's adoption of cool pose in specific circumstances reinforces his connection with the 'hood and defines his reality as different from the other characters in the series.

As Gunn becomes more integrated into the storylines throughout Season Two, his identity is challenged by Angel. While Gunn accepts working for Angel because he needs the money and likes the hunt, he and Angel struggle against each other for power and control in their group. This is evident from their first interaction in 'War Zone' (1:20), where Angel stumbles upon Gunn and his gang of vampire-hunters. Gunn's hatred of vampires is intrinsically linked with his distrust of whiteness. This distrust appears when Angel warns Gunn not to rush after the group of vampires that took his sister hostage. In this scene, Angel offers to help Gunn find his sister, but Gunn responds, 'I don't need no advice from some middle-class white dude that's dead!' emphasizing the importance of class between the men. Angel is privileged in Gunn's eyes, and could not possibly 'know what my life is!' Gunn goes on to stress that this is a fight he must do on his own, while Angel seems puzzled as to why Gunn will not accept his help. Angel's plea to 'do this together' is countered by Gunn's distrust, as he exposes Angel to sunlight and charges him to 'figure it out'. Obviously this is a reference to Angel being a vampire and Gunn being human; however, Gunn's reaction to Angel can also be read as a rejection of whiteness and white attempts to solve problems for black communities.

Gunn's continued rejection of Angel as an authority figure produces tension throughout the second season. In 'First Impressions' (2:3), the Angel team goes to meet an informant, Jameel, who is supposed to help with a case that Gunn brings to the office. During the interaction, Angel and Gunn disagree on how to approach the case, representing the growing power-struggle between the two. As previously seen, Gunn does not entirely trust Angel on account of his being a vampire, and being white. In this scene, Gunn's approach to getting information from Jameel emphasizes physical violence, while Angel opts to provide money for the information. Gunn links his 'beat it out of him' approach to 'survival of the fittest', reinforcing the association of the 'hood with implicit violence. The interaction between Jameel and Gunn highlights cultural aspects of the 'hood, particularly as Jameel notes that he 'ain't looking to make no new enemies'. Jameel's appearance then is a sign of respect for the position Gunn holds in the community, despite his unwillingness to share the information. Gunn justifies his violent approach with claims that 'people are dying!' and 'this is my case' – both of which Angel refutes, ultimately claiming that 'now it's mine'. As Gunn defers to Angel's power of decision making, he begins to assimilate with the members of the Angel team.

'I Would Do Anything for You But It's Not Enough': The Investment in Whiteness on Angel

As Gunn becomes a regular member of Angel Investigations, he begins to shed his blackness and adopt qualities of white culture. He modifies his identity through his association with Angel by adapting his speech patterns and clothing to be more consistent with his white counterparts, and spending less time with his 'posse' from the 'hood. While Gunn's dialogue mimics that of his gang for the majority of the second season, these linguistic patterns are dropped from frequent use as the series progresses. In fact, as Gunn's manner of speaking becomes more like his white counterparts, his original linguistic phrasing is used as a comic relief on the series. For example, in 'Waiting in the Wings' (3:13), Gunn learns that Angel has purchased tickets to the ballet instead of a rock concert:

> *Gunn:*   You got ballet on my Mahta Hari tickets?

Angel: This is the Blinnikov World Ballet Corps.

Gunn: No. No! This is not Mahta Hari. This is tutus, and guys with their big-ass packages jumping up and down. This is just ... I will never trust you again. The trust is gone.

Angel: Guys, seeing real ballet live it's – it's like another world. Gunn, these guys are tight, and you're gonna be trippin' out.

Gunn: Don't be usin' my own phrases when we lost the trust.

This interaction displays Angel appropriating Gunn's speech patterns. Gunn's reaction to this violation is comic, as it refers not to Angel's cultural use of the phrases, but the context of the interaction. The reason for the appropriation and use of Gunn's black dialect is that Angel bought tickets to the ballet, not that he and Gunn have mutually agreed upon communicative codes.

The linguistic erasure of Gunn's dialect leads to a second, more insidious method of whitening throughout the series: Gunn's romantic relationship with a white woman, Fred. Gunn and Fred begin dating in the third season, and are presented as a happy couple. The representation of black men and white women together is not inherently problematic, though this particular type of relationship suffers from a long-held stereotypical belief that black men frame interpersonal relationships with white women as key to gaining social status.[11] In *Angel*, the black man/white woman relationship becomes enormously problematic when Fred discovers in 'Supersymmetry' (4:5) that her former physics professor is responsible for sending her to a hell dimension. Fred wants to kill the professor to avenge her lost time, but Gunn pleads with her to reconsider, admitting that in the past he would resort to violence to solve Fred's problem, but at the same time acknowledging that he is a different person at this point in the narrative. He emphasizes that 'we help people', referring to his devotion to Angel Investigations' mission, and that the psychological demons that surface after an act of murder are worse than the real demons Angel's team deals with on a regular basis. Fred disagrees, but Gunn insists that she should not let the professor define her current identity, a plea resembling Gunn's own choice to leave his past behind and his transition into his new life.

Although Fred lets the conversation drop, she later turns to Wesley for help. She confronts the professor by holding him hostage at the point of a crossbow, and opens a portal to another dimension. Just as she is about to enact her revenge, Gunn finds her:

> Gunn: Fred, don't let him do this to you … I promise, we'll stop him. We'll find some other way.
>
> Fred: He'll never stop! He'll do it again!
>
> Gunn: If you kill him, I'm gonna lose you.

Just as Gunn says this last line, he grabs the professor from behind and breaks his neck with his bare hands, then tosses the professor's dead body into the portal before them. Fred stares at Gunn, startled. The viewer is led to believe that Gunn has committed murder in the past, and thus he believes that by killing for Fred he preserves her innocence and spares her from the potential torment of her own conscience. In essence, Fred's whiteness is preserved and Gunn's blackness absorbs the evil threatening Fred's perfection.

This scenario reifies what Lipsitz calls 'the possessive investment in whiteness' or maintaining a social order that privileges whiteness as a positive feature of social life.[12] Gunn even admits to as much when he notes 'If you kill him, I'm gonna lose you.' This act becomes a defining feature of their relationship, eventually leading to its demise. Fred is taken aback by Gunn's action, and begins to withdraw from the relationship. Gunn's act of killing the professor breaks the fragile colour-blindness in their relationship, causing Fred to re-examine whether or not she can truly be intimate with a black man. This strips Gunn of his confidence and Fred, his reason for being.

Shortly thereafter, Gunn undergoes a crisis in framing his identity. Killing the professor repositions Gunn as violent and this association with violence continues throughout the fourth season. The narrative frequently emphasizes Gunn's physical strength over his emotional or intellectual abilities. In 'Players' (4:16), Gunn even claims 'Hey, I'm the muscle' while a minor character, Gwen – commenting on how Gunn's white counterparts at Angel Investigations consistently use him for fighting and recon, but do not include him on research or strategy – observes 'Man, they have done a number on you. You really believe this "I'm the muscle" crap.' This link continues when Gunn is 'chosen' by the 'big cat' at Wolfram & Hart in 'Home' (4:22). The cat's choice to communicate with Gunn reinforces cultural stereotypes of the animalistic nature of black masculinity, further linking Gunn to black stereotypes, although his speech and mannerisms adapt to the white culture that surrounds him.

Perhaps the most defining moment of Gunn's struggle to 'become white' occurs in Season Five when Wolfram & Hart approach him about his 'untapped potential'. Much like Gwen, the Senior Partners of the law firm see that Gunn has more to offer than muscle, and they authorize a 'mind dump' that provides Gunn with superior legal knowledge. This act whitens Gunn further by allowing him access to something he did not previously have – education. bell hooks notes that social systems rob black men of critical-thinking skills and intellectual knowledge because black men do not have access to the means of education and, furthermore, are encouraged by a capitalist system to flee school for the streets where more money is to be made with less effort.[13] Gunn becomes comfortable in his role as a lawyer, but his identity hits another crisis as his mind dump begins to fade. He goes to the doctor who implanted the education in his brain and begs for an upgrade. Gunn refuses to go 'back to who [he] was', negating his own blackness. By receiving access to education, he experiences what it is like to be privileged and respected for intellectual pursuits rather than sheer muscle, and losing this newfound respect scares him immensely. Thus, Gunn makes a deal with the doctor to release a package stuck in customs in exchange for a permanent upgrade of education. When the package turns out to be the spirit of a dead goddess who kills Fred by invading her body and destroying her soul, Gunn realizes the consequences of his action. In 'Shells' (5:16), Gunn wrestles with his choice when Wesley confronts him:

Gunn: It was just a piece of paper. I was losing it. Every-
         thing they put in my head, everything that made
         me different – special. And he could fix it. Make it
         permanent. So I signed a piece of paper. It was a
         customs release form. I didn't think anyone would
         get hurt.
Wesley: Nothing from Wolfram & Hart is ever free. You
         knew that.
Gunn: I couldn't go back to being just the muscle. I—I
         didn't think it would be one of us. I didn't think it
         would be Fred.

Wesley refuses to forgive Gunn for his actions and stabs him in the stomach. Later in the episode, Harmony is the only character who visits Gunn in the hospital. She inquires:

Harmony: How could you do that? To your friends? To Fred?
Gunn: Because I was weak. Because I wanted to be some-
         body that I wasn't. Because I don't know where I
         fit. Because I never did. Because a thousand other
         reasons that don't mean a damn 'cause she's gone.
         She's gone and she's not coming back because of
         me. I did this, and I'm sorry [sobs] I'm sorry.

After his constant attempts to whiten himself fail, Gunn resigns himself to an ugly fate. His guilt over his actions comes to a head in 'Underneath' (5:17) where he volunteers to stay in a hell dimension, doomed to relive every day having his heart cut out by demons. The remainder of the series depicts Gunn's struggle for redemption, ultimately surfacing in the series' finale. Gunn agrees to stand with the Angel team to fight the coming apocalypse, knowing full well that it is a suicide mission. Although Gunn does not die on screen, Illyria (the goddess who consumed Fred) comments that he has less than ten minutes to live just as the team gears up for the final battle and the series fades to black.

'I've Spent Most of this Year Trapped in What I Can Only Describe as a Turgid Supernatural Soap Opera'. The Stakes of Televisual Representations of Black Male Identities

Although *Angel* was one of the first series on the WB to include a black male within an ensemble cast, this shift was not nearly as progressive as many hoped. Through the analysis presented in this chapter, we see that Gunn's representation is problematic because he is whitened throughout the series. Audiences and scholars should question the progressiveness of representing black men on television in roles that function to recreate the possessive investment in whiteness. Harper claims that the media cause anxiety for black men because they produce multiple challenges for the construction of a black masculine identity.[14] Moreover, Magubane observes that when black media personas are whitened, this troubles identity formation for black men on and off the screen.[15] In other words, there are cultural stakes of representing Gunn in a manner that supports the possessive investment in whiteness.

Given this representation, viewers are presented with two potential interpretations. The writers and directors of the series clearly meant to problematize Gunn's identity formation. Throughout the series, Gunn is represented as making sacrifices to become part of the Angel Investigations team – staking his sister, leaving his friends behind and agreeing to function in a subservient role to Angel. Gunn is not accepted at face value by the white characters in the series; he must continually struggle to prove himself as a worthy member of the team. His sacrifices are rewarded with 'white privilege' – obtaining a white girlfriend, and receiving education. Throughout these trials, Gunn struggles to negotiate his black masculinity with the political economy of 'whitening'. This representation can be read as 'deep' in many respects, as it articulates a process of negotiation between dominant and non-dominant cultures.[16]

On the other hand, the whitening of Gunn as the series progresses poses critical implications. Gunn's position in the ensemble cast does not encourage positive social change towards representing black men in media, but rather reinforces the stereotype that black characters will be subsumed by white narratives. Butler suggests that 'gender is [a] performative accomplishment which the mundane social audience, including the actors themselves, come to believe and to perform in the mode of belief'.[17] In the series, Gunn performs according to what he perceives others anticipate from him. His definition of himself as 'just the muscle' capitalizes on stereotypes of black men possessing superior physical prowess to white men. Moreover, his willingness to categorize himself in white terms is problematic because this act condemns him to the process of whitening. His quest for a white woman, followed by his selfless preservation of her whiteness harks back to what many scholars see as a culture teaching black men to loathe themselves, to see the street as their only home, and the 'hood as their only community.[18] Gunn's inability to effectively 'blend in' with white culture ultimately leads to an implicit rejection of the constraints placed upon Gunn's identity at the end of the series. The final episode depicts Gunn as returning to his original speech patterns, and it is the first time in over a year his character appears happy – even as he is about to die.

Racialized representations in the media, both visual and written, provide the viewing audience with powerful cues for identity formation, and in the case of Gunn, black masculinity is specifically questioned.[19] The lack of black characters in mainstream media contributes to the limitations imposed on black youth, specifically limiting their ability to dream existences other than mediated stereotypes.[20] Actor J. August Richards experienced this limitation himself prior to starting his acting career. When a reporter compared the dynamic relationship between Gunn and Angel to cultural icons Luke Skywalker and Han Solo, Richards claimed this was an excellent correlation. He then goes on to state, 'I'm a Harrison Ford fanatic as well as a *Star Wars* junkie. I used to always want to be Han Solo when we played *Star Wars* as kids, but they always made me be Lando Calrissian.'[21] Richards' own experiences of being forced into the 'black' role in the famous narrative rings true to his own struggles to become visible in mainstream television. The stakes of that visibility, however, are ultimately debatable.

NOTES

1 G. Levin, 'Citing "Whitewash", NAACP Reaffirms Plan to Boycott Major Network', *USA Today*, 4 November 1999, p. 3D. See also R. Graham, 'Life in the Pop Lane: Blacks' Biggest TV Trouble is at Home', *Boston Globe*, 28 August 2001, p. E1.

2 N. Johnson, 'Hot and Tangi', *Herald Sun*, 22 March 2002, p. H03.

3 A. White, 'Straight Shooter', *Courier Mail*, 5 April 2001, p. 7.

4 'Must be Talking to an Angel', *Dominion Post*, 18 March 2003, p. 3.

5 E. Guerrero, *Framing Blackness: The African American Image in Film* (Philadelphia: Temple University Press, 1993); T. Nakayama, 'The Significance of "Race" and Masculinities', *Critical Studies in Media Communication*, 17 (2000), pp. 111–14.

6 E. K. Ginsberg, 'Introduction: The Politics of Passing', in E. K. Ginsberg (ed.), *Passing and the Fictions of Identity* (Durham, NC: Duke University Press, 1996), p. 8.

7 M. Henry, 'He is a "Bad Mother *$%@!#"': *Shaft* and Contemporary Black Masculinity', *Journal of Popular Film and Television*, 30: 2 (2002), p. 114.

8 K. Chan, 'The Construction of Black Male Identity in Black Action Films of the Nineties', *Cinema Journal*, 37: 2 (1998), pp. 35–48.

9 R. C. Rowland and R. Strain, 'Social Function, Polysemy, and Narrative-Dramatic Form: A Case Study of *Do the Right Thing*', *Communication Quarterly*, 42 (1994), pp. 213–28.

10 R. Majors and J. M. Billson, *Cool Pose: The Dilemmas of Black Manhood in America* (New York: Lexington Books, 1991), p. 4.

11 For example, see J. A. Brown, 'Casework Contacts with Black–White Couples', *Social Casework: The Journal of Contemporary Casework*, 26 (1987), pp. 24–9; M. Kalmign, 'Trends in Black/White Intermarriage', *Social Forces*, 72 (1999), pp. 119–46.

12 G. Lipsitz, 'The Possessive Investment in Whiteness: How White People Profit from Identity Politics', in K. E. Rosenblum and T. Travis (eds), *The Meaning of Differences: American Construction of*

Race, Sex and Gender, Social Class and Sexual Orientation (Boston: McGraw-Hill, 2000), pp. 351–80.

13   b. hooks, *We Real Cool: Black Men and Masculinity* (New York: Routledge, 2004).

14   P. B. Harper, *Are We Not Men? Masculine Anxiety and the Problem of African-American Identity* (New York: Oxford University Press, 1996).

15   Z. Magubane, 'Black Skins, Slack Masks or "The Return of the White Negro": Race, Masculinity, and the Public Personas of Dennis Rodman and RuPaul', *Men & Masculinities*, 4 (2002), pp. 233–58.

16   M. P. Orbe, 'Constructions of Reality on MTV's "*The Real World*": An Analysis of the Restrictive Coding of Black Masculinity', *Southern Communication Journal*, 64 (1998), pp. 32–48.

17   J. Butler, *Gender Trouble* (New York: Routledge, 1990), p. 141.

18   hooks, *We Real Cool*.

19   N. Terkildsen and D. F. Damore, 'The Dynamics of Racialized Media Coverage in Congressional Elections', *Journal of Politics*, 61 (1999), pp. 680–99.

20   b. hooks, *Bone Black: Memories of Girlhood*, (New York: Henry Holt, 1996); M. P. Orbe and M. C. Hobson, 'Looking at the Front Door: Exploring Images of the Black Male on MTV's "*The Real World*"', in J. Martin, T. Nakayama and L. Flores (eds), *Readings in Intercultural Communication: Experiences and Contexts* (Boston: McGraw-Hill, 2002), pp. 219–26.

21   D. Hood, 'Gunn Fires Up *Angel*', *Herald Sun*, 15 April 2001, p. X09.

13

'Nobody Scream ... or Touch My Arms': The Comic Stylings of Wesley Wyndam-Pryce

STACEY ABBOTT

> *Cordelia:* What are you doing?
> *Wesley:* Knocking things over. Driving away business. You
>   know ... the usual.
>
> ('Guise Will Be Guise', 2:6)

*A*ngel, often discussed in terms of its darker themes of alienation and redemption, has been described in this volume and elsewhere as drawing from such genres as horror, superhero, film noir, the vampire film and the detective narrative. While each of these genre categories are valid, and like *Buffy the Vampire Slayer* (*BtVS*) before it, act as a testament to the series' commitment to genre hybridity, *Angel* is rarely discussed as comedy. Yet humour, as with *BtVS*, is one of its defining characteristics. Jane Espenson, one of the writers for *BtVS* and *Angel*, confirmed this when she told Roz Kaveney in an interview:

> [...] I still find it scary when I look at a page and don't see funny on it. When you finish a script your first instinct is to hold it in your hand and are just about ready to turn it in, almost everybody will flip it over a couple of times and read a page and try to see it from Joss's eyes. If he looked at this page is there funny? Is there anything that would make him chuckle? And it's scary if you open it and there's not.[1]

When comedy is taken into consideration it is usually a particular kind of humour that is discussed. Steven Wilson, in one of the few articles on *BtVS* that overtly discusses the role of humour, put together a list of categories of jokes used within the series, which include: buffoonery, world-weary disaffection, sight gags, non sequiturs, literary allusions, pop culture references, puns, pratfalls, irony, deconstruction or self-parody, 'really weird dialogue' and creating their own language.[2] Out of these twelve categories, nine apply to verbal humour while three apply to visual humour: buffoonery, sight gags and pratfalls.

When discussing humour in relation to these shows we seem to equate it with the spoken word. This should not be surprising in a medium that is lead by the writer and our own attraction to these one-liners should be equally understandable given that it is easier to quote a line than a sight gag. Visual humour, however, remains fundamental to both series in terms of style and performance. Nowhere is this more apparent then in the characterization of Wesley Wyndam-Pryce. When asked whether he misses 'goofy Wesley' in the face of his new and darker persona, Alexis Denisof confirmed that 'yeah, I must say, I am one for enjoying the odd banana peel and double take [...] but this is exciting too. To have a character that contains both is a rarity. I sometimes yearn for the days when he was just clowning around, but they may not be gone. I know Joss has some ideas about how to find that again.'[3] Whedon's ideas for Wesley came in the form of 'Spin the Bottle' (4:6), a comedy episode in Season Four in which a spell causes all of the characters to think they are seventeen again, thus returning to their adolescent personas. Wesley is therefore once again presented as awkward, gangly and bumbling. Whedon confirms that this script began with a desire 'to see Alexis fall down again'.[4]

The absence of slapstick within discussions of humour in *BtVS* and *Angel* seems to reflect the common perception of visual humour as low, physical comedy in contrast to the more cerebral wit of verbal comedy. One is a baser form of humour while the other requires 'intelligence'. I will, however, argue in this chapter that the style and use of slapstick by Alexis Denisof as Wesley on *Angel* actually serves to redefine his character from the one first introduced on *BtVS* and reorient our sympathies with Wesley, instead of against him.[5] The bumbling image of Wesley that is reprised in 'Spin the Bottle' is not the same comic character that was introduced on *BtVS*. Comedy also establishes the series' preoccupation with the concept and representation of masculinity, in contrast to *BtVS's* feminist concerns.

On *BtVS*, Wesley was first presented as a parody of Giles' British reserve and upper-class priggishness. In his first appearance in 'Bad Girls' (B3:14), both Buffy and Faith enter the library, look him up and down and ask Giles 'New Watcher?' Wesley is instantly recognizable as a Watcher because of his clipped British accent, his formal manners and his enthusiasm for historical detail when recounting the background to a particular demon; in other words, because of his similarity to Giles. The similarity is punctuated to comic effect by ending his first scene with both Giles and Wesley watching Buffy leave the library as they each absent-mindedly remove a handkerchief from their pockets and begin to clean their glasses in unison. Every fan will remember that this is a recurrent motif of Giles. Despite this similarity, Anthony Stewart Head argues that 'Wesley was everything that Giles resented and was determined not to be like.'[6] Their difference comes from the fact that Giles was more experienced with the supernatural through his own past as Ripper then Wesley, who clearly lacks the experience of Buffy or even of her friends. As a result, despite his clear knowledge of demon lore, Wesley is often portrayed in 'Bad Girls' and later episodes as frightened and cowardly.

Wesley was also introduced into the series as a comic foil for Buffy. Denisof explains that he saw his character as being there to 'set off Giles, set off Buffy and annoy everyone'.[7] Wesley overcompensates for his lack of experience in comparison with Buffy, Giles and the Scoobies by being overly authoritarian, stern and, significantly, without humour. As a result he is mercilessly mocked and ignored by the Scooby

Gang. Narratively his role as a foppish and powerless representative of the Watchers' Council, is to prepare Buffy and the
audience for her 'graduation' from the Council by first rebel-
ling against Wesley, as in 'Choices' (B3:19) when Buffy ignores
Wesley's orders and exchanges the Mayor's Box of Gavrok for
the kidnapped Willow.

The source of much of Wesley's humour on *BtVS* is at the
expense of his authority and masculinity for, as Peggy Davis
explains, Wesley's function is to act 'as comic relief by insti-
gating funny – though barbed – comments from the Scooby
Gang, of which he is obviously *not* a member, due to his
prissy and girlish demeanour'.[8] Buffy tells Wesley that she
will call him if they need 'someone to scream like a woman';
he awkwardly and embarrassingly pursues Cordelia like a
lovesick teenager, which climaxes in their fumbled kiss in the
library; and we last see Wesley strapped to a gurney after the
battle with the Mayor, having been knocked down and
stepped on, groaning and begging for painkillers ('Graduation Day Part II', B3:22). Wesley is, from his first appearance
to his last, a figure of humour but the joke is always on him
rather than with him.

On *Angel*, however, his character was necessarily re-
invented for the new series as he was to play sidekick to
Angel rather than foil. While humour is still central to his performance, there is increased focus upon physical humour
right from the start. He is introduced in 'Parting Gifts' (1:10)
as a faceless hunter, dressed in leather and driving a motorcy-
cle, pursuing a seemingly innocent demon who comes to
Angel for help. Each shot of this unidentified stalker is accompanied by dark, oppressive music and he is presented as an
impressive and formidable opponent for Angel, potentially
dangerous and with unknown motives. When they finally
come face to face, the stalker, poised for attack with a crossbow aimed at Angel, emerges from the shadows to reveal that
it is Wesley. Wesley maintains his stance until Angel effortlessly and speedily knocks the crossbow out of his hands and
regains authority.

There are two visual jokes going on here. The first is the quick disarmament of Wesley by Angel after the slow build-up to this confrontation. The second visual gag is the incongruity between Wesley the failed Watcher and the threatening image of the leather-clad stalker, an incongruity that is reinforced when he later tells Cordelia that he is walking funny because the leather pants 'tend to chafe the leg'. While he was instantly recognizable as a Watcher on *BtVS*, on *Angel* we are given misdirecting visual clues as to the stalker's identity, all of which result in comic surprise at Wesley's arrival in LA.

This type of visual humour, while effective, is not wholly unique to *Angel*.[9] Where Wesley truly stands out on *Angel* is in the consistent use of slapstick comedy to accentuate the clumsiness of his character and to effect his transformation from foil to sidekick. According to Alan Dale, 'the essence of a slapstick gag is a physical assault on, or collapse of, the hero's dignity; as a corollary, the loss of dignity by itself can result in our identifying with the victim.'[10] He further argues that slapstick emerges when the character is unable to control their surroundings or even their own body: 'slapstick is a fundamental, universal, and eternal response to the fact that life is physical. [...] It's the body that we can see interacting with physical forces and objects, and our intense exasperation that this interaction doesn't run smoother.'[11]

This is a further contrast with the verbal comedy that is so prevalent in both *BtVS* and *Angel* for, as Jana Riess explains, '[verbal] humour not only entertains fans but also signals which of the characters is in control'.[12] In a series in which the main protagonist, Angel, is a handsome, suave superhero who is always in control of his body, emotions and even bloodlust, slapstick is used to contrast Wesley's insecure image of masculinity with Angel. Wesley, in Season One, is rarely in control, physically or verbally.[13] His character is built around his acknowledgment of his cowardice and failure as a Watcher and his desire to atone for this failure by working with Angel. Much of his slapstick humour is generated by his over earnestness to be of help to Angel being undermined by his clumsiness. In 'Parting Gifts' he prepares for attack by taping a knife to his ankle, only to later fall over when he tries to pull it out to save Cordelia; in 'Expecting' (1:12) Cordelia's flirtatious friends cause him to nervously swing an axe while trying to seem cool, only to get it stuck in the wall; and in 'The Ring' (1:16) his courageous decision to find the missing Angel by intimidating a local bookie is punctuated by his dramatic removal of a crossbow from the weapons store but undercut by the fact that all of the other weapons get pulled out along with it.

Wesley's clumsiness, however, is only part of the equation. It is the contrast between Wesley and Angel that draws much humour as well. After being rescued at the end of 'Parting Gifts', Cordelia embraces and thanks Angel, ignoring Wesley, much to his disappointment. Angel then tells Cordy that he 'was lucky he had a rogue demon-hunter on his side', allowing Wesley a brief moment of pride. Furthermore, David Boreanaz's performance as Angel is the perfect opposition to Denisof. In contrast to Angel's stillness, Wesley's gestures and pratfalls seem all the more extreme. Boreanaz articulates himself through the most minimal gestures while Denisof's movements are huge and exaggerated. To further emphasize their differences, both actors are often shot in the same frame. In 'Expecting', when Wesley attempts to pull the axe out of the wall and subsequently falls over, Angel is silently watching him through the window at the back of the office. Later, when they accidentally track a demon to the wrong house, it is Wesley who bursts through the door ordering the quiet middle-aged couple innocently watching television to tell him where they lay their eggs, while Angel stands silently in the background and realizes their error. Finally in 'She' (1:13) Wesley is introduced dancing like a maniac at Cordelia's house party. His movements are broad, jerky and result in him falling over. While the actors are not shot in the same frame, the two are still contrasted by intercutting Wesley's dancing with shots of Angel, who is absolutely still except for the movement of his eyes as he looks on. Wesley's physical ineptitude in the face of Angel's self-control is, as Dale argues, an assault on his dignity but an assault that results in our sympathy for and identification with him. He is no longer pompous and annoying but rather earnest and inexperienced.

This is not to deny David Boreanaz's capacity for physical humour, for later in the party sequence we see one of his great moments of physical comedy when he imagines himself dancing. It is a shocking moment of physical release as Angel grooves around the floor in mock disco dance steps. This fantasy, or nightmare, is more than simply a comic romp for it serves to emphasize Angel's characteristic stillness in contrast, and it demonstrates Angel's control of himself for the fantasy abruptly cuts back to Angel turning down the invitation to dance by saying 'I don't dance.' While Angel avoids embarrassment, Wesley, who has no such control, embraces it. Ironically, this is one of the few moments where their differences serve to Wesley's benefit, for the next day Cordelia describes Angel as a 'giant black hole of boring despair' and points out that at her party Wesley 'was cooler'. It should, of course, be noted that she says this not to compliment Wesley but to point out the extent of Angel's inadequacy.

The way in which the two actors create quite disparate images of masculinity owes much to the comedic partnership of Dean Martin and Jerry Lewis who were similarly based upon 'a split or division [that] is fundamental to the comic promise, as two assuredly different representations of masculinity co-exist'. As Scott Bukatman argues 'the displacement of the control function onto the adult figure of "sexy," "virile" Dean Martin serves to disguise the sexual conflicts that remain latent in spastic, juvenile Jerry.'[14] This is not to say that Angel and Wesley perform the same kind of comedy as Martin and Lewis, but rather that they offer a similarly intertwined image of masculinity that is often played out through comedy. This is particularly significant in 'Guise Will Be Guise', a key episode that marks Wesley's transition from comic buffoon to hero, but at the expense of Angel's self-image.

The episode begins with a series of classic Wesley pratfalls. Alone in the office, Wesley tries to open the filing-cabinet. Applying too much force, he pulls the drawer out and its contents fly onto the floor. As he bends down to pick the papers up, someone approaches, startling him and as a result he bangs his head on the filing-cabinet drawer. Trying to maintain his decorum and authority, he offers to help the potential client in Angel's absence. When pressed to know his supernatural credentials, Wesley informs the client that 'I was a rogue demon-hunter so I know how to handle myself when things get rough'. This attempt at self-confidence, which is underscored by his puffed up posturing, is punctured by him slipping on the papers, falling to the floor and resulting in his driving the customer away. That Wesley's masculinity is under question in this sequence is reinforced by the fact that the scene ends with Cordelia entering the office with a plan to find Angel and asks Wesley 'do you have any clothes a man would wear?'

Further on in the episode, when he is forced to pretend to be Angel in order to save Cordelia, the disguise is initially awkward and unfamiliar, highlighting Wesley's inability to step into Angel's hero shoes. Now wearing Angel's coat, he enters the office, announcing 'I'm Angel', and promptly stumbles across the threshold. Later, in a single long shot, he mistakenly walks through the entrance to his abductor's house before being invited. Realizing his error, Wesley quickly leaps backward and calmly re-enters as the invitation is uttered. Finally, when he meets Virginia, the daughter of a businessman who has kidnapped Angel/Wesley to be her protector, he squeals in horror at the sight of his own reflection in a mirror. Increasingly, however, in pretending to be Angel, Wesley gains physical confidence, as in the sequence when two thugs try to kidnap Virginia. He challenges the henchmen by saying:

> I'm Angel [*throws his glasses away*] the vampire with a soul. … [*pauses with uncertainty*] fighting for my redemption with … with … [*pause for dramatic effect*] killing evil demons. That's right. … scourge of the demon world. Don't worry boys, I don't kill humans … [*looks away and the turns back threateningly*] unless I'm angry. … You're going to leave now. Then you're going to tell Linear … [*pause to spike up his hair*] forget about the girl.

By playing the Angel role, Wesley overcomes his insecurities and physical ineptitude, which enables him to save and seduce Virginia, or as Cordelia puts it: 'One day as Angel ... one day and he's getting some.'

However, as Wesley becomes increasingly Angel-like and confident, Angel is transformed into a comic character whose own masculinity is undercut through a series of attacks on his persona. Cordelia mocks his brooding obsession with penance: 'This is Angel. "Oh no, I can't do anything fun tonight, I have to count my past sins and alphabetize them ... oh, by the way, I'm thinking of snapping on Friday"'. Later, when he is sent by the Host to see a swami to help him deal with his growing obsession with Darla, the swami accuses Angel of being preoccupied with his image, attacking his choice of car: 'vampire living in a city known for its sun, driving a convertible. Why do you hate yourself?'; his clothing – 'so why all the layers of black?' – and even his hair gel: 'How many warriors slated for the coming apocalypse do you think are going to be using that hair gel? Don't get me wrong. You're out there fighting ultimate evil, you're going to want something with hold.' All of which forces Angel to admit that his 'persona is a little affected'. The comic punchline, however, comes at the climax of the episode, when during their rescue of Virginia from a ritual sacrifice organized by her father, it is revealed that she is impure and therefore not suitable for the incantation. Her father, shocked to find that she is no longer a virgin, explains that the only reason he hired Angel to protect her was because he is a eunuch, a plan that failed due to Wesley's masquerade. While Cordelia reels at the concept that Wesley had sex, and Virginia informs her father that it is has been a long time since she was a virgin, much to Wesley's relief, Angel tries to clarify this misconception by repeatedly piping in that he is not a eunuch. He is ignored. So, in an episode that sees Wesley play the hero and get the girl, Angel becomes the figure of humour, reinforcing their comic duality, but more importantly driving home a complex representation of these characters that challenges our conventional understanding of masculinity or, as Steven Cohan and Ina Rae Hark describe it, 'the cultural fiction that masculinity is not a social construction'.[15] Looked at in isolation each character suggests a one-dimensional stereotype, the masculine hero and the feminized buffoon. Together, however, they demonstrate that masculinity is a far more fluid and changing concept, a theme of the series that is enhanced by the expansion of Angel Investigations to include Charles Gunn, Lorne and eventually Spike, each of whom contributes a new and distinct image of masculinity into the gender mix. Like the series' characteristic moral ambiguity, *Angel* similarly highlights that there is no black and white in terms of gender construction, only differing shades of grey.

So we come back to 'Spin the Bottle'. As Wesley became increasingly placed within the role of leader of Angel Investigations (AI) in Season Two, followed by his kidnapping of Connor and subsequent ejection from AI in Season Three, his comic buffoonery was substantially reduced. As a result 'Spin the Bottle' is the only major comedy episode to feature Wesley's slapstick techniques since the second season.[16] Peggy Davis argues that '[b]y Season Four the audience can barely remember a time when Wesley was a harmless, comical fop so thoroughly has he transformed into the darkly brooding hero'.[17] I would argue, however, that 'Spin the Bottle' was specifically designed to remind us of the old Wesley. In this episode, Whedon wanted to use the memory-spell narrative as a means to mix old- and new-school Wesley together, highlighting Denisof's ability to 'go from James Bond to Peter Sellers at the drop of a hat'.[18] As a result, Wesley embodies both the hero in complete control and the comic oaf out of control, meaning he takes on both the Angel and the Wesley roles.

Two scenes introduce us to the dark crusader that Wesley has become. The first is when he skilfully tests out a new weapon hidden within his sleeve until triggered to unfold and extend into an elegant sword. The second scene is a confrontation with Gunn. Angered by Wesley's relationship with Fred, Gunn questions his intentions, threatening him should he make an advance on her. When Wesley responds with a cool dismissal of his threat, Gunn grabs him, causing a wooden stake to thrust out menacingly from Wesley's sleeve into Gunn's face. Wesley explains: 'Not all of us have muscle to fall back on.' When he walks away, Gunn asks him 'what happened to you, man?' Wesley pauses before responding, 'I had my throat cut and all my friends abandoned me.' In both these sequences, Wesley is equated with Angel the superhero and anti-hero. He deftly uses the kind of hidden gadgets that Angel used in the first season of the series. In the scene with Gunn, he is incredibly reminiscent in his darkness to the Angel of Season Two, both through his parting remark to Gunn but also the way in which in their confrontation the hidden stake seems to be a physical response to Wesley's anger and hostility, much like Angel's 'game face'. While Wesley does not intentionally trigger it, he still seems in complete control.

When the spell goes wrong, though, we are reunited with the Wesley of days gone by and this Wesley is a combination of the one from *BtVS* and the one from *Angel*. Upon discovering himself in an isolated location with a group of strangers, all claiming to be teenagers, Wesley plays the pompous head boy of the Watchers' Academy. As on *BtVS*, his pretence at superior knowledge and experience is, however, undercut by Gunn's actual experience, and humorous tensions ensue. Mixed in with his pompous performance is the return to classic slapstick and Wesley's lack of physical control, as when Wesley attempts to save Cordelia from Angel by running to her rescue in the basement. His body betrays him as he topples down the stairs in a startling feat of physical contortion. If Whedon's desire in writing and directing this episode was to see Alexis fall down, Denisof delivers this with style.

In another scene, his earlier confrontation with Gunn is reprised, but to comic effect. Annoyed by Wesley's attempts to take charge, Gunn threatens to turn him into 'headless boy if you don't get out of my face'. Wesley responds by demonstrating his 'skill' in karate, thrusting his arms about in a series of mock 'martial art' stances and gestures, until one forward thrust results in the wooden stake once again popping out, this time demonstrating his lack of control. Pushing the stake back into his sleeve, Wesley inadvertently triggers the release of his sword, which alarmingly flies out just as Fred screams. Wesley, no longer exhibiting the same control over his weapons, freezes, holding his arms and legs extended, and yells out a warning to the others: 'Nobody scream … or touch my arms.' In this sequence, it is both Wesley's body out of control and his recognition that his body is a threat to himself and potentially others that generates the humour as he delicately lifts his trouser legs to see if there are any further weapons. Furthermore, he is not simply betrayed by his body but by the accoutrements of the new Wesley, thoroughly undermining his James Bond-like image.

While the episode offers a gleeful return to the goofy Wesley of the past, the comedy now serves a different purpose. He is no longer a comic foil nor a sidekick. He contributes equally to the investigation into why they are in the hotel and, while he is often nervy or jumpy, he does not demonstrate any of his past cowardice. When Angel is revealed as a vampire and threatens Cordy and Fred, Wesley acts as protector. Similarly, the slapstick moments no longer generate sympathy or identification; Wesley's response to these pratfalls is not embarrassment or self-deprecation but, rather, he continues the fight. For instance, after his pratfall down the stairs in his attempt to save Cordy, he does not skulk away in embarrassment but rather remains in charge by directing Connor to kill Angel. He may be out of control, but there is no loss of dignity. Instead these slapstick moments generate nostalgia for the lighter days of the series when Wesley was both comic and central to the group, not a brooding and isolated 'Byronic Hero'.[19] Whedon and Denisof approached this episode out of nostalgia for the 'days when he was a complete idiot [...] a bumbling moron', and it does offer a jubilant reprieve from Wesley's dark persona of Seasons Three and Four.[20] But, by using scenes of comedy to mirror and mock scenes of his 'brooding heroism', it also offers a critique of this persona. Peggy Davis argues that on *Angel* Wesley can 'embody masculine heroism or feminine comic figure, but not both',[21] an observation supported in 'Orpheus' (4:15) when Wesley himself establishes an opposition between his darkness and sense of humour by telling Willow that he thinks his 'sense of humour [like Angel's soul] is trapped in a jar somewhere', and that he has seen a darkness in himself. In 'Spin the Bottle', however, his humour/soul is temporarily released and he is briefly able to embody both, demonstrating that comedy allows for a space in which the conventions of masculinity can be undermined, challenged and redefined.

NOTES

1 Jane Espenson, cited by Roz Kaveney, 'Writing the Vampire Slayer: Interviews with Jane Espenson and Stephen S. DeKnight', in Roz Kaveney (ed.), *Reading the Vampire Slayer: The New Updated Unofficial Guide to Buffy and Angel*, new edition (London: I.B. Taurus, 2004), pp. 102–3.

2 Steve Wilson, 'Laugh, Spawn of Hell, Laugh', in Roz Kaveney (ed.), *Reading the Vampire Slayer: An Unofficial Companion to Buffy and Angel* (London: I.B. Taurus, 2001), pp. 78–97.

3 Alexis Denisof, cited by David Richardson, 'Sleeping with the Enemy', *Starburst Slayer Special*, 53 (2002), p. 38.

4 Joss Whedon, DVD commentary for 'Spin the Bottle', *Angel Season Four DVD Collection* (F1-DGB 24796DVD) Region 2.

5 For an analysis of the role of comedy in *Buffy the Vampire Slayer* in relation to the character development of Spike, see Michele Boyette, 'The Comic Anti-hero in *Buffy the Vampire Slayer*, or Silly Villain: Spike is for Kicks', *Slayage: The Online International Journal of Buffy Studies*, 4 (2001). At http://www.slayage.tv/essays/slayage4/boyette.htm.

6 Anthony Steward Head, cited by Anthony C. Ferrante, 'Paranormal Protectors', *Fangoria*, 196 (2000), p. 47.

7 Alexis Denisof, cited by Ian Spelling, 'Alexis Denisof', *Starburst Special*, 50 (Yearbook 2001), p. 12.

8 Peggy Davis, '"I'm a Rogue Demon-hunter": Wesley's Transformation from Fop to Hero on *Buffy the Vampire Slayer* and *Angel*', paper given at the *Slayage* Conference on *Buffy the Vampire Slayer*. Nashville, TN, 28–30 May 2004, p. 1.

9 See 'Hush' (B4:10), which features numerous visual jokes including Buffy's miming the act of staking, which is misinterpreted by her friends, and the misleading signifiers that lead to Xander thinking that Spike has fed from Anya.

10 Alan Dale, *Comedy is a Man in Trouble: Slapstick in American Movies* (Minneapolis and London: University of Minnesota Press, 2000), p. 3.

11 Ibid., pp. 10–11.

12 Jana Riess, *What Would Buffy Do? The Vampire Slayer as Spiritual Guide* (San Francisco: Jossey-Bass, 2004), p. 42.

13 When Wesley's humour is derived from verbal articulations it is not through wit and confidence but rather it is his stammering, nervousness and inarticulateness that gets the laughs, the verbal equivalents of a pratfall. A good example of this takes place in 'She'. While at Cordelia's party an attractive woman asks Wesley if his sweater is hand-woven to which he replies, after briefly choking on a party snack, 'Certainly not by me.' When she explains that she simply wanted to compliment the sweater he responds: 'I'll pass that on then … to the person who knit it … I mean I would if I knew who did … but I don't … so I won't pass it on to anyone, will I?'

14 Scott Bukatman, 'Paralysis in Motion: Jerry Lewis's Life as a Man', in Andrew S. Horton (ed.), *Comedy/Cinema/Theory* (Berkeley, LA and Oxford: University of California Press, 1991), pp. 190, 191.

15 Steven Cohan and Ina Rae Hark, 'Introduction', in Steven Cohan and Ina Rae Hark (eds), *Screening the Male: Exploring Masculinities in Hollywood Cinema* (London and New York: Routledge, 1993), p. 3.

16 'Waiting in the Wings' (3:13) was to feature a classic sequence of Wesley buffoonery but it was cut as its comedic tone did not fit with the overall seriousness of the episode (it is now available as an extra on the *Angel Season Three DVD Collection*). In this sequence, Wesley, attending the ballet with the rest of the AI team, imagines Fred on stage in the ballerina role with himself as her dance partner. The romantic atmosphere of the ballet and the gracefulness of Fred's dancing is undercut by Wesley's entrance as he oafishly bounds across the stage. Denisof delivers a fearless comedic performance as he leaps, pirouettes and prances across the stage with little grace and elegance, while also slipping, falling, pulling a hamstring and barely being able to catch Fred as she leaps into his arms.

17 Davis, '"I'm a Rogue Demon-hunter"', p. 8.

18 Whedon, DVD commentary, 'Spin the Bottle'.

19 Davis, '"I'm a Rogue Demon-hunter"', p. 7.

20 Whedon, DVD commentary, 'Spin the Bottle'.

21 Davis, '"I'm a Rogue Demon-hunter"', p. 8.

14

Angel's Monstrous Mothers and Vampires with Souls: Investigating the Abject in 'Television Horror'

MATT HILLS AND REBECCA WILLIAMS

The generic hybridity of *Angel*'s 'parent' show *Buffy the Vampire Slayer* (*BtVS*) has been much remarked upon. Writers such as Lisa Parks have reflected on how *Buffy* draws on 'conventions of the soap opera, horror, comedy, music video, action and sci-fi genres', suggesting that this creates 'tonal variation' where the conventions of one genre, such as horror, may be taken seriously in one moment and then parodied in the next.[1] In direct contrast to *BtVS*, *Angel* has been thought of as more clearly generic: 'in its iconography, *Angel* predominantly draws on references to the hard-boiled conventions of film noir. It's this that makes it different to *Buffy*.'[2] Given its status as a *Buffy* spin-off, critics have appeared keen to mark out possible lines of division between *Buffy* and *Angel*, with Jennifer Stoy going so far as to suggest that *Angel* has 'reinterpreted its parent show' in terms of themes of family.[3] However, by setting up generic and thematic contrasts between *Buffy* and *Angel*, critics have failed to reflect on major points of overlap between the two shows such as their shared, distinctive use of horror genre conventions. In this chapter we therefore want to focus on how *Angel* works not as noirish detection but rather as 'television horror',[4] considering how the rhetorics of horror film are reconstructed for prime-time television audiences.

Although some analysis has been made of *Buffy* in relation to Carol J. Clover's (1992) work on slasher movies,[5] we will apply another key theory of horror film to *Angel's* television horror, focusing on Barbara Creed's work on 'abjection'.[6] *The Monstrous-Feminine* borrows this idea from Julia Kristeva's *Powers of Horror*.[7] Abjection can be defined as any process or ritual that is concerned with protecting the self's 'clean and proper body' from polluting bodily wastes or emissions.[8] Such wastes, classified as not-self matter, must be excluded from the self, being cast out across the self/not-self boundary that demarcates the clean and proper body. As Creed puts it: 'The place of the abject is [...] the place where "I" am not. The abject threatens life; it must be "radically excluded" from the place of the living subject, propelled away from the body and deposited on the other side of an imaginary border which separates the self from that which threatens the self'.[9] Horror film 'abounds in images of abjection' of this type, representing the violent expulsion of vomit (*The Exorcist*, William Friedkin, 1973), pus (*Demons*, Lamberto Bava, 1985), menstrual blood (*Carrie*, Brian De Palma, 1976), and so on.[10] More broadly, abjection is concerned with the cultural construction and maintenance of borders; the border separating self and not-self; the border separating tabooed foods or substances; even the borders of cultural categories and 'laws'.[11] By challenging cultural norms of the bounded self and body, abjection depicts selves in states of physical dis-integration and mental/spiritual 'possession'.[12]

Creed suggests that abjection and the abject are commonly represented in horror films in graphic, gory detail, and Rebecca Bell-Metereau has recently developed this idea, analysing the preponderance of special effects (SFX) slime and threateningly viscous fluids in contemporary horror films.[13] However, due to discursive constructions of television as a 'domestic' or 'family' medium, the depiction of 'disgusting fluids or revolting images'[14] is arguably far less commonplace in 'television horror'. It has been argued that examples of imaginary abjection typically occur on television within more positive and body-healing narratives rather than within threatening, body-disintegrating representations.[15] We will suggest here that the abject is variously figured in *Angel* via a range of characters such as Cordelia, Darla, Angel, Spike and Fred/Illyria. The abject is not fully made safe or positive in *Angel*, given the show's links to the horror genre, but neither does *Angel*'s television horror entirely replicate analyses of horror film and abjection. In the following section we will focus on how abjection is often visually and narratively restricted in the televisual mise-en-scène of *Angel*. We will then move on to consider how *Angel*, as television horror, depicts processes of abjection in more complex ways than arguments drawn from horror-film theory would predict.

RESTRICTED VERSIONS OF ABJECTION: CORDELIA AND DARLA

Positing that the horror film frequently depicts women as monstrous in relation to notions of the border, the mother–child relationship and the female body, critic Barbara Creed has formulated the theory of the 'monstrous-feminine' in the horror movie. Creed notes that '[w]hen woman is represented as monstrous it is almost always in relation to her mothering and reproductive functions' and suggests that the female is abject because maternal functions such as 'menstruation and childbirth are seen as [...] two events in woman's life which [...] place [...] her on the side of the abject'.[16] Creed has further argued that, given this powerful symbolic equation of abjection with maternity and femininity, where male characters are represented as monstrously abject (their bodies violated or threatened with disintegration, their self-identities confused or destabilized) then they too are coded as feminine.

We shall now examine the ways in which Cordelia and Darla code the 'monstrous-feminine' via their representation as monstrous wombs or mothers. Cordelia Chase is frequently constructed as an example of the monstrous feminine, and hence coded as abject across the first four seasons of *Angel*. This character has been increasingly demonized and aligned with monstrosity and the grotesque, as in her literal diegetic demonization in 'Birthday' (3:11), but also in episodes where Cordelia is portrayed as what Creed terms a 'monstrous womb'. More so than any other character on *BtVS* or *Angel*, Cordelia has suffered and been threatened with bodily invasion and rape, either symbolically or literally. Cordelia is first impregnated with demon offspring in 'Expecting' (1:12), and is next assaulted in 'Epiphany' (2:16) when she is attacked by Skilosh demons who, using a phallic-shaped weapon, inject their demonic seed into the back of her head.

Even when in another dimension, Cordelia cannot escape the threat of demon rape and impregnation. After being appointed ruler of the dimension Pylea in 'Through the Looking Glass' (2:21), she is informed that she must mate or 'com-shuck' with the Groosalugg in order to pass her visions onto him. Cordelia herself bemoans her status as a violated and devalued character, commenting 'If you ever figure out how to get us out of here, I want you to find me a dimension where some demon doesn't want to impregnate me with its spawn! I mean, is that just too much to ask?'

Given this tendency to portray Cordelia as a monstrous womb, it is the fourth season episode 'Inside Out' (4:17) that makes it most explicit. Utilizing actress Charisma Carpenter's real-life pregnancy, Cordelia becomes pregnant with (and gives birth to) the demonic power Jasmine, thereby becoming the 'big bad' of Season Four. The very title of the episode in which Cordelia gives birth relates to Creed's theory of horror and abjection. Creed argues that the notion of a decisive inside/outside binary is compromised by the monstrous womb, commenting that 'the act of birth is grotesque because the body's surface is no longer closed, smooth and intact – rather the body looks as if it may tear apart, open out, reveal its innermost depths'.[17]

Angel thus seemingly displays a tendency to narratively restrict its depictions of abjection, gendering these in line with Creed's work on the 'monstrous-feminine'. And yet, at the same time, Cordelia's depiction as a 'monstrous womb' is rendered far less graphically than comparable representations in horror film (e.g. in the *Alien* franchise). Although 'Expecting' refers to *Alien* through its representation of powerfully acidic amniotic fluid (recalling the corrosive effect of the alien's blood), Cordelia never actually gives birth to her demonic brood, while an ultrasound image of her seven or more demon babies is withheld from the audience's gaze. Where horror film would use these as key instances to display spectacular SFX of abjection, *Angel*'s television horror is marked by the absence of such set pieces. Furthermore, via the use of knowingly symbolic imagery, Cordelia's abject state is twice represented in 'Expecting' through the smearing of viscous fluids (lipstick and blood) around her mouth. Her coding as monstrous-feminine is thereby translated into a displaced image of voracious, primal femininity/maternity, becoming suitable for prime-time television.

Although Cordelia is repeatedly figured as a monstrous womb, on the one occasion where she brings her offspring to term ('Inside Out'), any possible imagery of bloodied and viscous abjection is entirely removed from the episode's visual representation of birthing. Instead, the climactic birth scene depicts cosmic radiance and a 'star-child' type of SFX, as Jasmine appears haloed by bright, white, supernatural light. The recurrent slime of horror film is displaced by a clean, spectral birthing, one imagined as an outburst of energy rather than as a messy, sticky disruption of the female body's borders. Where *Angel* does depict the sliminess of abjection (as in 'Expecting' and 'Epiphany') it tends to use slime as a less objectionable stand-in for imagery that, it is implied, would be far more revolting. In 'Expecting', the fight between Wesley, Angel and a Tarval demon occurs off-screen, with the camera being pointedly positioned outside the house where the fight occurs. The audience is shown a series of indexical signs of the struggle, such as yellowy gloop (the demon's 'lifeblood') sprayed across a window, or Wesley being hurled out of the building before returning to the fray. What is *not* shown is as significant as what is. Rather than slimy goo presaging the graphic representation of abjection (and images of a demon's body being hacked apart), slime is used as a part standing in for the whole of the battle. 'Epiphany' offers a very similar non-spectacle; in this case, Angel's hacking apart of a Skilosh demon is masked by the positioning within the frame of a couch, as well as by the lower edge of the frame. Again, it is the spraying upwards into shot of greenish goo that symbolically substitutes for and indicates the demon's abject demise, which is implied as being even more gruesome than what is shown onscreen. Unlike much horror film, the television horror of *Angel* appears to be marked by its use of abject bodily fluids as stand-ins for images of actual bodily dismemberment and disintegration, as well as by its withholding, or symbolic translation, of full-blooded representations of abjection. This is *not* to say that television horror isn't 'real' horror. Rather, we are arguing that there are distinct limits to the visual pleasures/repulsions of abjection in *Angel*.

Cordelia's escapades do not exhaust representations of the 'monstrous womb' in *Angel*. For, when Angel's sire Darla returns to LA in 'Offspring' (3:7) she is pregnant with his child and quickly becomes perhaps the most monstrous-feminine character in the show. Darla's pregnancy is monstrous for many of the same reasons as Cordelia's, but her status as a vampire further complicates the issue. All of the vampires featured on *Angel* can be considered abject since they 'cross back and forth over boundaries that should otherwise be secure' such as dead/alive, and human/animal.[18] For Creed though, the female vampire is particularly abject since 'she disrupts identity and order; driven by her lust for blood, she does not respect the dictates of the law which set down the rules of proper sexual conduct. Like the male, the female vampire also represents abjection because she crosses the boundary between the living and the dead, the human and the animal.'[19]

Thus, the female vampire is more monstrous than the male, as she subverts typical feminine norms of behaviour and sexual activity. Darla's status as both a vampire and a pregnant woman cements her monstrosity and liminality. These two elements are fused in scenes in 'Offspring' when Darla bites Cordelia and later tries to bite a child, admitting she craves the pure blood of children because her baby has a soul. Both Cordelia and Darla therefore seemingly fulfil the archetype of Creed's monstrous-feminine, but what of the show's male vampire characters, Angel and Spike?

ELABORATED VERSIONS OF ABJECTION: ANGEL, SPIKE ... AND FRED/ILLYRIA

As vampires, Spike and Angel are monstrous for many of the same reasons as Darla. They too are border-crossers. However, their unique status as vampires with souls means that they must be considered abject and monstrous in a different way to the usual or generic vampire written about by the likes of Barbara Creed and Noel Carroll.[20] Creed argues that the monstrosity of the vampire depends on its lack of a soul. She comments that:

> the corpse is [...] utterly abject. It signifies one of the most basic forms of pollution – the body without a soul. As a form of waste it represents the opposite of the spiritual, the religious symbolic. In relation to the horror film, it is relevant to note that several of the most popular horrific figures are 'bodies without souls' ([e.g.] the vampire) [...][21]

But how, then, might we explain the monstrosity and abjection of Angel and Spike? Given that Angel's soul was not sought by him (unlike Spike's situation), being forcibly returned, it is not difficult to read this re-insertion of the soul as a symbolic rape violating the boundaries of Angel(us)'s self. This potentially supports a reading of Angel as emasculated and feminized via his abjection. However, as well as being a creature who straddles borders between life and death, good and evil, Angel subverts typical theories of the vampire. Stacey Abbott has noted that:

> the idea of a vampire with a soul is a complex concept that has been more fully explored on the new series *Angel* [...] It

is only when Angel is moved from peripheral love interest to the central protagonist of a new series that his representation breaks from strategically polarizing his good and evil sides. In *Angel*, as a means of developing the character to sustain its own serial narrative and to shape future narrative arcs, the many ways in which Angel and Angelus merge are examined.[22]

Since he is 'a curious hybrid between human and vampire',[23] we want to suggest that Angel is doubly abjected. He is the vampire that crosses the border between life and death, but as a vampire with a soul he is also narratively and semiotically humanized, and given the free will to choose not to harm others. That is, unlike the 'bestial' and generically monstrous vampire driven by its bloodlusts, Angel has a conscience and a sense of social justice/law (or the symbolic). Although Angel's abjection as a blood-thirsty vampire would seem to place him in line with many of Creed's arguments, the character's soulfulness repositions him as a version of caring yet potent masculinity. Far from being clearly feminized, Angel acts as a sometimes conservative version of law-enforcing and paternal masculinity; although he is repeatedly shown to be uneasy with his newfound role as CEO of Wolfram & Hart in Season Five, he is arguably more comfortable with his position as head of the 'family' of protagonists. Angel's narrative agency in the series is indeed highly complex; he is both monster and victim (subject to the rages and rampages of Angelus, and to the caprices of events that periodically remove and restore his soul), both occasionally feminized and often highly conventionally masculinized. On the rare occasions that Angel is more obviously feminized and abjected, these representations are coded as 'unreal' in order to partly defend the character from the fuller connotations of feminized masculinity. For example, in 'Soul Purpose' (5:10) a parasite is attached to Angel's body, inducing hallucinations and fever dreams, one of which involves Fred opening up Angel's body to remove his internal organs, heart and soul. This scene is a powerful condensation of images of the opened-up and abjected/feminized male body, but its tone (via incidental music and performance codes) is very much one of comedic surrealism and dream logic. Fred removes increasingly absurd (and impossibly large) objects from Angel's gaping chest cavity, before peering inside Angel's body, which is represented as a cavernously vast, empty black hole. The scene is devoid of bloody mess or other viscous bodily fluids, as if Angel's abject bodily disintegration is akin to the tidy opening of a box or vessel. This rather disembodied vision of abjection and the comedic colouration of the scene both serve to limit the feminization of Angel's abject masculinity (as well as limiting television horror). Rather than neatly fitting into Creed's arguments for a restricted abjection that is highly gendered as feminine, Angel's representations across the series refuse to settle into clearly feminized masculinity, or even clear monstrosity. His doubled abjection seems to almost cancel itself out, with his ensouled status rendering him somewhat sanctified rather than abjectly polluted. The character of Angel therefore represents a knowing twist on vampiric images and narratives; he does not simply represent cultural abjection (i.e. violating cultural categories such as dead/alive), but instead represents a meta-level of genre abjection (i.e. violating established categories and norms of what it means to be a vampire within the horror genre itself). Barbara Creed's arguments operate only at the first level of abjection, assuming that horror films offer us images of cultural abjection, but failing to consider how new levels of abjection may emerge through violations of the horror genre's own codes and archetypal narratives/monsters.

If Angel is doubly or generically abject because he is a vampire with a soul, then from his first appearance on *Angel*, Spike's position is even more complex due to his status as a ghost. Spike's liminality straddles life and death on two levels – not only is he the complicated hybrid of a ghost of a vampire, but he too possesses a soul.

Ghosts themselves have been subject to much critical analysis, and Samuel Chambers has argued that ghosts are particularly liminal signifiers.[24] For Chambers, 'the constant appearance of ghosts [...] thereby marks a queer space in the most general sense: the realm of the spectre is a place in which characters renegotiate boundaries' and such identity work 'can only go on in the liminal realm inhabited by ghosts, spectres and assorted "others"'.[25] Also addressing spectrality, Katherine Fowkes has argued that although the corpse in horror can be considered abject because it is a body without a soul, the abject zombie/vampire nevertheless 'lacks precisely what the returning dead possess in ghost films – a soul'.[26] Spike's ghostly status hence aligns him more with this anti-abjection archetype than with that of the vampire. As Fowkes notes, 'the figure of the ghost rejects the abject corpse as a thematic of death, and instead plies the possibilities of connecting across forbidden boundaries by erasing, expelling or disavowing the abject'.[27] Despite this, we would suggest that vampire-ghost Spike can readily be analysed as a version of abjected and feminized masculinity, although once again this does not exhaust the character's relationship to the abject.

The episode 'Hell Bound' (5:4) sees Spike fighting to avoid being pulled into hell by a spirit named Pavayne who lives at Wolfram & Hart. Afraid that this means he is damned for his previous evil deeds, Spike is haunted by gruesome images of dead employees, some of whom slice off their fingers or have large shards of glass protruding from their eyes. This is one of *Angel*'s more horrific episodes, and the horror serves to highlight Spike's status as a confused monstrous figure. For much of the episode, he is invisible to other characters and unable to communicate, a trait which Fowkes notes 'makes the ghost a humiliated and impotent subject and becomes a delaying tactic in the narrative'.[28] Spike's impotence and emasculation in this episode are furthered when Pavayne strips him of his clothing and forces him to fight naked. The spectacle of Spike's naked body symbolically castrates him and subjects him to the possibility of the 'female gaze'. In Fowkes' reading of the gendering of ghosts she argues that:

> Although a male ghost may take up a feminine position in a narrative, this feminine position must be reconciled with the physical presence of the actor playing the role [...] The visual presence of gender is precisely what makes the gen-

der switching aspect of the ghost compelling to film [authors' note: or television] as opposed to a non-visual medium. The visual presence of a male actor playing an ineffectual character establishes the incontrovertible evidence of maleness, which is necessary to establish the fantasy of [gender] reversal in the first place.[29]

It is precisely Spike's masculinity that makes his feminization possible. Accordingly, the ineffectual and decorporealized vampire-ghost Spike (of the early part of Season Five) is both masculine and feminine as 'by casting male actors as ineffectual and feminized ghosts [...] male and female viewers [can] accept a feminized male without impugning the masculinity of the protagonist'.[30]

If 'Hell Bound' depicts Spike as emasculated and feminized via his ghostliness, the later Season Five episode 'Damage' (5:11) represents a rather different type of abjection. For here, a recorporealized Spike is attacked by the psychotic slayer Dana, who hacks Spike's arms off as punishment for what she believes he has done to her family. Becoming abject in the sense of losing bodily integrity, Spike is shown as accepting this fate.[31] Although he is not guilty of the exact crime Dana accuses him of, Spike muses on the fact that he has been guilty of similar transgressions countless times across his existence as an embodied and marauding vampire. Angel and Spike discuss their monstrous status at the episode's conclusion: Angel contrasts Dana, as an 'innocent victim', to the monstrosity represented by himself and Spike. Disputing this, Spike concludes that both ensouled vampires were also innocent victims 'once upon a time', implying an abject collapse of the distinction, or crossing of the boundary, between monster and victim. In this sense, Angel and Spike are thus abjected at the level of their narrative agency or generic and narrative role, as well as being abjected in the more usual ways that vampires and ghosts are. Both characters are a compounded series of abjections – vampire/ensouled/ghost – as well as becoming abject at the level of their (horror) genre identity as monsters *and* victims.

What we are terming 'elaborated abjection' is, then, abjection that does not merely represent the collapse of cultural classifications such as dead/alive, inside/outside, or self/other, but which instead challenges established generic and narrative classifications (i.e. what it means to be a vampire; whether characters are clearly defined as good/evil, or as monsters/victims). A further instance of elaborated abjection occurs in Season Five's representation of Fred. In this case, yet again a leading female character is possessed or taken over by demonic forces (the Old One, Illyria). This appears to reinforce our earlier argument that abjection is highly gendered in *Angel* – like the Cordelia of Season Four before her, Fred's self-identity is invaded, undermined and expelled from her body. Creed quotes Julia Kristeva on this type of ultimate abjection, where 'nothing remains in me [...] It is no longer I who expel. "I" is expelled.'[32] It is not just the case that Fred is possessed, but rather that she is effectively transformed from one 'good' character into another 'evil' one. And yet, the continuity of the actress involved (Amy Acker) means that Illyria is, physically at least, a re-versioning or partial continuation of Fred. The episode 'The Girl in Question' (5:20) presents the narrative possibility that Illyria can transform herself into Fred (that is, Illyria playing Fred, rather than Fred 'herself'), setting up a complex conundrum with regard to identity. For this narrative event is very much *not* represented as the abjection of two identities existing in one body (the typical 'possession' horror narrative). Instead, this episode suggests that Fred's memories and physical appearance can be used by Illyria to experiment in human social intercourse. In one sense, then, Illyria represents Fred's death – and the ultimate abjection of the corpse, body without a soul or material self without the self of personality and spirit – but, at the same time, traces of Fred are preserved within the Other that is Illyria. *Angel* uses the narrative possibilities of horror-fantasy to question where the boundaries around self-identity actually *are*, not simply border crossing, but challenging (or if you like, deconstructing) the very notion of such borders and boundaries upon which abjection otherwise depends. Such challenges to the existence of 'the bounded self' also occur in other episodes where major reality shifts are depicted within the diegesis, and where characters' memories are rebooted or rewritten, as in Connor's story arc from 'Home' (4:22) through to 'Origin' (5:18) and 'Not Fade Away' (5:22). These types of abjection, where characters are radically reworked or rewritten – treated as blank slates to be fantastically re-engineered or re-created within the show's narrative universe – are not simply representations of cultural categories coming under abject attack. They are instead genre-dependent (because 'fantastic') reworkings of narrative possibility and identity; types of generic rather than purely cultural abjection.

We have argued here that although monstrous and abject characters can be found in *Angel*, such abjection often occurs in contrast to Creed's assertion that the abject is represented onscreen (in horror films) in graphic and gory detail, with an emphasis on bodily wastes as 'images of blood, vomit, pus, shit etc, are central to our culturally/socially constructed notions of the horrific'.[33] Such images are rarely possible on television shows outside the realm of medical drama because of stricter norms of television censorship and the notion of television as a 'family' medium. Regardless of this, we have suggested that *Angel* should not be thought of as failed or inauthentic horror because of its visual and narrative restrictions of abjection (*contra* Levine and Schneider).[34] Instead, we have argued that through characters such as Angel and Spike, *Angel* the series represents abjected and feminized masculinity in a way that has often characterized horror-film imagery. At the same time, the series qualifies its feminized masculine characters, seeking to restore more conventional masculinity. *Angel* also uses its serial narrative[35] to complicate theories of abjection by semiotically layering levels of the abject over one another (vampire/with a soul/head of demonic law firm; vampire/with a soul/returned as a ghost). Through its serialized and generic abjection, *Angel* moves beyond the notion that the horror genre is just about portraying the culturally abject (opened bodies, corpses, spilt blood etc). As television horror, and despite being visually restricted in terms of gore and slime, *Angel* puts forward doubled or extended notions of abjection that violate generic categories (e.g. 'the vampire', 'the ghost', 'the monster', 'the victim') rather than simply putting grue and goo on screen.

NOTES

1 Lisa Parks, 'Brave New *Buffy*: Rethinking "TV Violence"', in M. Jancovich and J. Lyons (eds), *Quality Popular Television* (London: BFI Publishing, 2003), p. 122; see also Catherine Johnson, '*Buffy the Vampire Slayer*', in G. Creeber (ed.), *The Television Genre Book* (London: BFI Publishing, 2001).

2 Karen Sayer, 'This Was Our World and They Made it Theirs: Reading Space and Place in *Buffy the Vampire Slayer* and *Angel*', in Roz Kaveney (ed.), *Reading the Vampire Slayer: The New, Updated Unofficial Guide to Buffy and Angel* (London and New York: I.B. Tauris, 2004), pp. 138–9.

3 Jennifer Stoy, 'Blood and Choice: The Theory and Practice of Family in *Angel*', in Kaveney (ed.), *Reading the Vampire Slayer*, p. 229.

4 See Matt Hills, *The Pleasures of Horror* (London and New York: Continuum, 2005).

5 See Holly G. Barbaccia, 'Buffy in the "Terrible House"', *Slayage: The Online International Journal of Buffy Studies*, 4 (2001), at http://www.slayage.tv/essays/slayage4/barbaccia.htm; Mary Hammond, 'Monsters and Metaphors: *Buffy the Vampire Slayer* and the Old World', in S. Gwenllian-Jones and R. E. Pearson (eds), *Cult Television* (Minneapolis: University of Minnesota Press, 2004), pp. 147–64; Kent A. Ono, 'To Be a Vampire on *Buffy the Vampire Slayer*: Race and ("Other") Socially Marginalizing Positions on Horror TV', in Elyce Rae Helford, *Fantasy Girls: Gender in the New Universe of Science Fiction and Fantasy Television* (New York: Rowman & Littlefield, 2000), pp. 163–86.

6 Barbara Creed, *The Monstrous-Feminine: Film, Feminism, Psychoanalysis* (London: Routledge, 1993).

7 Julia Kristeva, *Powers of Horror: An Essay on Abjection*, trans. Leon S. Roudiez (New York: Columbia University Press, 1982).

8 Ibid., p. 72.

9 Creed, *Monstrous-Feminine*, p. 9.

10 Ibid., p. 10.

11 Ibid., pp. 10–11.

12 Carol J. Clover, *Men, Women and Chainsaws* (London: BFI Publishing, 1992), p. 78.
13 Rebecca Bell-Metereau, 'Searching for Blobby Fissures: Slime, Sexuality and the Grotesque', in M. Pomerance (ed.), *Bad: Infamy: Darkness, Evil and Slime on Screen* (New York: State University of New York Press, 2004), pp. 287–99.
14 Ibid., p. 287.
15 Jason Jacobs, *Body Trauma TV* (London: BFI Publishing, 2003), p. 69.
16 Creed, *Monstrous-Feminine*, pp. 7, 50.
17 Ibid., pp. 48, 58.
18 Ken Gelder, *Reading the Vampire* (London: Routledge, 1994), p. 70.
19 Creed, *Monstrous-Feminine*, p. 61.
20 Noel Carroll, *The Philosophy of Horror* (New York and London: Routledge, 1990).
21 Creed, *Monstrous-Feminine*, p. 10.
22 Stacey Abbott, 'Walking the Fine Line Between Angel and Angelus', *Slayage*, 9 (2003), at http://www.slayage.tv/essays/slayage9/Abbott.htm.
23 Ibid.
24 Samuel A. Chambers, 'A Telepistemology of the Closet; or, The Queer Politics of *Six Feet Under*', *Journal of American and Comparative Cultures*, 26: 1 (2003), p. 29.
25 Ibid., pp. 29, 31.
26 Katherine A. Fowkes, *Giving Up the Ghost: Spirits, Ghosts, and Angels in Mainstream Comedy Films* (Michigan: Wayne State University Press, 1998), p. 58.
27 Ibid., p. 59.
28 Ibid., p. 54.
29 Ibid., p. 117.
30 Ibid., p. 123.
31 Creed, *Monstrous-Feminine*, p. 11.
32 Julia Kristeva, quoted in Creed, *Monstrous-Feminine*, p. 9.
33 Ibid., p. 13.
34 Michael Levine and Steven Jay Schneider, 'Feeling for Buffy: The Girl Next Door', in J. B. South (ed.), *Buffy the Vampire Slayer and Philosophy* (Chicago: Open Court, 2003), pp. 294–308.
35 Barbaccia, 'Buffy in the "Terrible House"'; Hammond, 'Monsters and Metaphors', p. 150.

PART FIVE:

'Let's Go to Work':
The Afterlife of
the Spin-off with a Soul

15

Afterword: The Depths of Angel *and the Birth of* Angel *Studies*

RHONDA V. WILCOX AND DAVID LAVERY

> *Angel:* If there's no great glorious end to all this ... if there's no bigger meaning, then the smallest act of kindness is the greatest thing in the world.
> ('Epiphany', 2:16)
>
> *Angel:* I kinda want to slay the dragon.
> (series' end, 'Not Fade Away', 5:22)
>
> *Doyle:* Violence is not going to solve anything. On the other hand, it's kind of festive.
> ('Lonely Heart', 1:2)

Angel and *Angel* show us something about being pulled in different directions. Crime drama, comedy, opera (soap or not); male, female, sweet old et cetera; determinism, destiny or free will; role-playing or the search for the real; sorrow or humour; kindness or violence. Some of these 'productive tensions' (to reapply Upstone's application of Homi Bhabha) can be seen in the epigraphs above. In Season Two, Angel spiralled downward to the point at which he discovered that the long elevator ride down to Wolfram & Hart's office – to moral hell – lands you exactly where you started. Hell is LA, and he is not out of it. But after Detective Kate Lockley's attempted suicide and Angel's self-destructive night of furious sex with a woman he could not save from evil – his vampire mother/lover Darla – he has what his demon friend the empath Lorne later calls 'a moment of clarity'. The series expresses, in Angel's subsequent comments to Kate, a variant of Christian existentialism: Heaven is where you make it, too; the meaninglessness constitutes freedom to invest his own choices, even the smallest kindnesses, with as much meaning as the grandest dragon-killing gesture. But of course Angel never stops wanting to kill the dragon.

This particular thematic tension (explored by Roz Kaveney) is one shared with *Buffy*; more than once the show reminds us, as both Buffy and Jonathan say in 'Superstar' (B4:17), that you can't make everything right with one big gesture – it 'takes work'. Of course the very last words of *Angel* are 'let's go to work': dragon-slaying is a job (or should it be 'a job is dragon-slaying'?) – a job that will continue. Compare Buffy's dying words at the end of *her* fifth season ('The Gift', B5:22): 'This is the work I have to do.' As Hills and Williams note, many critics are concerned with establishing the separate nature of the two shows. It is understandable that admirers of the newer series in particular would be concerned about individuation from the series that sired it; and of course *Angel* and *Buffy* are different in many ways. But it must also be admitted that the two shows bleed into each other. It is possible to watch *Angel* without ever having watched *Buffy*; and, in fact, many people do. Some feel less drawn to the youthful protagonists of *Buffy*; some feel more drawn to the greater visual and moral darkness of the more noir *Angel*. But if we grant as a given that *Angel* has the strength to stand on its own as a series, then a greater richness of the *Angel* text can be discovered through a consciousness of the two series joined.

DEPTH OF FIELD

The years (1999–2001) when the WB ran two hours of *Buffy* and *Angel* back-to-back in the US offered some remarkable crossovers which comprised, in effect, two-hour movies. Yet these two successive hours contained the different flavours of the different series and showed different points of view. The 'Fool for Love' (B5:7)/'Darla' (2:7) combination, in particular, provided this television-*Rashomon* sort of effect. In the first hour, we see a visually spectacular slow-motion, transcendently scored shot of the vampires Angel, Darla, Spike and Drusilla striding through the fire of a Boxer Rebellion riot on the night Spike killed his first slayer. Angel is grim-faced; and as we follow the story told by Spike in *Buffy*, Angel seems to be the most hardened of vampires. But in the next hour – in the series devoted to his character – we see the same scene (exactly the same shot, exactly the same music) with a different understanding: Angel's grimness is the result of his trying to forget the soul with which he's just been cursed. The meaning is completely different from the other series' point of view; and this comprehension of our lack of understanding is part of the point. In the *Angel* episode 'Sanctuary' (1:19), Buffy shows her worst side in her fury at seeing Angel comfort Faith soon after she had possessed Buffy's body (the possession being known only by those who had watched the relevant *Buffy* episodes). By the end of the episode Angel tells off Buffy, and she tells him she loves Riley (something she never says to Riley). Angel is in control of the scene and kicks her out of his town. In the succeeding week, Angel comes to *Buffy*'s Sunnydale in 'The Yoko Factor' (B4:20), in which he apologizes, he and Buffy laugh and restore their friendship, and she tells him to call before coming to her town. The narrative weight goes to the protagonist, as the law of fictional gravity dictates. *Angel* favours Angel, just as *Buffy* favours Buffy. But the story is different when the elements of the two series are joined, when the viewer sees both.

Even after *Buffy* went to United Paramount Network (UPN) in 2001, the combination of certain elements continued. Phil Colvin's discussion of the episodes in which Eliza Dushku guest-starred as Faith provides some impressive examples (not least in terms of their structuring of the overall narrative). But the humorous connections are as important as the great drama. There are few funnier moments than the time just before Angel returns from his reunion with Buffy after her second (and more serious) death: Charisma Carpenter and Alexis Denisof play Cordelia Chase and Wesley Wyndam-

Pryce playing Buffy and Angel – 'Kiss me!', 'Bite me!' ('Fredless', 3:5). Perhaps one funnier is James Marsters' rendition of
Spike mocking Angel from a rooftop in 'In the Dark' (1:3):
'Helping those in need's my job and working up a load of sexual tension and prancing around like a big poof is truly
thanks enough'. Or consider the minor but very significant
serious recurring character Anne, who runs a shelter in LA.
Roz Kaveney notes that, for what may be his last day on
earth, Charles Gunn chooses to spend time with 'Annie' at the
shelter – enacting those small kindnesses that Angel praises in
'Epiphany'. As Kaveney notes, Anne (who with her shelter
saves many) represents the potential for good deeds done by
any one person who is saved. Anne, with her ordinary name
and humble work, represents the ordinary hero. However,
there is a much deeper back-story to Anne, known by viewers
of both shows in tandem but never overtly expressed in
Angel. The choice to leave the story unexpressed allows viewers to experience the sense that in this world there are many
stories of lives unexpressed: the narrative constructs an experience of the theme within the viewer. What the *Angel* series
chooses never to express – despite numerous scenes with
characters who might have made the connection – is that
Anne, under the poignantly humorous name of Chanterelle,
was first saved by Buffy in 'Lie to Me' (B2:7). She reappeared
in LA calling herself Lily in the *Buffy* episode 'Anne' (B3:1) –
so named because as a runaway in LA Buffy Anne Summers
wasn't using her first name – and by the end of the episode
the blonde Lily had chosen to take the name 'Anne'. In other
words, Anne is Buffy's middle name – that is to say, *Angel*'s
everyday hero is an avatar of Buffy, just as there are many versions of Angel in the show (as many critics here have noted).
The shot of a lonely woman standing in an almost empty LA
street at night, which has always been in the credits sequence
of *Angel*, comes not from this series but from 'Anne', the LA
episode of *Buffy*. Those who view both series can see the
transfusion. Both the long-term development of characters
and the physical sense of a different place and time where the
reality of this world still exists give a depth of field to the

presentation of both series. But perhaps *Angel*, as the second series, benefits more from this sense of opening farther doors into a world already there.

TELEVISION CHIAROSCURO

Not since *The X-Files* has a series so consistently made beautiful use of darkness as the chiaroscuro of *Angel*. As David Greenwalt and Joss Whedon recall in a Season One DVD commentary,

> We had a terrific Director of Photography named Herb Davis who ... had been a camera operator on *Buffy* and the DP on *Buffy*, Michael Gershman, nipped at our heels for months to give Herb a shot to light *Angel* and quite frankly, the show wouldn't still be on the air if he hadn't. He's really fast and good and makes beautiful sort of moody frames and you really get a sense of the loneliness of his [Angel's] place. I love when the fridge was open, you know, and just the blood [packets inside]. He knows where to put the light and where to give us the nice darks because *Angel* has to have nice darks.

Angel's head limned with light in the darkness of his apartment in 'City Of'; Angel sitting in the dark at the beginning and end of 'Lonely Heart' (1:2); Angel and Fred in the blue light of the sewers in 'Fredless'; Spike naked in the dark depths of Wolfram & Hart ('Hell Bound', 5:4) – *Angel* is full of such moments of beautiful dark.

Of course the dark is not just visual but emotional and moral. Many critics have noted *Angel*'s connection to noir (Stacey Abbott having pointed out the variations), and of course noir is everywhere, from Boreanaz's big-city dick voice-over in 'City Of' ('It started with a girl') to Lorne in a trench-coat shooting Lindsey in a dive in 'Not Fade Away'. In *Angel*, noir is real. We want to add to the discussion, however, the term 'chiaroscuro' – a shading to show depth – to recognize the Caravaggio candle of light in the dark. You have to know where to put the light to see the darkness, to see in the darkness. The noir world, however, seems more unrelievedly dark than *Angel*, which exhibits a different take on morality and a different sense of humour.

Most of *Angel*'s main characters are both heroic and seriously flawed. They are also, thanks to both the writers and the versatile actors, capable of great humour – of which, more later. They wound, kill and commit moral incest. Yet time and again characters struggle to do right (in a very un-noirish fashion). Light and dark mix exquisitely when Darla stakes herself so her unborn child may live ('Lullaby', 3:9), and so she will not once again become the horror that she was. The re-formation of the broken family in *Angel* is, time and again, an act of heroism and a source of genuine joy. Even after a reverse-Oedipal curse/prophecy ('The father will kill the son'), Angel manages to reconnect with both his blood son Connor and his moral brother Wesley (Connor's 'Uncle Wesley', as Angel calls him in 'Loyalty', 3:15); Cordelia, having in effect died in childbirth, manages to reconnect with Angel even after she dies. Heroines in *Angel* don't fare much better than in an Edgar Allan Poe story; but that is only in terms of statistical mortality, not character development. Cordy, Lilah and Fred, even Darla, all manage to have significant presence after their deaths (the posthumous women of *Angel* would be fun to analyse).

Angel nonetheless has unquestionable moments of darkness. One of the most poignant is developed slowly, and fulfilled in the series' last scene for Lorne. As played by Andy Hallett, Lorne is an excellent example of the series' enhancement of a secondary character in whom actor, writing and direction successfully merged. Lorne functions well as a simple spectacle, with horns, Vegas suits, lively green skin and a notable nose that, over the seasons, grows shorter – more human? – as we get to know the character better. He can 'read' people's natures and futures when they sing, and is certainly a plot convenience. But, he insists 'I'm not some mystical vending machine here to spit out answers every time you waltz in with a problem' ('Fredless'). As Stan Beeler notes, Lorne represents the entertainment community, the gay community and minorities in general, but he is far more than a token; he is a character with a voice of his own, in every sense of the word. The owner of Caritas ('mercy', he tells us it means in his very first appearance), where violence has no place, Lorne is the gentlest soul in the series – even more so than Fred, who, after all, tasers the teenaged Connor. And, if it can be said that Fred spent five years as a slave in the brutal warrior world of Pylea, it must be remembered that Lorne grew up there. Lorne has always responded strongly to the usually gentle Fred; 'I really like her', he says after she repudiates 'destiny' as 'evitable' – this coming from a man who hears the echoes of the future in the voices of others. Thus his movement towards moral ambiguity is all the more significant. After Fred's death, he sinks farther and farther into emotional shadow. One of the darkest moments of the series comes soon after, when Lorne loses his innocence of deadly violence and, at Angel's behest, shoots Lindsey in cold blood. Because his moral family has asked him, he does so; but he then cuts himself off from them. His lengthy development as a character shows emotional depth; his final action shows another kind of depth and darkness. Both show the chiaroscuro of *Angel*.

Yes, the darkness is there. But in that same episode Charles Gunn helps Anne. Illyria, the monster that subsumed Fred, comforts the mortally wounded Wesley. Perhaps even more importantly, the episode is lightened when Connor makes fun of his father: 'You girl' he calls him when Angel offers his good penmanship as a way to help Connor with a resumé. If *Buffy* is about (among other things) the strong woman, *Angel* is about (among other things) the loving, nurturing man: as Cordelia tells Wes in 'Parting Gifts' (1:10), 'After an all-nighter of fighting the lurking evil, we get eggs. [Angel's] a good cook for someone on a liquid diet.' *Buffy* and *Angel* also both use the extreme feminine and masculine gender stances. At the same time, they display the potential complexity of such roles. In many ways the two series are mirrors, shadows, of each other. As Stacey Abbott says, 'Comedy also establishes the series' preoccupation with the concept and representation of masculinity, in contrast to *BtVS*'s feminist concerns'. The series explore these preoccupations in different fashions. For instance, while *Buffy* directly shows a significant long-term lesbian romance, *Angel* more often uses the queer text method of frequent textual games with the characters' sexual and gender roles – especially for Angel himself: 'Seriously, I wasn't hitting on you' is the kind of explanation he keeps having to make ('Lonely Heart'). Each of the characters is, to some degree or other, made more sympathetic by being made the subject of humour. Anyone who knows the series has only to think of Angel dancing or Angel singing to understand the importance of humour here (see above, Chapter 13, and remember the Xander dance from *Buffy*). During Seasons Two and Three, the Mutant Enemy closing 'Grr, argh' was followed by the sound of Boreanaz's faux-Elvis 'Thank you, thank you very much' – Boreanaz laughing, Angel laughing, and the series laughing all at once. Humour suspends pain. And humour spins perspective. Doyle – who sacrificed himself in as big a flash of burning light as Buffy or Spike – says 'Violence is not going to solve anything. On the other hand, it's kind of festive', turning a head-slam into slapstick, moving the nature of meaning in the series. This shift in attitude, superficially so different from Angel's as expressed in the first epigraph above, is in a way about the same thing. Doyle changes the moment from drama to comedy for himself and the viewers, changes the way he is experiencing the world just as surely as Angel does; and just as surely as the series does as it shifts from moment to moment. *Angel* contains multitudes.

Less than three years old, the multi-disciplinary, hybrid discipline of *Buffy* Studies constitutes one of the most surprising academic phenomena in recent memory. Who would have thought, back in 1997, when a disappointing camp movie became a television programme with a silly name on a fledgling network, that critics and scholars throughout the English-speaking world and in several foreign countries as well would find in *Buffy* enough (and more than enough) worthy of investigation to inspire scores of essays, at least a dozen books, and four international conferences? At the most recent of these, held in Nashville, Tennessee in May 2004, over 180 papers were presented in perhaps the largest scholarly conference ever devoted to a single television show. *Buffy* students come from a wide variety of backgrounds: literary critics, classicists, psychologists, lawyers, military historians, philosophers, ethicists, lexicographers, folklorists, media scholars, physicists, vampirologists, political (and library) scientists, Foucauldians, Lacanians, Jungians … they may fight turf battles on campus but are united in their intellectual passion for the Buffyverse.

The spin-off of *Angel* Studies, at least until now, has lagged behind. When we began work on our book *Fighting the Forces* during the first season of *Angel*, we didn't receive a single essay proposal on *Angel* and probably wouldn't have included one anyway. When we started *Slayage: The Online International Journal of Buffy Studies* (http://www.slayage.tv/) in 2001, our rules for submission only allowed writing about *Buffy*'s sibling if 50 per cent of the text was devoted to big sis. At 2004's *Slayage* Conference, only sixteen papers presented included *Angel* in their title, but in three days of fervid dialogue only days after 'Not Fade Away' had faded away, *Angel* seemed, for the first time, to be a subject of comparable interest to *BtVS*. *Angel* seemed itself to be the dragon ready to be slain (aka 'investigated').

Now that we scholars of the Buffyverse have this rich collection, we need not feel quite so outnumbered as Team Angel in that fatal alley behind the Hyperion. The work of investigating Angel has just begun.

16

'We'll Follow Angel to Hell ... or Another Network': The Fan Response to the End of Angel

STACEY ABBOTT

On 13 February 2004 in a now famous press release, the Warner Brothers (WB) network announced the decision to cancel the Mutant Enemy television series *Angel*. It would be allowed to finish its fifth season with enough notice to 'wrap up the series in a way befitting a classic television series'.[1] As news began to circulate about this decision, three different friends emailed to inform me of the devastating news. With each email, I still couldn't believe the decision. It didn't seem possible that a series that had really hit its stride in terms of storyline and characterization – despite, as Phil Colvin and Roz Kaveney have documented here, making considerable alterations to its format at the bequest of the network – could be so easily abandoned. My next thought was that, like *Buffy the Vampire Slayer* (*BtVS*) after its fifth season, it would be picked up by another network. *Angel* would continue.

Fast forward to 30 May 2004, I am at the *Slayage* Conference on *Buffy the Vampire Slayer* in Nashville, sitting on a panel, discussing the cancellation of *Angel* only a week after the transmission of the series' finale, 'Not Fade Away' (5:22) in North America. The room is filled with *Angel* fans, many of whom have specifically come to the conference out of an interest in *Angel*, all desperate to discuss the series and its finale, and to rail against its demise. What becomes clear to me from this session at the conference is that despite its recent end, life still remains in *Angel* through its vibrant and committed fan base, eager to fight for the series both in terms of its place within the canon of Quality Television and its space on the networks. This is no real surprise, however, as the period in between the network's announcement and the *Slayage* Conference had witnessed a phenomenal campaign by fans to save the series. *Angel* would not be allowed to fade away without a fight.

The Saving Angel Campaign, spearheaded by the slogan 'Looking for a few (million) good viewers? We'll Follow *Angel* to Hell ... Or Another Network', was designed to force the network to take notice of the millions of loyal viewers who would be lost if *Angel* vanished from the air or who could be gained by another network should they choose to pick up the series. The campaign took numerous and often quite creative forms, including: online petitions; a WB call-in campaign, in which fans were urged to telephone their local network during *Angel*'s commercial breaks to remind them of all the viewers who would vanish with the series' cancellation; and a regular flood of postcards to the network and advertisers. Through donations by fans, the campaign raised a total of $41,217.84 to cover the expenses of a live rally on 31 March 2004 in Los Angeles in conjunction with an online rally worldwide; advertisements demanding the restoration of the series placed in the *Hollywood Reporter* (9 March 2004) and *Variety* (15 March 2004); and the now famous AngelMobile, a mobile billboard in Los Angeles featuring the campaign slogan. Additionally, the campaigners took Angel's mission statement to 'help the helpless' to heart and demonstrated that fans of the series are not only loyal but also generous by donating the remaining funds, a total of $13,000, to the International Committee of the Red Cross. The Saving Angel Campaign also ran blood drives, sent stuffed toys to children's hospitals and raised a further $15,000 for the Los Angeles Regional Food Bank.[2]

This amazing attempt to save *Angel*, as he has saved so many before him, demonstrates more than fan devotion to the vampire with a soul, but is a further indication of the evolving fan relationship to quality television. Often described as 'must-see' television, series such as *Angel* demand and receive an incredible amount of emotional investment from their viewers. As Mark Jancovich and James Lyons explain, 'television has traditionally been discussed in terms of habitual viewing and televisual "flow"', while must-see TV is 'distinguished by the compulsive viewing practices of dedicated audiences who organize their schedules around these shows'.[3] Viewers do not watch television passively, but rather engage with a selection of series on an emotional and intellectual level. While in years gone by fans of series like *Star Trek* were often viewed as sad and obsessive (otherwise known as the 'get a life' syndrome), it is apparent by the increasing devotion of fans to series such as *Buffy the Vampire Slayer, Angel, The Sopranos, ER, The X-Files, Six Feet Under* and *Sex and the City*, to name but a few recent examples, that the 'obsessive' fan is making a qualitative comment on the nature of television. As the organizers of Saving Angel declare, '[o]ur fight has been one not only for a particular show, but for the ideal of Quality Television against an ever-expanding wasteland of "reality" programming, and the disappearance of well-written scripted dramas from the small screen.'[4] This is not to deny the generic and fan pleasures of cult television, of which there are many, but rather to recognize that the perception of television and its fans has evolved, a shift that was acknowledged by Peter Kramer when he declared that 'American fictional television is now better than the movies' and 'a life is what you get when there is nothing on television'.[5] If series such as *Angel* continue to vanish from our screens, then we may have to 'get a life' after all.

While rumours abound as to possible TV movies, at the time of writing the fate of *Angel* remains undetermined. That is not say that the fight has been lost but simply that the fight is ongoing. But then again, that is what the series was about, wasn't it? At least according to series creator and co-producer, Joss Whedon:

The message we always tried to give with the show is that redemption is really hard and it takes your whole life, and it involves fighting all the time, sometimes against things that can't be beaten. The last episode of *Angel* will reflect that strongly. And the fact that through all the years of trying to find the format and trying to find the regulars and trying to find the relationships that we held true to that promise and, in fact, have come full circle to it, means to me that we really had something there. The whole time, in all the various incarnations, we always had the thing that I wanted, which was an exciting, strong, tough, funny, melodramatic show about the idea of redemption and how frickin' hard it is to be a human being.[6]

Need I say more?

NOTES

1 Warner Brothers press release cited on the BBC Cult homepage, 'Angel Cancelled: Warners Pulls Plug on Whedon's Joy', at http://www.bbc.co.uk/cult/news/buffy/2004/02/16/9502.shtml.

2 Saving Angel Campaign newsletter and website, at http://www.savingangel.org.

3 Mark Jancovich and James Lyons, 'Introduction', in Mark Jancovich and James Lyons (eds), *Quality Popular Television* (London: British Film Institute, 2003), p. 2.

4 Saving Angel Campaign organizers, at http://www.savingangel.org.

5 Peter Kramer, cited by Jancovich and Lyons, 'Introduction', p. 1.

6 Joss Whedon, 'Look Back in *Angel*', interview by Ed Gross, *SFX* (July 2004), p. 64.

Appendices

Episode Guide

Episode   *Title*   *Original Airdate*

SEASON ONE

1:1   **'City Of'**   **5.10.1999**
writer (w.) David Greenwalt & Joss Whedon.
director (d.) Joss Whedon.

1:2   **'Lonely Heart'**   **12.10.1999**
w. David Fury.
d. James A. Contner.

1:3   **'In the Dark'**   **19.10.1999**
w. Douglas Petrie.
d. Bruce Seth Green.

1:4   **'I Fall to Pieces'**   **26.10.1999**
story: Joss Whedon & David Greenwalt.
teleplay: David Greenwalt.
d. Vern Gillum.

1:5   **'Rm w/a Vu'**   **2.11.1999**
story: David Greenwalt & Jane Espenson.
teleplay: Jane Espenson.
d. Scott McGinnis.

1:6   **'Sense and Sensitivity'**   **9.11.1999**
w. Tim Minear.
d. James A. Contner.

1:7	**'The Bachelor Party'**	**16.11.1999**
	w. Tracey Stern.	
	d. David Straiton.	

1:8	**'I Will Remember You'**	**23.11.1999**
	w. David Greenwalt & Jeannine Renshaw.	
	d. David Grossman.	

1:9	**'Hero'**	**30.11.1999**
	w. Howard Gordon & Tim Minear.	
	d. Tucker Gates	

1:10	**'Parting Gifts'**	**14.12.1999**
	w. David Fury & Jeannine Renshaw.	
	d. James A. Contner.	

1:11	**'Somnambulist'**	**18.1.2000**
	w. Tim Minear.	
	d. Winrich Kolbe.	

1:12	**'Expecting'**	**25.1.2000**
	w. Howard Gordon.	
	d. David Semel.	

1:13	**'She'**	**8.2.2000**
	w. David Greenwalt & Marti Noxon.	
	d. David Greenwalt.	

1:14	**'I've Got You Under My Skin'**	**15.2.2000**
	story: David Greenwalt & Jeannine Renshaw.	
	teleplay: Jeannine Renshaw.	
	d. R. D. Price.	

1:15	**'The Prodigal'**	**22.2.2000**
	w. Tim Minear.	
	d. Bruce Seth Green.	

1:16	**'The Ring'**	**29.2.2000**
	w. Howard Gordon.	
	d. Nick Marck.	
1:17	**'Eternity'**	**4.4.2000**
	w. Tracey Stern.	
	d. Regis B. Kimble.	
1:18	**'Five by Five'**	**25.4.2000**
	w. Jim Kouf.	
	d. James A. Contner.	
1:19	**'Sanctuary'**	**2.5.2000**
	w. Tim Minear & Joss Whedon.	
	d. Michael Lange.	
1:20	**'War Zone'**	**9.5.2000**
	w. Garry Campbell.	
	d. David Straiton.	
1:21	**'Blind Date'**	**16.5.2000**
	w. Jeannine Renshaw.	
	d. Thomas J. Wright.	
1:22	**'To Shanshu in LA'**	**23.5.2000**
	w. & d. David Greenwalt.	

SEASON TWO

2:1	**'Judgement'**	**26.9.2000**
	story: Joss Whedon & David Greenwalt.	
	teleplay: David Greenwalt.	
	d. Michael Lange.	
2:2	**'Are You Now, or Have You Ever Been'**	**3.10.2000**
	w. Tim Minear.	
	d. David Semel.	

2:3	**'First Impressions'**	**10.10.2000**
	w. Shawn Ryan.	
	d. James A. Contner.	

2:4	**'Untouched'**	**17.10.2000**
	w. Mere Smith.	
	d. Joss Whedon.	

| 2:5 | **'Dear Boy'** | **24.10.2000** |
| | w. & d. David Greenwalt. | |

2:6	**'Guise Will Be Guise'**	**7.11.2000**
	w. Jane Espenson.	
	d. Krishna Rao.	

| 2:7 | **'Darla'** | **14.11.2000** |
| | w. & d. Tim Minear. | |

2:8	**'The Shroud of Rahmon'**	**21.11.2000**
	w. Jim Kouf.	
	d. David Grossman.	

2:9	**'The Trial'**	**28.11.2000**
	story: David Greenwalt.	
	teleplay: Douglas Petrie & Tim Minear.	
	d. Bruce Seth Green.	

2:10	**'Reunion'**	**19.12.2000**
	w. Tim Minear & Shawn Ryan.	
	d. James. A. Contner.	

2:11	**'Redefinition'**	**16.1.2001**
	w. Mere Smith.	
	d. Michael Grossman.	

2:12	**'Blood Money'**	**23.1.2001**
	w. Shawn Ryan & Mere Smith.	
	d. R. D. Price	

2:13   **'Happy Anniversary'**   **6.2.2001**
        story: Joss Whedon & David Greenwalt.
        teleplay: David Greenwalt.
        d. Bill Norton.

2:14   **'The Thin Dead Line'**   **13.2.2001**
        w. Jim Kouf & Shawn Ryan.
        d. Scott McGinnis.

2:15   **'Reprise'**   **20.2.2001**
        w. Tim Minear.
        d. James Whitmore Jr.

2:16   **'Epiphany'**   **27.2.2001**
        w. Tim Minear.
        d. Tom Wright.

2:17   **'Disharmony'**   **17.4.2001**
        w. David Fury.
        d. Fred Keller.

2:18   **'Dead End'**   **24.4.2001**
        w. David Greenwalt.
        d. James. A. Contner.

2:19   **'Belonging'**   **1.5.2001**
        w. Shawn Ryan.
        d. Turi Meyer.

2:20   **'Over the Rainbow'**   **8.5.2001**
        w. Mere Smith.
        d. Fred Keller.

2:21   **'Through the Looking Glass'**   **15.5.2001**
        w. & d. Tim Minear.

2:22   **'There's No Place Like Plrtz Glrb'**   **22.5.2001**
        w. & d. David Greenwalt

SEASON THREE

3:1	**'Heartthrob'**	**24.9.2001**
	w. & d. David Greenwalt.	
3:2	**'That Vision Thing'**	**1.10.2001**
	w. Jeffrey Bell.	
	d. Bill Norton.	
3:3	**'That Old Gang of Mine'**	**8.10.2001**
	w. Tim Minear.	
	d. Fred Keller.	
3:4	**'Carpe Noctum'**	**15.10.2001**
	w. Scott Murphy.	
	d. James A. Contner.	
3:5	**'Fredless'**	**22.10.2001**
	w. Mere Smith.	
	d. Marita Grabiak.	
3:6	**'Billy'**	**29.10.2001**
	w. David Greenwalt.	
	d. Turi Meyer.	
3:7	**'Offspring'**	**5.11.2001**
	w. David Greenwalt.	
	d. Turi Meyer.	
3:8	**'Quickening'**	**12.11.2001**
	w. Jeffrey Bell.	
	d. Skip Schoolnik.	
3:9	**'Lullaby'**	**19.11.2001**
	w. & d. Tim Minear.	
3:10	**'Dad'**	**10.12.2001**
	w. David H. Goodman.	
	d. Fred Keller.	

3:11	**'Birthday'**	**14.1.2002**

w. Mere Smith.
d. Michael Grossman.

| 3:12 | **'Provider'** | **21.1.2002** |

w. Scott Murphy.
d. Bill Norton.

| 3:13 | **'Waiting in the Wings'** | **4.2.2002** |

w. & d. Joss Whedon.

| 3:14 | **'Couplet'** | **18.2.2002** |

w. Tim Minear & Jeffrey Bell.
d. Tim Minear.

| 3:15 | **'Loyalty'** | **25.2.2002** |

w. Mere Smith.
d. James A. Contner.

| 3:16 | **'Sleep Tight'** | **4.3.2002** |

w. David Greenwalt.
d. Terrence O'Hara.

| 3:17 | **'Forgiving'** | **15.4.2002** |

w. Jeffrey Bell.
d. Turi Meyer.

| 3:18 | **'Double or Nothing'** | **22.4.2002** |

w. David H. Goodman.
d. David Grossman.

| 3:19 | **'The Price'** | **29.4.2002** |

w. David Fury.
d. Marita Grabiak.

| 3:20 | **'A New World'** | **6.5.2002** |

w. Jeffrey Bell.
d. Tim Minear.

3:21 **'Benediction'**   **13.5.2002**
w. & d. Tim Minear.

3:22 **'Tomorrow'**   **20.5.2002**
w. & d. David Greenwalt.

SEASON FOUR

4:1 **'Deep Down'**   **6.10.2002**
w. Steven S. DeKnight.
d. Terrence O'Hara.

4:2 **'Ground State'**   **13.10.2002**
w. Mere Smith.
d. Michael Grossman.

4:3 **'The House Always Wins'**   **20.10.2002**
w. David Fury.
d. Marita Grabiak.

4:4 **'Slouching Toward Bethlehem'**   **27.10.2002**
w. Jeffrey Bell.
d. Skip Schoolnik.

4:5 **'Supersymmetry'**   **3.11.2002**
w. Elizabeth Craft & Sarah Fain.
d. Bill Norton.

4:6 **'Spin the Bottle'**   **10.11.2002**
w. & d. Joss Whedon.

4:7 **'Apocalypse, Nowish'**   **17.11.2002**
w. Steven S. DeKnight.
d. Vern Gillum.

4:8 **'Habeas Corpses'**   **15.1.2003**
w. Jeffrey Bell.
d. Skip Schoolnik.

4:9   **'Long Day's Journey'**   **22.1.2003**
w. Mere Smith.
d. Terrence O'Hara.

4:10   **'Awakening'**   **29.1.2003**
w. David Fury & Steven S. DeKnight.
d. James A. Contner.

4:11   **'Soulless'**   **5.2.2003**
w. Sarah Fain & Elizabeth Craft.
d. Sean Astin.

4:12   **'Calvary'**   **12.2.2003**
w. Jeffrey Bell, Steven S. DeKnight & Mere Smith.
d. Bill Norton.

4:13   **'Salvage'**   **5.3.2003**
w. David Fury.
d. Jefferson Kibbee.

4:14   **'Release'**   **12.3.2003**
w. Steven S. DeKnight, Elizabeth Craft & Sarah Fain
d. James A. Contner

4:15   **'Orpheus'**   **19.3.2003**
w. Mere Smith.
d. Terrence O'Hara.

4:16   **'Players'**   **26.3.2003**
w. Jeffrey Bell, Elizabeth Craft & Sarah Fain.
d. Michael Grossman.

4:17   **'Inside Out'**   **2.4.2003**
w. & d. Steven S. DeKnight.

4:18   **'Shiny Happy People'**   **9.4.2003**
w. Elizabeth Craft & Sarah Fain.
d. Marita Grabiak.

4:19   'The Magic Bullet'   16.4.2003
        w. & d. Jeffrey Bell.

4:20   'Sacrifice'   23.4.2003
        w. Ben Edlund.
        d. David Straiton.

4:21   'Peace Out'   30.4.2003
        w. David Fury.
        d. Jefferson Kibbee.

4:22   'Home'   7.5.2003
        w. & d. Tim Minear.

SEASON FIVE

5:1   'Conviction'   1.10.2003
        w. & d. Joss Whedon.

5:2   'Just Rewards'   8.10.2003
        w. David Fury.
        d. James A. Contner.

5:3   'Unleashed'   15.10.2003
        w. Elizabeth Craft & Sarah Fain.
        d. Marita Grabiak.

5:4   'Hell Bound'   22.10.2003
        w. & d. Steven S. DeKnight.

5:5   'Life of the Party'   29.10.2003
        w. Ben Edlund.
        d. Bill Norton.

5:6   'The Cautionary Tale of Numero Cinco'   5.11.2003
        w. & d. Jeff Bell.

5:7   **'Lineage'**   **12.11.2003**
          w. Drew Goddard.
          d. Jefferson Kibbee.

5:8   **'Destiny'**   **19.11.2003**
          w. David Fury & Steven S. DeKnight.
          d. Skip Schoolnik.

5:9   **'Harm's Way'**   **14.1.2004**
          w. Sarah Fain & Elizabeth Craft.
          d. Vern Gillum.

5:10   **'Soul Purpose'**   **21.1.2004**
          w. Brent Fletcher.
          d. David Boreanaz.

5:11   **'Damage'**   **28.1.2004**
          w. Steven S. DeKnight & Drew Goddard.
          d. Jefferson Kibbee.

5:12   **'You're Welcome'**   **4.2.2004**
          w. & d. David Fury.

5:13   **'Why We Fight'**   **11.2.2004**
          w. Drew Goddard & Steven S. DeKnight.
          d. Terrence O'Hara.

5:14   **'Smile Time'**   **18.2.2004**
          w. Joss Whedon & Ben Edlund.
          d. Ben Edlund.

5:15   **'A Hole in the World'**   **25.2.2004**
          w. & d. Joss Whedon.

5:16   **'Shells'**   **3.3.2004**
          w. & d. Steven S. DeKnight.

5: 17   **'Underneath'**   14.4.2004
         w. Sarah Fain & Elizabeth Craft.
         d. Skip Schoolnik..

5:18   **'Origin'**   21.4.2004
         w. Drew Goddard.
         d. Terrence O'Hara.

5:19   **'Time Bomb'**   28.4.2004
         w. Ben Edlund.
         d.Vern Gillum.

5:20   **'The Girl in Question'**   5.5.2004
         w. Steven S. DeKnight.
         d. David Greenwalt.

5:21   **'Power Play'**   12.5.2004
         w. David Fury.
         d. James A. Contner.

5:22   **'Not Fade Away'**   19.5.2004
         w. Jeffrey Bell & Joss Whedon.
         d. Jeffrey Bell.

FURTHER READING

Abbott, Stacey. 'Walking the Fine Line between Angel and Angelus', *Slayage: The Online International Journal of Buffy Studies*, 9 (August 2003), at http://www.slayage.tv/essays/slayage9/Abbott.htm.

Alderman, Naomi and Annette Seidel-Arpaci. 'Imaginary Para-Sites of the Soul: Vampires and Representations of "Blackness" and "Jewishness" in the *Buffy/Angelverse*', *Slayage: The Online International Journal of Buffy Studies*, 10 (November 2003), at http://www.slayage.tv/essays/slayage10/Alderman_&_Seidel-Arpaci.htm.

Alexander, Jenny. 'A Vampire is Being Beaten – De Sade Through the Looking Glass in *Buffy* and *Angel*', paper given at the *Slayage* Conference on *Buffy the Vampire Slayer*, Nashville, TN, 28–30 May 2004, at http://www.slayage.tv/SCBTVS-Archive.htm.

Andrews, Scott. 'California Demon', *Starburst Slayer Special*, 53 (2002): pp. 42–5.

Anon. 'Behind the Scenes featuring Darling Violetta: Creator and Performer of the *Angel* Theme', *City of Angel* (October 2000), at http://www.cityofangel.com/behindTheScenes/bts/musicDV1.html.

Battis, Jess. *Blood Relations: Chosen Families in* Buffy the Vampire Slayer *and* Angel (Jefferson, NC: McFarland, forthcoming 2005).

Bernstein, Abbey. 'Apocalypse Now', *Dreamwatch*, 118 (2004), pp. 35–6.

Blanco, Theresa. '"You're Beneath Me": The Stigma of Vampirism in *Buffy* and *Angel*', paper given at the *Slayage* Conference on *Buffy the Vampire Slayer*, Nashville, TN, 28–30 May 2004, at http://www.slayage.tv/SCBTVS-Archive.htm.

Comeford, AmiJo. 'Structural Identity, or Saussure Visits Buffy/Angel's World: An Oppositional View of *Angel*', paper given at the *Slayage* Conference on *Buffy the Vampire Slayer*, Nashville, TN, 28–30 May 2004, at http://www.slayage.tv/SCBTVS-Archive.htm.

Cummings, Jean. 'Heavenly Body: Interview with David Boreanaz', *Starburst*, 271 (2001), pp. 58–62.

Darlington, David. 'And it's Goodbye from Him', *Shivers*, 113 (2004), pp. 15–16.

Davis, Peggy. '"I'm a Rogue Demon-Hunter": Wesley's Transformation from Fop to Hero on *Buffy the Vampire Slayer* and *Angel*', paper given at the *Slayage* Conference on *Buffy the Vampire Slayer*, Nashville, TN, 28–30 May 2004.

DiLullo, Tara. 'Inside Out: Interview with Steve DeKnight', at http://cityofangel.com, 2003.

——. '"Not Fade Away": Interview with Jeffrey Bell and David Fury', *Dreamwatch*, 118 (2004), pp. 30–2.

Dowling, Jennifer. '"We Are Not Demons": Homogenizing the Heroes in *Buffy the Vampire Slayer* and *Angel*', *Refractory: A Journal of Entertainment Media*, 2 (2003), at http://www.refractory.unimelb.edu.au/refractory/journalissues/vol2/vol2htm.

Ferrente, Anthony C. 'Angel Flies Solo', *Fangoria*, 229 (2004), pp. 20–4.

Fitzpatrick, Caroline. 'Monsters and Mean Streets: *Angel* and the Legacy of Noir', paper given at the *Slayage* Conference on *Buffy the Vampire Slayer*, Nashville, TN, 28–30 May 2004.

Gallagher, Diana G., and Paul Ruditis. *Angel: The Casefiles Volume 2* (New York and London: Pocket Books, 2004).

Gross, Ed. '*Angel* Evolutions', *Cinefantastique*, 35: 5 (2003), pp. 54–9.

———. 'Look Back in *Angel*: Interview with Joss Whedon', *SFX Magazine* (July 2004), pp. 56–64.

Halfyard, Janet K. 'Love, Death, Curses and Reverses (in F Minor): Music, Gender and Identity in *Buffy the Vampire Slayer* and *Angel*', *Slayage: The Online International Journal of Buffy Studies* 4 (2001), at http://www.slayage.tv/essays/slayage4/halfyard.htm.

——.'The Greatest Love of All: Cordelia's Journey of Self-Discovery', paper given at the *Slayage* Conference on *Buffy the Vampire Slayer*, Nashville, TN, 28–30 May 2004, at http://www.slayage.tv/SCBTVS-Archive.htm.

Hill, Annette, and Ian Calcutt. 'The UK Marketing and Reception of *Buffy the Vampire Slayer* and *Angel*', *Cult Media*, at http://www.cult-media.com/issue1/Ahill.htm.

Holder, Nancy, Jeff Mariotte and Maryelizabeth Hart. *Angel: The Casefiles Volume One* (New York and London: Pocket Books, 2002).

Jankiewicz, Pat. 'Angelic Host: Interview with Andy Hallet', *Starburst*, 272 (2001), pp. 24–7.

Jowett, Lorna. 'The Problem of Romance and the Representation of Gender in *Buffy* and *Angel*', paper given at the *Slayage* Conference on *Buffy the Vampire Slayer*, Nashville, TN, 28–30 May 2004, at http://www.slayage.tv/SCBTVS-Archive.htm.

Joy, Nick. 'The Two Gentlemen of Pylea', *Starburst*, 289 (2002), pp. 60–5.

Kaveney, Roz (ed.). *Reading the Vampire Slayer: An Unofficial Critical Companion to Buffy and Angel* (London: I.B. Tauris, 2001).

——(ed.). *Reading the Vampire Slayer: The New, Updated Unofficial Guide to Buffy and Angel* (London: I.B. Tauris, 2004).

——. '"She Saved the World. A Lot": An Introduction to the Themes and Structures of *Buffy* and *Angel*', in Roz Kaveney (ed.), *Reading the Vampire Slayer: The New, Updated Unofficial Guide to Buffy and Angel* (London: I.B. Tauris, 2004), pp. 1–82.

——. 'Writing the Vampire Slayer: Interviews with Jane Espenson and Steven S. DeKnight', in Roz Kaveney (ed.), *Reading the Vampire Slayer: The New, Updated Unofficial Guide to Buffy and Angel* (London: I.B. Tauris, 2004), pp. 100–31.

Lee, Patrick, 'David Greenwalt's *Angel* Takes Wing', at http://www.scifi.com, 2000.

Nazzaro, Joe. 'Creatures of DeKnight: Interview with Steven DeKnight', *TV Zone*, 167 (2003), pp. 52–7.

Nazzaro, Joe. 'Reflections of the Undead: Interview with David Boreanaz', *Starburst Angel Special*, 57 (2003), pp. 8–16.

Ndalianis, Angela. '*Buffy, Angel* and the Palimpsest Apocalypse', paper given at 'Staking a Claim: Exploring the Global Reach of *Buffy*', University of South Australia, Adelaide, Australia, July 2003.

Nevitt, Lucy, and Andy William Smith. '"Family Blood is Always the Sweetest": The Gothic Transgressions of Angel/ Angelus', *Refractory: Journal of Entertainment Media*, 2 (2003), at http://www.refractory.unimelb.edu.au/refractory/ journalissues/vol2/vol2htm.

O'Hare, Kate. '*Angel* Finale Offers Endings and Beginnings', at http://tv.zap2it.com, 2003.

———. 'Producer Admires *Angel* from Afar', at http:// tv.zap2it.com, 2003.

Reading, John. 'Street Hunter: Interview with J. August Richards', *TV Zone*, 145 (2001), pp. 40–3.

Richardson, David. 'Sleeping with the Enemy', *Starburst Slayer Special*, 53 (2002): pp. 36-41.

Riess, Jana. *What Would Buffy Do? The Vampire Slayer as Spiritual Guide* (San Francisco: Jossey-Bass, 2004).

Sayer, Karen. 'This Was Our World and They Made it Theirs: Reading Space and Place in *Buffy the Vampire Slayer* and *Angel*', in Roz Kaveney (ed.), *Reading the Vampire Slayer: The New, Updated Unofficial Guide to Buffy and Angel* (London: I.B. Tauris, 2004), pp. 132–55.

Schiffren, Mara. 'On Escherian Dualism and the Metaphysics of the Middle Way: Interpreting the Spatial Architecture of *Angel*', paper given at the *Slayage* Conference on *Buffy the Vampire Slayer*, Nashville, TN, 28–30 May 2004.

Siemann, Catherine. 'Ethics or Legal Ethics? Wolfram and Hart and the Code of Professional Responsibility', paper given at the *Slayage* Conference on *Buffy the Vampire Slayer*, Nashville, TN, 28–30 May 2004.

Smith, Jim. 'This Hollywood Life', *Starburst*, 283 (2002), pp. 20-7.

Spelling, Ian. 'To Live and Thrive in LA: Interview with Amy Acker', *Starburst*, 280 (2001), pp. 34–7.

———. 'Alexis Denisof', *Starburst Special*, 50 (2001), pp. 10–13.

Stoy, Jennifer. 'Blood and Choice: The Theory and Practice of Family in *Angel*', in Roz Kaveney (ed.), *Reading the Vampire Slayer: The New, Updated Unofficial Guide to Buffy and Angel* (London: I.B. Taurus, 2004), pp. 220–32.

Sutherland, Sharon, and Sarah Swain. '"If a Vampire Bites a Lawyer is it Cannibalism?": The Demonisation of Lawyers in *Angel*', paper given at the *Slayage* Conference on *Buffy the Vampire Slayer*, Nashville, TN, 28–30 May 2004.

Topping, Keith. *Hollywood Vampire: The Unofficial Guide to Angel* (London: Virgin, 2000).

Waldon, David. 'Magic and Loss: Interview with Joss Whedon', *Starburst*, 312 (2004), pp. 20–5.

Wardell, Velinda. 'Shooting Angel: Interview with Ross Berryman ACS', *Australian Cinematographer*, 17 (2002), pp. 11–17.

INDEX